The Western Territories in the Civil War

Edited by LeRoy H. Fischer

Oppenheim Regents Professor of History

Oklahoma State University

ISBN 0-89745-000-0

Sunflower University Press

BOX 1009   •   MANHATTAN, KANSAS 66502, USA

The Western Territories in the Civil War

LeRoy H. Fischer, Editor

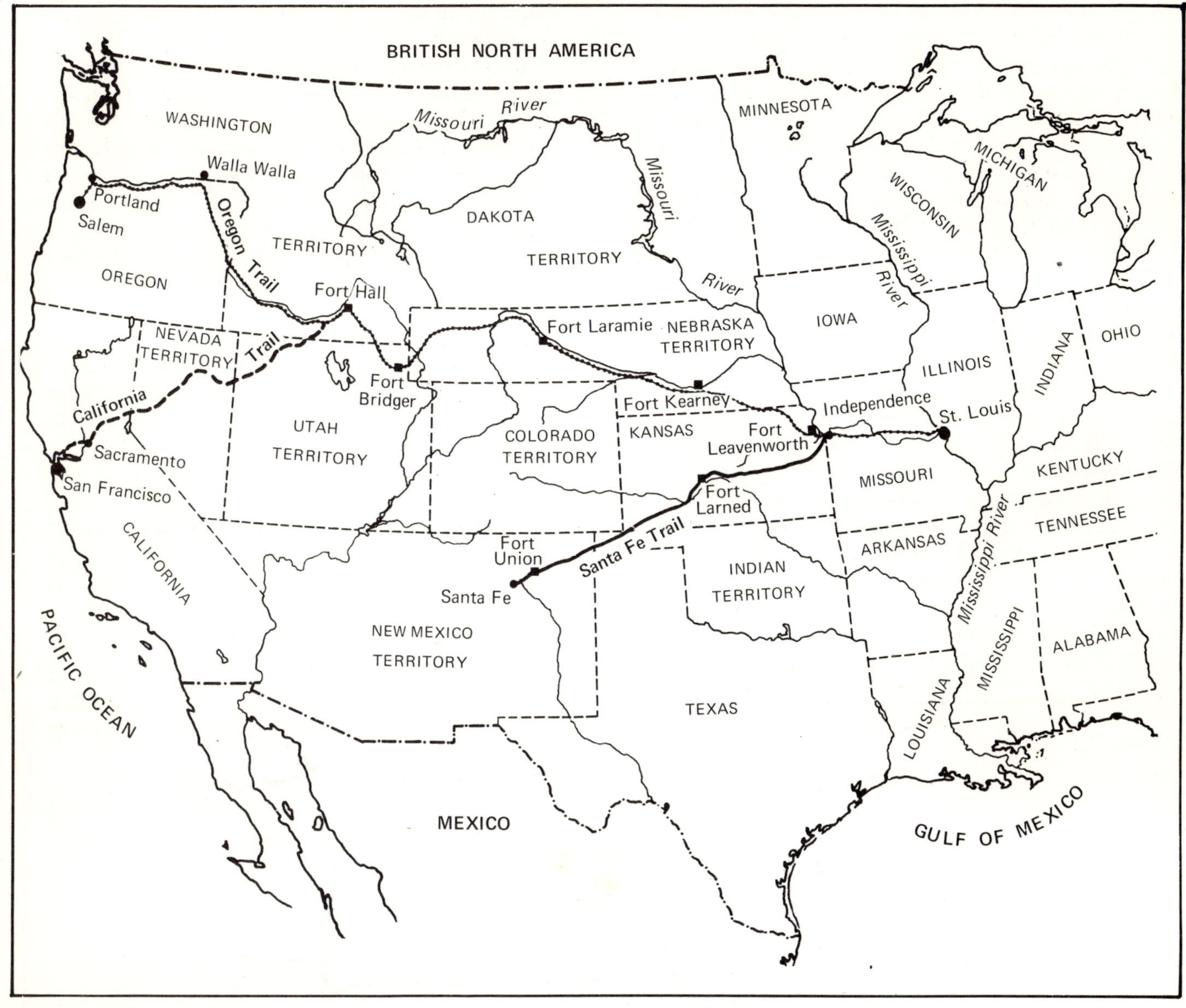

The Trans-Mississippi West at the Beginning of the Civil War

Map Drafted by Georganne T. Bartow

INTRODUCTION

The Western Territories in the Civil War
By LeRoy H. Fischer
Oppenheim Regents Professor of History
Oklahoma State University
Guest Editor-in-Chief

For nearly a century public interest in the Civil War focused on the primary areas of military combat in the South, the Southeast, and the North. During the centennial commemoration of the conflict, this attention broadened to include the war in the West, the vast region beyond the Mississippi River. Collectively, this includes nine states and eleven territories. Because the states involved were treated earlier in similar context (LeRoy H. Fischer, Guest Editor-in-Chief, "The Western States in the Civil War," *Journal of the West*, Vol. XIV, No. 1, January, 1975, pp. 1-184), the present study is limited to the eleven territories of the trans-Mississippi West of the Civil War years. A few specialized studies have appeared, notably biographical and military accounts, concerning the war in the West, but the contributions and problems of the eleven territories during the conflict have not been considered collectively before this presentation. Every effort is made herein to treat the total history and culture of each of the territories for the Civil War period in their varied aspects.

In the enormous reaches beyond the Mississippi River, seven organized territories existed at the beginning of the Civil War. These were Dakota, Washington, Nevada, Utah, Colorado, Nebraska, and New Mexico territories. During the war, three new territories were organized: Arizona, on February 24, 1863; Idaho, on March 3, 1863; and Montana, on May 26, 1864. Although named the Indian Territory, the area in which the Five Civilized Tribes (the Cherokees, Chickasaws, Choctaws, Creeks, and Seminoles) resided as independent Indian nations during the Civil War, this area was not wholly organized by the United States until the state of Oklahoma won admission in 1907. Meanwhile, during the Civil War, Nevada became a state on October 31, 1864, in time to participate in the presidential election of 1864, just as President Abraham Lincoln had planned. He carried the new state by a comfortable majority. Various boundary changes and adjustments in the Western territories continued throughout the Civil War and after, as indicated on the accompanying map, due to the creation of new territories and local conditions.

Most of the territories remained unknown except by name to Easterners. The trans-Mississippi West straddled the great overland trails that followed the Platte and North Platte rivers on their course from Independence, Missouri, and Council Bluffs, Iowa, to the West Coast via Fort Bridger and Salt Lake City, both in Utah Territory. Proud Indians, who cared little for the Union or the Confederacy, roamed the prairies, occupied the mountains and deserts, and feared for their way of life as frontiersmen encroached on their domain to settle and organize United States territories.

A few white men successfully carved out settlements in the vast interior of the West. The old and new prospered, like Santa Fe, New Mexico Territory, one of the earliest settlements in the United States, and Salt Lake City, Utah Territory, by comparison established but recently. Some settlements were former fur trading posts, like Fort Hall on the bank of the Snake River, in Washington Territory and others were established as military outposts like Fort Laramie in Nebraska Territory. A few developed overnight in the wake of the discovery of precious metals, such as Denver, Colorado Territory, and Virginia City, Nevada Territory.

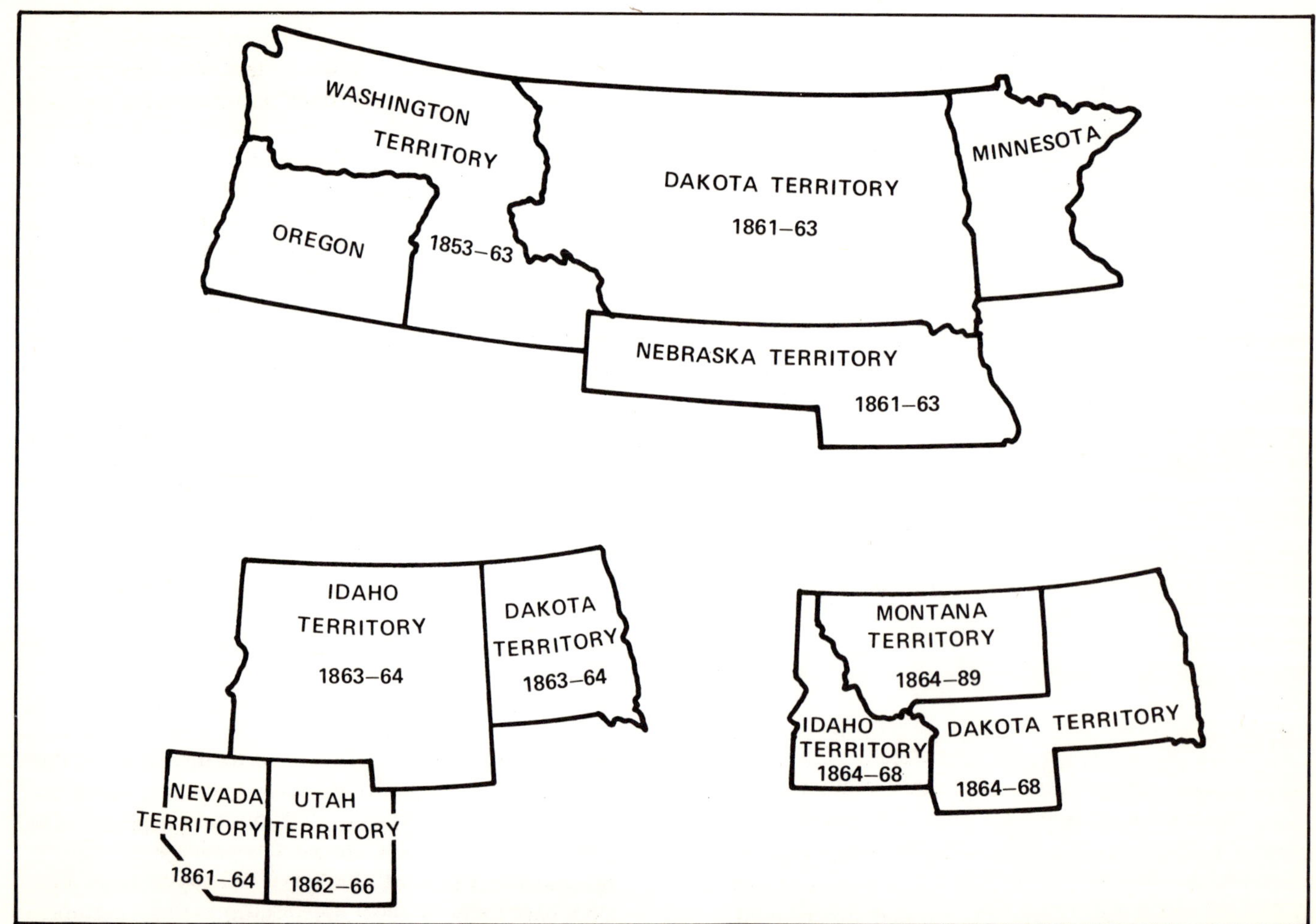

Territorial Additions and Boundary Changes During the Civil War

Map Drafted by Georganne T. Bartow

Whatever the background of the territorial settlements, the restless Indians and the drifting whites of this frontier were drawn into the vortex of war as North and South clashed from 1861 to 1865. As a result, several significant engagements of the war took place in the Western territories.

The Civil War in the Western territories was distracted by an element, the Indians, not a concern at the time east of the Mississippi River. They were not a new factor in the wars of the United States. As the French and the British had fought to win the American continent in the eighteenth century, the various tribes had rarely remained neutral. During the American Revolutionary War, they sided with the British, and in the nineteenth century they kept the United States Army occupied almost continually, first east of the Mississippi River and finally in the territorial reaches of the West. Overall, the Indians of the West turned the problems created by the Civil War to their own benefit and usually ignored pleas for support of the United States or the Confederate States. The only significant variation from this pattern was in the Indian Territory.

In the remote reaches of Dakota and Montana territories, many of the basic political questions arising during the Civil War were a strong part of the national scene. The slavery controversies in the legislature of Dakota Territory and the "Bloody Shirt" accusations in Montana Territory were reflections of general Civil War issues.

The most devastating impact of the Civil War in Dakota Territory was the effect it had on Indian uprisings. At the beginning of the war, some of the most important rebellious Indian leaders heard rumors that Union forces were being defeated by the Confederates. These same Indian leaders also were aware of the decreased number of United States Army forces stationed in their midst. These forces at the beginning of the war had been withdrawn to areas in the East considered more crucial, leaving Dakota and Montana basically unprotected. But the United States government soon corrected this situation by supplying more forces than ever before. Likely the soldiers who responded to the Sioux Indian attacks may have assembled more quickly than under peacetime circumstances because the war already had provided practice in recruiting and organizing troops. The Dakota Cavalry Regiment played an important role in the Sioux Indian campaigns and constituted almost one fourth of the troops used in Dakota Territory.

Economically, Dakota Territory suffered severely during the Civil War. Growth slowed and part of it saw a retreat in the line of settlement due to Indian uprisings during the war years. In 1862, 1863, and 1864 nature combined with Indians to destroy most of the crops; in fact, agriculture probably suffered more than at any other time. Montana Territory, on the other hand, thrived because of the mining of precious metals; the major problem there was inadequate transportation.

To the west of Dakota and Montana territories, the inhabitants of Washington and Idaho territories largely were preoccupied during the Civil War with developing into a viable part of the Pacific Coast. Population increased rapidly, due primarily to the discovery of gold. When United States Army units were transferred east at the beginning of the war, militia volunteers numbering 964 men performed the work of keeping peace and pacifying Indians. Although these militia units were completely inexperienced, they learned as they performed and functioned satisfactorily. Even Indian unrest was relatively insignificant, perhaps no greater than in peacetime. Thus the war was not a current, realistic issue because there was no militia involvement outside the two territories, communications of the day were slow, and the major battles in the East and South were geographically remote. Little was experienced of the tragedy of the war itself.

Amazingly, Washington Territory feared Confederate invasion from the Pacific Ocean. Only San Francisco, California, of the many coastal settlements was fortified, and the loss of that city would have signaled the loss of the entire Pacific Coast. Fearful of this, Congress enacted the Northwest Coastal Defense Plan in July of 1862, and allotted a total of $300,000 for fortifications. At Cape Disappointment in Washington Territory, renamed Fort Cape Disappointment in 1864, a unit of the coastal defense system was constructed. Perhaps Washington Territory had reason for its fear, for treasure ships left California loaded with rich cargoes bound for the East Coast and Europe, tempting targets for Confederate naval vessels. Captain James I. Wadell secured the sleek and modern *Shenandoah* from England in October of 1864, and was soon operating in the waters of the Pacific Northwest; there he captured thirty-eight merchant vessels flying the flag of the United States. Wadell allowed eight ships to go free, carrying the crews of all thirty-eight; the other vessels were burned or scuttled. Wadell's actions caused much apprehension in Washington Territory, especially due to the many steamers that traveled from Puget Sound to the state of Oregon and San Francisco. This threat not only frightened many sea travelers, but also added to the pro-Union attitude in Washington Territory.

Although Nevada Territory was a neighbor to the south of Washington and Idaho territories, it experienced a more active political climate in terms of national issues during the war years. Perhaps the statehood movement, which achieved its goal in 1864, was responsible for this. In order for the new state to participate in the presidential election of November of that year, Governor James W. Nye decided to send the constitution to Washington, D.C., by telegraph. The message not only established a record for the longest telegram, but its cost of $3,000 was the highest price ever paid for a single transmission.

At the beginning of the war, United States Army troops stationed in Nevada were ordered to crucial military areas in the East. Without law enforcement in the territory, the nationally important Overland Mail Route connecting with the Pacific Coast was subject to attacks by Indians and highwaymen. The trail soon became the only route that people, merchandise, and mail could take overland from the East Coast to the West Coast. Indians soon were killing some cattle and attacking a few wagons on the route. The basic problem was that the white population had destroyed or curtailed many of the food sources of the Indians. Because the major streams and lakes made excellent sites for building communities and locating industries, the Indians were driven to the more arid sections of the territory. In addition, the fish habitat began to be curtailed and the game that had been plentiful before the coming of the whites was killed or chased away. Governor Nye suggested to the commanding general of the Department of the Pacific that food be passed out to the Indians along the Overland Mail Route to pacify them.

Nye was soon given 60,000 rations of flour and 40,000 rations of meat for distribution to these Indians.

To offset the loss of troops at the beginning of the war, Governor Nye was ordered to raise a regiment of infantry and one of cavalry for duty in Nevada itself. These men were used to guard the Overland Mail Route, garrison the forts of the territory, and generally provide law and order. By the end of the war, 1,180 men had served in the militia forces of Nevada Territory.

The precious metal resources of Nevada Territory enabled the Union to maintain its credit and finance the war. Nevada produced $45 million in gold and silver bullion during the war years alone. The Civil War indirectly brought about the territory's somewhat premature admission to the Union, but with statehood came better order in the mining section and production increased. After the war the resources of Nevada again were called upon to provide the financial backing necessary to reconstruct the nation.

Aerial view of Fort Union National Monument. Star Fort (also called Second Fort Union, 1861-1863) in the foreground. Post of Fort Union is to the right in rear of the Star Fort, and the Depot is to the left in the photo. Construction of the Post and Depot was begun in 1864, and completed in 1869. The white structure in the upper right corner of the photo is the stone Territorial Prison.

To the east of Nevada Territory, the Mormons in Utah created a situation distinctly different from any other Western territory. Although an organized territorial government was functioning, actual authority rested with the Mormon Church and Brigham Young, its leader. Because the Mormons had been persecuted elsewhere, they had settled in the Great Salt Lake Valley in an effort to escape restrictions and regulations by gentiles and governments. The Mormons did not support either North or South during the Civil War. Their purpose at the time was to perfect a theocratic state and prepare themselves for economic self-sufficiency.

The Civil War brought no military combat to Utah Territory, for Confederate troops did not invade it, but the war touched its development in several ways. The removal of United States Army troops from Utah Territory for service in the East at the beginning of the war permitted the Mormon Church more latitude and caused territorial officials additional concern. As a result, the United States government decided to reassign troops to Utah Territory in 1862 and Congress passed an Anti-Bigamy Act that same year. This brought to Utah Colonel P. Edward Connor, the commanding officer of the Third California Volunteer Infantry Regiment, a man obsessed with breaking the theocratic control of the Mormons. The many tensions among civil, military, and religious authorities in Utah Territory during the Civil War years generally resulted from Connor's attitudes and actions.

Rapid economic development was the most important result of the Civil War in Utah Territory. The outbreak of the conflict caused the United States to remove the transcontinental mail and telegraph routes from the potentially unfriendly Southwest to Utah Territory. In addition, the Mormon desire for economic self-sufficiency made Utah an agricultural center for gold and silver mining communities in surrounding territories. Although the Mormons were not conscientious objectors to war, combat in the East likely influenced the decision of many of them to migrate to Utah Territory, thus increasing its population and economic productivity.

To the east of Utah Territory lay Colorado Territory. The Civil War adversely affected its economy by intensifying a depression caused originally by a slump in gold mining. Placer gold deposits had been exhausted, and techniques for processing rock ore remained unperfected. Labor needs for the mines went unheeded, for the war effort absorbed any excess labor in the East and local Indian uprisings hampered immigration. During the war the territory suffered a major loss of population. Nevertheless, the potential of the mines of Colorado was obvious to Congress, and in 1862 it voted to establish a branch of the United States mint in Denver.

Territorial organization came to Colorado concurrent with the beginning of the Civil War. Local leadership seemed disorganized and turbulent, and even the United States government did not move effectively for some months to organize the territory, although local citizens sided almost wholly with the Union. Unfortunately the territory's first chief executive, Governor William Gilpin, proved a poor choice. Visionary and impractical, he poorly managed military affairs and aroused resentment among the population.

Yet Gilpin's military organization checked Brigadier General Henry H. Sibley's invasion of New Mexico in 1861-1862. Otherwise, a Confederate victory in the Southwest would have cost additional lives and prolonged the war. Victory for the Union at Glorietta Pass was Colorado Territory's major military contribution. The engagement also created a hero, Colonel John M. Chivington, who later did much damage to his home territory by perpetrating offenses against humanity during the Indian massacre at Sand Creek. Colorado forces also served ably in clearing the Indian Territory of Confederate forces and in operations against guerrillas and regular Confederate units in Missouri.

Thus Colorado Territory gave much to the war effort but suffered extensively in return. The war decreased immigration, disrupted an already depressed economy, increased political rivalries, and brought an Indian war that continued after the sectional conflict ended. Colorado paid dearly for territorial organization.

Located on the northern border of Colorado Territory, Nebraska Territory also stood ready to support the Union war effort vigorously. The territory furnished an amazing 3,157 men during the war out of a population of somewhat less than 30,000. Perhaps as many as 2,000 more Nebraskans fought for the Union in surrounding state units, while a few fought for the Confederacy. Regiments from Kansas, Missouri, Iowa, and Illinois usually had a small number of Nebraskans. The First Nebraska Infantry Regiment proved itself outside of the territory at the capture of Fort Donelson and the Battle of Shiloh.

Nebraska Territory provided its greatest war service, however, on the home front. Thousands of immigrants migrated west on its roads, and it gave them safe and dependable travel. Without its cooperation, the movement of people and provisions to the West virtually would have halted. It was Nebraska Territory's roads that took over when the Southern trails closed at the beginning of the war. Although the territory was hurt economically at the outset of war by the loss of its close ties with Southern financial interests and markets, Nebraska quickly increased its agricultural production to help feed the North. In addition, the territory welcomed thousands of Union sympathizers as settlers following their dispossession of homes and farms owing to guerrilla fighting and military activity in the border and Southern states.

Overall, Nebraska benefited in a number of ways from the Civil War. Its population increased impressively, its political status improved to the point of receiving invitations to statehood, and its economy thrived for the first time. Before the war, subsistance farming was usual, but profitable markets opened during the war. In the short run of the war, the Homestead Act of 1862 was of some value to the territory, but its major boost in population from this legislation would come in the years following the war. Had it not been for the war, many gains and improvements for the territory would have been delayed for years.

To the southwest the inhabitants of New Mexico and Arizona territories faced an early invasion by Confederate forces. On June 30, 1861, 2,466 men and officers of the United States Army garrisoned the area. For years they had carried on continuous and semi-effective warfare against determined nomadic Indians and were scattered in small forts across the territories for the purpose of keeping the main routes to California open.

The Confederate government gave considerable attention to the strategic location of New Mexico Territory. Control of it would limit Union communication with California and the Pacific Coast and impede the flow of gold to the North. If New Meixco Territory fell, the secessionist element in southern California likely would control that area. Thus the South would acquire needed precious metal and specie, as well as Pacific Ocean seaports. If these efforts failed, warfare in New Mexico would open an additional theater of military operations and divert some Federal strength from concentrating east of the Mississippi River. Confederate leaders also speculated that the Mormons in Utah Territory, who did not appreciate their attachment to the Union, would join the Confederacy if New Mexico fell. Then Colorado, containing many Southerners working its gold fields, could be invaded from west and south. The fall of New Mexico Territory also would make it possible for Texans to acquire the north Mexican states of Chihuahua and Sonora for purposes of expanding slavery. To accomplish this, Confederate Brigadier General Henry H. Sibley invaded New Mexico Territory in 1861-1862, but failed completely to achieve his purposes.

Political factionalism resurfaced within the territory following the withdrawal of Sibley's forces. These struggles, however, were between the Republican office holders appointed by President Lincoln and the Democratic leaders who had controlled the territory before the war. Republicans generally attempted to gain economic advantage in the territory for Eastern financial interests. Office seeking politicians in Washington, D.C., created Arizona Territory in 1863, a development welcomed by the inhabitants of both territories.

To the east of New Mexico Territory, the Five Civilized Tribes of the Indian Territory experienced the Civil War in its severest form: total devestation and guerrilla warfare. In other ways the territory also was distracted. Political wrangling among both Federal and Confederate officers flourished in both commands, and neither Union nor Confederate forces obtained the supplies they needed from their governments.

Yet the Civil War had a positive side for the forces and civilians of the Indian Territory. The military ability of several commanders emerged. Major General James G. Blunt and Colonel William A. Phillips of the Union forces proved dynamic and agressive leaders, while the hit-and-run tactics employed so effectively by Confederate Brigadier General Stand Watie provide a textbook for successful guerrilla warfare. The common soldiers — Indian, Negro, and white — fought as bravely and as capably as their counterparts in the North and South. Strangely the devestation of war brought new employment to the territory's Indians in the ranks of the Federal and Confederate armies.

On a larger front the Civil War in the Indian Territory affected in major ways the strategy of the North and the South. The forces of the United States helped block Confederate expansion to the west through intervention in the territory, thereby breaking a primary link between New Mexico Territory and the South and simultaneously thwarting a major Confederate offensive into the state of Kansas. Although the South was largely neutralized by the presence of Federal forces in the Indian Territory, Confederate troops in the same area prevented Union forces from invading and possibly occupying Texas, thus severing that significant supply state from the Confederacy.

In the end the Five Civilized Tribes of the Indian Territory needed not only to reconstruct their society and economy as a result of total devastation caused by the Civil War, but also to mend their wartime political divisions as well. The many changes the war brought left the Indian Territory an easy target for the expansion of the white man's frontier.

Overall, the Civil War had a greater impact on the Western territories than is usually realized and acknowledged. Although the territories did not affect the outcome of the war, the war affected the territories, some severely. As regular United States Army forces were withdrawn from the territories for service in the East, untrained volunteer militia units took their place, inviting Indian uprisings. War stories and Confederate victories also excited the Indians, and continued white migration to the West gave them additional motivation. The manpower demands of the larger war sometimes played havoc even with the skeleton protection of the volunteer militia forces when they were sent to other territories or to states for military service as campaigns developed. On the frontier, horses for cavalry use were frequently in short supply because of the insatiable need for military mounts in the East. Wagons and harness also continued in short supply, as did sufficient arms to go around. Thus many soldiers, both Union and Confederate, carried whatever weapons they could find or went unarmed; sometimes hostile Indians in the territories were better armed. In almost every conceivable way, military operations on the territorial frontier were minimized by the war in the East, and the territories suffered accordingly.

Acknowledgments

The studies that follow were prepared by graduate students in my research seminar at Oklahoma State University. To these people I am deeply grateful, especially for their cooperation and dedication. Much appreciation is also extended to Odie B. Faulk, professor and chairman of the history department at Oklahoma State University, for his encouragement and interest in this undertaking. At Oklahoma State University, Norman N. Durham, dean of the Graduate College, George A. Gries, dean of the College of Arts and Sciences, Donald W. Grace, director of research of the College of Arts and Sciences, and Neil J. Hackett, Jr., director of the School of Social Sciences, likewise contributed substantially. Lending additional encouragement were Elisabeth Oppenheim, Joan Oppenheim, the late Leo Oppenheim, Edgar R. Oppenheim, and the late George H. Shirk, all of Oklahoma City, Oklahoma. Martha, my wife, aided materially throughout the preparation of the papers for publication and for her able assistance I am most grateful. For the interest and careful work of Robin Higham and Dean Coughenour of Manhattan, Kansas, in bringing the materials to the light of print, special thanks are due. Lastly, without the vast holdings of the Oklahoma State University Edmon Low Library and the cooperation of its capable staff, especially Heather M. Lloyd and Vicki D. Phillips, the studies could not have been completed.

LeRoy H. Fischer
Oppenheim Regents Professor of History
Oklahoma State University

Dakota And Montana Territories
By Kenny L. Brown

The remote territories of the Far West seemed to have little in common with the embattled states east of the Mississippi during the Civil War. This was particularly true of such areas as Dakota Territory and its offspring Montana Territory. Nevertheless, many events within these areas were at least nominally related to problems arising from the Civil War. The Sioux uprising in August of 1862 which started in Minnesota and spread to Dakota Territory would have normally received much more attention. Because of the Civil War, however, protection of the frontier settlers became secondary. The situation was sufficiently critical for Dakota Territory's Governor William Jayne to complain to military officials, saying "Family after family are leaving our Territory and whole settlements are about to be broken up. We must have immediate aid and assistance from you or else our Territory will be depopulated."[1] On the other hand, the indirect consequences of the Civil War were much less important in Montana Territory, the main problem being controversial politics permeated with accusations of Copperheadism and disloyalty. Whether or not related to the vast struggle between the states, other important events also attracted the attention of settlers in the region. A fluctuating population, disastrous weather, flour shortages, and turbulent frontier politics, along with the Indian uprisings, made the Civil War period a very critical time for Dakota and Montana territories.

At the outbreak of the Civil War, Dakota Territory encompassed a vast region which included all of present-day North Dakota and South Dakota and a large portion of present-day Montana and Wyoming. Throughout the war years, the boundaries changed several times. In March, 1863, Congress granted the new Idaho Territory which subtracted the Wyoming and Montana portions from Dakota Territory, thereby reducing it to the area of North Dakota and South Dakota. Another change occurred in May, 1864, when Idaho Territory was broken up and Montana Territory was created. At this time a large portion of Wyoming was also transferred back to Dakota Territory.[2]

The Indian population of this enormous area was substantial. Although reduced in numbers during the bloody war years, it totaled over 50,000 in 1865. This included several major tribes such as the Sioux, Poncas, Arapahoes, Cheyennes, Assiniboines, Crows,

Black Feet, Mandans, and Flatheads. In contrast, only a few whites lived in Dakota Territory at the beginning of the war. In 1860, the census indicated that 2,576 whites inhabited the settled portion of it. The census of 1870, the first such enumeration following the Civil War, showed that approximately 45,000 lived in Montana, Wyoming and Dakota territories. Although the growth of the region was somewhat large, the white population only roughly equalled that of the Indians even five years after the Civil War.[3]

William Jayne, President Abraham Lincoln's family physician and neighbor in Springfield, Illinois, was appointed by Lincoln as the first governor of Dakota Territory.

When Dakota Territory was formed in 1861, the oldest town was Pembina, located on the Red River in the far northeastern corner of the territory and originally established as a trading post in 1801. Because it was not included within the boundaries of the new state of Minnesota in 1858, the residents of Pembina asked Congress to establish a territorial government for the area. Pembina alone had over 1,000 inhabitants and would have been a logical choice for a capital of a new government. Nevertheless, the embryo towns developing to the south would become the center of future settlement and would quickly surpass the Red River district in importance.[4]

Much of this southern region was still under the control of the Indians prior to 1858. John B. S. Todd, a typical enterprising frontiersman, recognized the opportunities of the area and led the movement to open it to settlement. Born in Lexington, Kentucky, on April 14, 1814, Todd was the cousin of Mary Todd, future wife of Abraham Lincoln. He attended the United States Military Academy and, after graduating in 1837, rose to the rank of captain and served in the Florida Indian Wars, the Mexican War, and along the Indian frontier. Accompanying Brigadier General William Harney, he came to the region that would become Dakota Territory. In the summer of 1856, Todd resigned shortly after Harney's forces built Fort Randall on the Missouri River. He left the army to become the sutler at the fort and soon formed a partnership with

Daniel Frost, a fur trader from St. Louis, Missouri. The firm of Frost, Todd, and Company was organized at Sioux City, Iowa, that summer. Before long, the company received the right to trade with the Indians in the area, establishing various posts within a short time.[5]

With settlements expanding from the east, it was evident that authorities would soon purchase the land west of Minnesota which belonged to the Yankton Sioux. Realizing the area would soon be open for settlement, Frost and Todd organized the Upper Missouri River Land Company in February, 1858. As Indian traders, they had exclusive rights to establish posts in the area, and they used this favorable position by building several trading centers which would later be claimed as townsites. To insure their success, Todd also became involved in negotiations with the Yankton Sioux to release their claims to the land. His efforts were successful, for the treaty, signed on April 19, 1858, allowed Todd and Frost to claim 160 acres at each post.[6]

Once Todd had accomplished his goal of getting a favorable foothold in the area, he then struggled to keep it. Other land corporations had also been formed to the northeast on the Big Sioux River. The officers of these companies wanted Sioux Falls, their principal town, to become the capital of the proposed territory. The villages of this region had been open to settlement before the treaty with the Yanktons; thus, because of their age, they had an advantage over the Todd and Frost com-

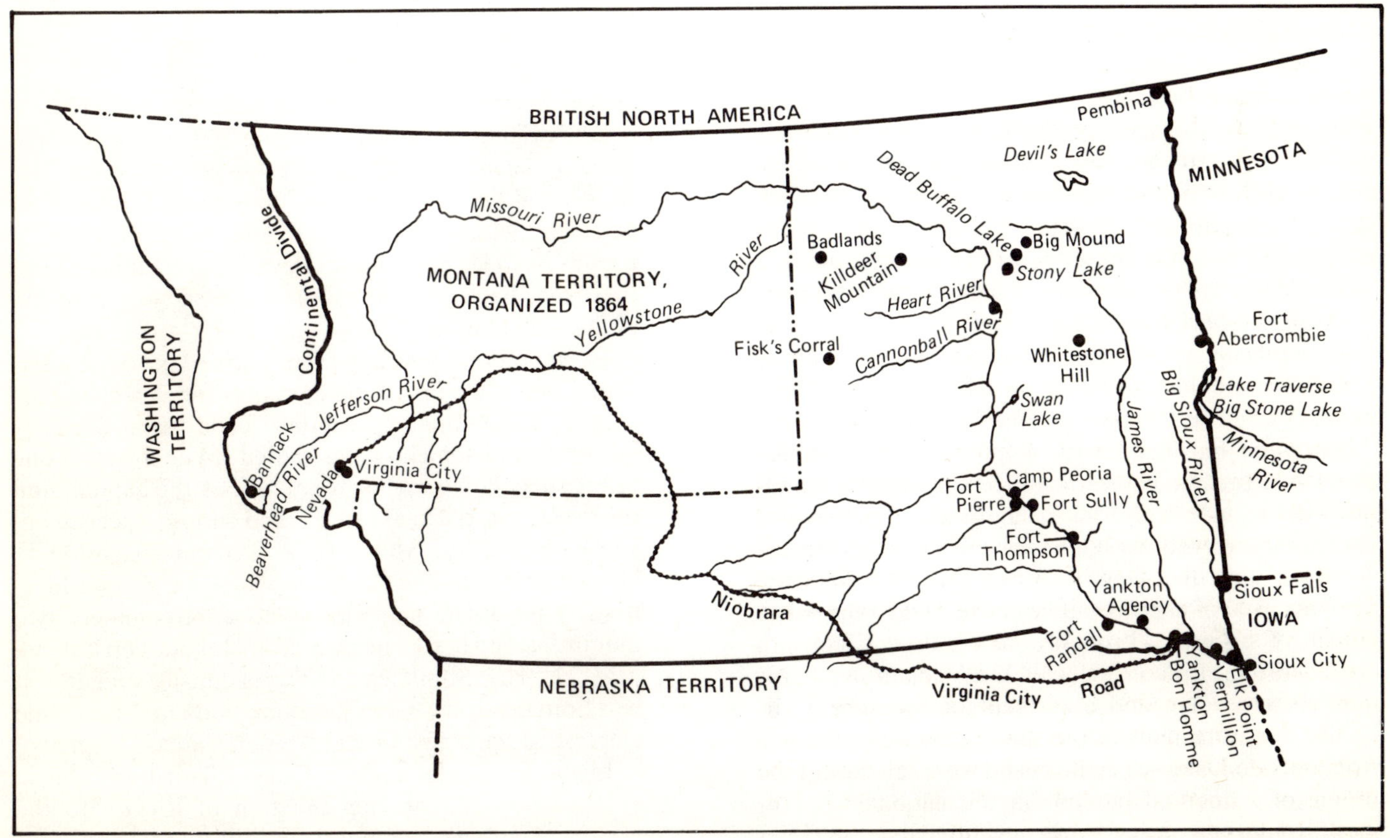

Montana and Dakota Territories During the Civil War

Map Drafted by Georganne T. Bartow

John B. S. Todd, a cousin of President Abraham Lincoln's wife, Mary Todd, settled in the 1850s in the area soon to become Dakota Territory.

Daniel M. Frost, a fur trader from St. Louis, Missouri, did much to develop Dakota Territory economically.

munities on the Missouri River. To allow his towns to grow and reach a parity, and with the hope of obtaining the capital, Todd went to Washington and lobbied for a delay in territorial organization. Congress, weary of the slavery question, inadvertently aided Todd in his scheme by avoiding the issue of organization of new territories. Finally, after some delay, which allowed Todd's Missouri River towns to grow, Congress authorized the establishment of Dakota Territory. President James Buchanan signed the act on March 2, 1861, two days before Lincoln assumed the presidency.[7]

Although burdened with a multitude of complex problems, Lincoln chose the officers of Dakota Territory within a month after his inauguration. The obvious choice for governor would have been Todd. However, Todd was an ardent Democrat, and Lincoln might have been accused of nepotism if he chose Todd, who was a cousin of his wife. Probably taking these facts into consideration, Lincoln selected Dr. William Jayne, his family's physician and a resident of Springfield, Illinois. The remainder of the appointees were likewise from outside Dakota Territory and were selected at the urging of influential persons in the national government. Important among those new officials were Chief Justice Philemon Bliss, a former abolitionist Con-

gressman from Ohio; Territorial Secretary John Hutchinson, originally from Minnesota but who had most recently been involved in government in Kansas Territory; and Surveyor General George Hill, a native of Michigan who would later sell surveying contracts to friends from his home state. Because of their positions, these men had a profound effect on the government and politics of Dakota Territory.[8]

Even before Governor Jayne arrived in the new territory, one of the first decisions confronting him was the choice of a temporary capital. Todd again used his influence and somehow persuaded Jayne to select one of his speculative towns, Yankton, as the capital until the first territorial legislature could choose a permanent site. Supposedly, Mary Todd Lincoln suggested to Governor Jayne that Yankton would be a good location. After Jayne's appointment, approximately two months passed before he arrived in Dakota Territory on May 27, 1861. Soon he called for a census, and after it was completed, issued a proclamation authorizing the election of the legislature and a delegate to Congress.[9]

In the initial elections in Dakota Territory, almost everyone agreed on the question of loyalty to the Union. Southern sympathizers, if there were any, either left the territory or kept their opinions to themselves. Sometimes the ideals of Radical Republicans, such as slavery, were opposed, but for the most part the public and politicians supported the Union and the war effort against the South. Before the attack on Fort Sumter, the *Dakotian* voiced an opinion which combined a call for loyalty with the frontiersman's desire for statehood. The newspaper proclaimed, "Our motto is — The Union with thirty-four stars, and as many more as shall apply for admission with republican institutions — always more, but never less."[10] Following the outbreak of hostilities, the *Dakotian* took a firm stand against the rebellion and condemned Northerners who sympathized with the South. The editor called for stern measures when he wrote, "If traitors cannot be persuaded, they can be hung. Rebellion can and will be crushed; and the memory of attempted Secession, like that of Nullification, must go down to posterity as an impracticable and exceedingly dangerous experiment."[11]

Anticipating the upcoming elections, many of the residents of Vermillion held the first political convention on June 1, 1861, within a week after the governor had arrived. This was the Union Party meeting, but was popularly called the Republican convention. Those attending nominated A. J. Bell, a new resident of Vermillion, for delegate to Congress; soon the *Vermillion Republican* supported him. On September 1, 1861, a convention of the People's Party held at Bon Homme chose Charles P. Booge, trader at the Yankton agency, as candidate for Congress. Todd, a Democrat, also ran as an "independent" but was not nominated by a territorial convention because he felt his chances would be better if he ran without such support. Each candidate proclaimed their allegiance to the Union and the war policy of Lincoln. Todd was no exception. The *Dakotian,* his newspaper ally, continually pointed to Todd's loyalty. The editors also contended that Todd was a natural choice because he had been responsible for the organization of the territory. Finally the newspaper explained that Todd should be chosen because of "his intimate relations at Washington with the Chief Executive."[12] With such emphasis, the campaign was one of personalities rather than issues, a trend which continued during the remainder of the territorial period. Also, the absence of true party organization particularly characterized the early Dakota elections during the Civil War.[13]

Also to be chosen in the approaching elections were the members of the territorial legislature. Various communities throughout the territory held mass meetings which nominated the candidates, a process which was much more controversial than the selection of delegates. On September 16, 1861, the election was held. Todd easily won over his two opponents; nine members of the Council and thirteen members of the House of Representatives were likewise chosen. Shortly after the election, Todd was commissioned a brigadier general of volunteers and was stationed in northern Mis-

souri. He stayed there only a short time before asking for leave to attend the ensuing session of Congress. After taking the oath of office on December 9, 1861, Todd carried out his duties as delegate and looked after the interests of the territory. In this term of Congress, he introduced several resolutions dealing with Dakota Territory. These included proposals for internal improvements such as railroads, public buildings, military roads, bridges, and development of mineral resources.[14]

While Todd was representing the territory in Congress, the legislature in Dakota Territory, which convened on March 17, 1862, was establishing the foundation of government and becoming enmeshed in heated controversies. Probably the most important contribution of the first legislature was the drafting of criminal and civil codes. Also, this first assembly organized the counties and provided for village governments in the territory. The greatest controversy arose over the selection of a territorial capital. Although Yankton had been chosen temporarily by Governor Jayne, the assembly was required to determine a permanent location. Jayne and Todd's allies in the legislature joined forces to persuade the legislature to select Yankton. Political deals were made and the pro-Yankton group prevailed after much difficulty and controversy. One observer reported, "A little blood was shed, much whiskey drank, a few eyes blacked, revolvers drawn, and some running done. A few kept sober, stood at the wheel, cleared the shoals, and steered the bill through the darkness."[15]

During the first legislative session, the question of slavery was considered; thus, Dakotans debated this issue which had led to the war being waged in the South and East. Jayne, in his first message to the legislature, explained that slavery had continually been a distracting dispute in the territories and that it should be prohibited in Dakota Territory. He hoped to see no dissenting votes against the law that he proposed which would forbid slavery or involuntary servitude. This attitude gained him the support of Radical Republicans in Congress. The Democrats of the territorial legislature, however, made a mockery of Jayne's pleas by introducing a bill which would have prohibited all Negroes from the territory. It stated, "No person of color, bond or free, shall reside upon the soil of Dakota Territory."[16] The Council passed the bill due to the majority of Democrats there, but the House of Representatives defeated the legislation because of the defection of two Democrats in that body. Although few people opposed the Union or the war effort, these legislators displayed their dislike for abolitionists on this occasion.[17]

Subsequent territorial legislatures of the Civil War years considered many more issues of major importance. The initial laws passed by the first legislature were revised and new legislation was passed to supplement the old. Justice, probate, and criminal codes were written; and laws concerning divorce, apportionment, and working hours for nonexistent industries were passed. Finally, the legislators continually memorialized Congress to appropriate funds for internal improvements for Dakota Territory.[18]

Whereas the territorial assembly seemed to accomplish much of the necessary work in establishing the government, the political campaigning during the same period was hectic and often divisive in the territory. This was particularly true of the congressional delegate contests. In Dakota Territory, no election was more controversial or troublesome than in 1862. The general election of 1861 had filled the elective offices of the territory for only one year, and it was necessary once again to elect not only the territorial legislature but also the delegate to Congress. Todd decided to run for reelection for that position; however, he was to face a much more difficult race than he had the previous year. Governor Jayne, evidently weary of the frontier conditions of Dakota Territory and desiring to go to Washington, D.C., had gained enough political strength to contest Todd.[19]

The ensuing campaign, like the first in the previous year, became one of personalities instead of issues. For the most part, the usual party identifications were ignored as both candidates gained support from coalitions of Democrats and Republicans. Impromptu parties, both with a Union label, were formed with Jayne receiving the nomination of the Republican and Union Party, while Todd accepted the endorsement of the People's Union Party. Even though disguised by these party names, Todd was generally recognized as a Democrat and Jayne a Republican. Both men declared loyalty to the Union and Lincoln's war policies. Likewise, both men emphasized their reputed influence with the chief executive — Jayne and his supporters reminded everyone that Jayne was a personal friend of the Lincoln family, but Todd and his allies explained that Todd's relationship to Mrs. Lincoln was more important. Todd's friends also emphasized his work for the territory in the past and claimed that Jayne was not worthy of election because he had been in the territory only a short time.[20]

The outbreak of the Sioux insurrection in Minnesota, and eventually in Dakota Territory, detracted some from the campaigning; nevertheless, the election was held on September 1, 1862. The Indian hostilities were not the only misfortunes that plagued the election, for overzealous partisans also stuffed the ballot boxes with fraudulent votes in several areas. Because of the threat of Indian attack, the delivery of the ballots from the Red River region to Yankton was delayed and arrived after the votes had already been canvassed and a winner had been named. Jayne was the victor by a small margin; but if the Red River votes had been included, Todd would have been the winner. Todd soon notified Jayne that he contested the election and memorialized Congress to that effect. Although Jayne was seated as delegate in 1863, Congress later ruled in favor of Todd on

June 11, 1864.[21]

The controversies of the election of 1862 had not been confined to the choice of the delegate. At least seven out of fifteen seats were contested in the territorial House of Representatives when the legislature convened in December of 1862. Two separate Houses of Representatives were formed, one with Todd's supporters and the other with Jayne's cohorts. Seventeen days of session passed before the opposing factions compromised, and the problem was solved. Thus, while arguments were being presented in regard to the delegate election, the dispute over the assembly election came to an end.[22]

Almost immediately after Congress made its decision in favor of Todd, the campaign for delegate in the election of 1864 began. Newton Edmunds, a new governor for the territory, used his influence to defeat Todd in this election. Jayne had resigned his governor's position in March, 1863, to defend himself over the contested delegate election. To replace him, in October President Lincoln appointed Edmunds, a Radical Republican who had a brother serving in Lincoln's administration. Edmunds joined forces with many of the other Republicans and soon gained political control of the territory. Their candidate for delegate was Walter A. Burleigh, the Yankton Indian agent who ran for office under the banner of the Republican and Union Party. Initially, Todd did not intend to enter the contest; thus, his supporters formed the Territorial Union Party and nominated Dakota Territory Chief Justice Philemon Bliss for delegate. After Congress designated Todd as the winner of the contested election of 1862, however, he decided to seek re-election. Many of his old friends deserted Bliss and began helping Todd while some of Bliss's supporters joined forces with Burleigh. Todd lost the election and was going to contest it but later dropped the matter. The outcome of this election indicated that the territorial Republicans had finally gained dominance over the embattled Todd.[23]

In this campaign, as well as others along the way, the Republicans repeatedly enhanced their chances for election by accusing their Democratic opponents of being "Copperheads" or "Secessionists." Democrats, such as Todd, tried to offset this tactic by creating a new party which had a cognomen of "union." Yet this diversion was not always successful, and Republicans still branded former Democrats as Copperheads or semi-secessionists. A good example of this was an editorial in the *Dakotian* in 1863 which praised the outcome of the election of the territorial legislature. The editor explained that a majority of those elected to the legislature were true loyalists while those who lost were Copperheads. He stated, "It was an earnest and persistent effort of the real friends of the Administration . . .and to put down the rebels wherever found, either North or South, —and against a combination of peace Democrats, semi-secessionists, and ballot box destroyers."[24]

Sometimes a specific individual would be accused of disloyal sentiments, often unjustly. Reuben Wallace, a member of the territorial house from Bon Homme, was accused of expressing such an attitude in the local saloon in Yankton. The Dakota Territory House of Representatives undertook a full scale investigation to determine the truth of the allegations, and Wallace's loyalty was proven beyond suspicion. Moses K. Armstrong, as observer and fellow legislator, later stated that Wallace simply had been debating for the sake of argument. Armstrong explained further: "The affair has raised a great smoke from a little fire, and a strong stench on a small matter."[25] Dakota Territory, like many other areas of the country, experienced the persistent accusations of Copperheadism.

While the inhabitants of eastern Dakota Territory had been creating a government, building homes, and fighting Indians, a steady stream of prospectors and would-be miners had been entering the goldfields in the mountains of western Dakota Territory and eastern Washington Territory. The first gold rush in the region was centered around the upper reaches of the Clearwater River on the western side of the Continental Divide in Washington Territory. The key discoveries were made in the summer and autumn of 1860, with a substantial number of miners entering the area the following year. Across the mountains to the east in Dakota Territory, Granville and James Stuart, pioneers who would help develop the area, were prospecting and found enough gold to build a sluicebox in 1861 on Gold Creek. Other prospectors soon scoured the area and found gold deposits on Grasshopper Creek, a tributary of the Beaverhead River, and founded the mining town of Bannack. Although the influx of people into the area was substantial, the Dakota territorial legislature created neither counties nor voting districts in this region. On March 3, 1863, the area was incorporated into the new Idaho Territory, which included the present-day states of Idaho, Montana, and Wyoming.[26]

In May, 1863, a new gold find was made at Alder Gulch, fifty miles east of Bannack, and the new town of Virginia City was established. These mining camps east of the Continental Divide were far removed from the government located at Lewiston, which was on the western edge of the territory. The difficulties of governing these eastern towns soon became apparent, and many inhabitants began calling for a new territory to be separated from Idaho. Accordingly, they sent a representative to Washington, D.C., to persuade the United States government to organize the desired territory. Their spokesman was Chief Justice Sidney Edgerton of Idaho Territory, and former Ohio congressman, who was living at Bannack. Edgerton encountered much difficulty when he arrived in Washington, D.C., early in 1864, for few people were concerned about the unknown region of the Far West. Instead, the Civil War captured most people's attention. The determined Edgerton resorted to theatrics to attract attention by laying a chunk of gold from Montana on a desk in the House of Representatives. The House of Representatives members and people in the gallery immediately were attracted to the glittering yellow metal Edgerton displayed. Undoubtedly, this incident had positive effects, because the members of the House of Representatives were awakened to the wealth of the area. However, the formation of Montana Territory was much more dependent on the support of important politicians. The Radical Republicans backed the idea, and President Lincoln even saw great prospects for the region when Edgerton showed him some Montana gold. "Talk about bankrupting this country; it can't be done, it can't be done," Lincoln explained. "There is gold enough in the Rocky Mountains to pay off our national debt in three years, if we could get it out."[27] With such support, Montana Territory was created on May 26, 1864, and, quite appropriately, Edgerton became the first governor. The newly appointed executive immediately initiated the necessary prerequisites for the government. He designated Bannack as the temporary capital, supervised a census, then called for an election of a legislative assembly and congressional delegate for the territory.[28]

Subsequent political battles indicated that even remote Montana Territory could not escape the effect of the Civil War. When the citizenry began to think about politics in 1864, there were three major and distinct groups in the territory: some Northern Republicans who were in the minority but were aggressive and active, many Northern Democrats who generally supported the Union cause but antagonized the Republicans, and a large number of former Southern sympathizers who had fled from the war but remained thoroughly Democratic in politics. The pro-Southern group consisted largely of former citizens of border states, particularly Missourians who had previously been associated with Confederate Major General Sterling Price's army. The influence of these recent arrivals was apparent in the names of some of the early settlements such as Confederate Gulch. Originally, Virginia City was named Varina City, after the wife of Jefferson Davis. The Confederate supporters in the territory had an even more important effect, as indicated by Thomas Francis Meagher, later secretary of the territory. Meagher explained: "Governor Edgerton, in the honest and intrepid discharge of his duties, had many embarrassments and vexations to encounter from this element." He complained further: "These sympathizers with the Rebellion acquired not only a strong majority in the territorial legislature, but the mastery, moreover, of the political action of the territory."[29]

Such criticism probably distorted the real situation, for Republicans during this time tended to exaggerate the strength and odious qualities of the Democrats. Even Meagher later changed his interpretation of the circumstances, explaining that much of the Southern element was dutiful and had caused trouble only after harasssment from Republicans in the territory. The *Montana Post,* the only territorial newspaper during the war and strongly Republican, undoubtedly caused much of the ill feelings between the two parties. Particularly during the campaigns of 1864, the newspaper equated Democrats with traitors, and Southern sympathizers were labeled "a breed of two-legged imitations of men."[30] Governor Edgerton added to the attack when he told the settlers at Virginia City that there were only two parties: one for the Union and one against it.[31]

This tactic of emphasizing the disloyalty of Democrats had adverse results, for many voters probably reacted against the Republicans (temporarily renamed the Union Party) and elected a Democratic delegate. On October 24, Samuel McLean, a Pennsylvanian, won this contest over the Union Party nominee, Wilbur Fisk Sanders, nephew of Governor Edgerton. The election of a Democrat-dominated legislature further dismayed Republicans. The *Montana Post* begrudgingly claimed that the Union Party would have won if it had not been for the votes of secessionists who openly claimed to be citizens of Dixie but voted as citizens of Northern states. The newspaper, showing an unbelievable amount of tolerance, later commented on the delegate election, saying, "Colonel McLean is our Territorial Delegate. Let us see what he will do for us and judge him by [his] acts."[32]

The question of loyalty again arose after the legislature of Montana Territory convened on December 10, 1864. Governor Edgerton informed the newly elected legislature that the law required each of them to take an "iron clad" oath of loyalty to the Union and the United States Constitution. With some showing great reluctance, all but one member of the legislature took the

oath. The one exception was John H. Rogers, who had previously fought with the Missouri militia under Major General Sterling Price. Missouri's governor had organized the militia to oppose any force, Union or Confederate, that might try to take control of the state government. When Price decided to join his men with the Confederate Army, Rogers quit and moved west. A phrase in the "iron clad" oath required Rogers to swear that he had never voluntarily taken up arms against the United States. Technically he had; therefore, Rogers declined to take the oath in its original form. The House of Representatives permitted him to take a revised version which excluded the phrase that Rogers refused to accept. Governor Edgerton, nevertheless, would have no communication with the legislature until Rogers took the original oath, which was necessary to properly organize the assembly. Rogers, realizing that no progress could be made otherwise, resigned.[33]

After Rogers ended this controversy, the legislature began its necessary work. As in Dakota, these first legislators found it necessary to lay the groundwork for territorial government and law enforcement. Accordingly, civil and criminal codes were drawn up, corporation charters were issued, water regulation was outlined, and laws on mineral claims were written. One of the most unpopular pieces of legislation was an anti-gambling act, an odious development to many of the hardened card players in this mining frontier. However, a more serious mistake of the first legislature was the failure of its members to complete a plan for creating voting districts. As a result of this neglect, much political haggling and turmoil followed when it was time to seat the second legislature.[34]

Although the problems of government were troublesome to the people of Montana Territory and Dakota

A drawing of Fort Randall, Dakota Territory, on the eve of the Civil War

Territory, they were overshadowed by the more threatening menace of the Sioux Indians in eastern Dakota. The scale of warfare in this frontier region was infinitesimal in comparison to the Civil War that the people of other areas were experiencing; yet the Sioux uprising, which began in 1862, became one of the most deadly in the history of Western expansion.

The difficulties of fighting the Indians were aggravated by insufficient numbers of troops stationed in the region. The United States Army had established four garrisons in the area where the conflict occurred: Fort Abercrombie on the Red River of the North about fifty miles above Lake Traverse, Fort Randall on the Missouri River about forty-five miles west of Yankton, and Fort Ripley and Fort Ridgely located nearby in Minnesota. On January 1, 1861, approximately nine hundred troops in fourteen companies of the regular army were stationed in the four posts. By the summer of 1862, the War Department had gradually withdrawn these troops so that they could be used in more strategic areas. Volunteer units, which were only about two-thirds of the strength of the original forces, replaced the regulars. The majority of the new troops came primarily from Iowa and Minnesota; Dakota Territory initially provided a company of volunteers. On December 7, 1861, Secretary of Dakota Territory John Hutchinson, acting as governor, issued a proclamation calling for enlistments. When doing so, Hutchinson appealed to the patriotism of his fellow citizens saying, "I trust you will take pride in proving to the country that you are ready to do your part in putting down the existing Rebellion by volunteering to guard and defend your own territory."[35]

By January, 1862, the number of recruits was sufficient to organize the first company of Dakotans and begin the necessary training. Officers were commissioned with Nelson Miner as captain. The volunteers reported to Yankton, where some local buildings served as headquarters for Company A. There they drilled and learned the basics of the soldier's life, and a few became indirectly involved in the capital location controversy which came before the territorial legislature. In March 1862, Governor William Jayne ordered that soldiers be sent to the state capital after George M. Pinney had requested that men be stationed there to keep order. Pinney had angered many of his fellow members of the legislature when he changed his position on the capital location — he had initially supported the Yankton site but switched to favor Vermillion. Several of the representatives threatened him, and he responded by asking for troopers to be sent to the House of Representatives. Captain Miner sent Second Lieutenant Frederick Ploghoff with ten men to keep order. No violent confrontation occurred, however, for a majority of the representatives walked out. Eventually, the whole affair resulted in an explanation from Governor Jayne and the replacement of Pinney as speaker. [36]

Although Company A of the Dakota Territorial Volunteer Cavalry Regiment spent its first few months being trained and used as a political pawn, its status soon changed when it was mustered into United States service on April 29, 1862. The company was immediately ordered to Fort Randall, where it remained a short time with three companies of the Fourteenth Iowa Volunteer Infantry Regiment. In July, the Dakotans left Fort Randall and were stationed at the major settlements in the area, including Vermillion, Sioux Falls, and Yankton.[37]

Almost immediately after the troops were dispersed,

Fort Randall, the major military post in Dakota Territory during the Civil War, from a Civil War era photograph.

they were called into action due to the Sioux uprising which began in neighboring Minnesota in August, 1862. Initially, the Santees, who were composed of four major bands of Sioux, rose up in response to their conditions and treatment, starting the war which spread to neighboring tribes in Dakota Territory. The complex reasons for the revolt were typical of the frontier. For sixty years, the Santees had been crowded into continually shrinking reserves and, by 1858, occupied only a 10 by 150 mile ribbon of land along the Minnesota River in southwestern Minnesota. Their white overseers were purposely trying to destroy their culture and way of life. The Sioux were well aware of this and resented the haughty attitude of the whites. Thomas J. Galbraith, the agent for these Indians, and Clark Thompson, the new superintendent of the Northern District, which included several agencies, did not improve the condition or temperament of the Santees. For instance, in 1861 they offered the Indians what appeared to be a bonus to the usual annuities, but turned out to be only an advance on the 1862 annuity. Also Galbraith and Thompson tried to substitute supplies and goods for money when they gave the annuity payments. In 1862, the yearly arrival of provisions was delayed for well over a month, resulting in a small confrontation which almost led to violence. Such frustrating circumstances continually irritated the Santees, and they evidently decided that the agreements of the white men were worthless.[38]

Although the usual frontier attitudes and conditions led the Indians to fight the white men, the far-off Civil War tended to have an indirect effect of encouraging the Indians to make war. Agent Galbraith realized this and reported, "The great rebellion, the war for the Union, has been a fruitful source of trouble among the Sioux, exciting inquiry, restlessness, and uneasiness."[39] He further explained that half-breeds and others told the Indians exaggerated stories. The Indians were informed that the "niggers" would take over, the Indians would get no more money, and the "Great Father" was whipped. Galbraith, perhaps trying to find a scapegoat for his problems, added that although there was no direct interference by Confederate emissaries, he was convinced that "rebel sympathizers did all in their power to create disaffection among the Indians."[40] Stephen R. Riggs, a missionary among the Sioux, did not mention rebel sympathizers but concluded that stories about the war had a profound effect on the Indians. He claimed that the Indians decided the time was opportune to strike when only women, children, and old men remained in the settlements.[41]

The Santees were not the only disgruntled Indians in the American West. The Chippewas and Winnebagos of Minnesota almost joined in the uprising; the Shoshones, Gros Utes, Mandans, Assiniboines, Blackfeet, and Teton Sioux to the west were either fighting or showing signs of belligerency. Some observers believed there was a conspiracy among all of the tribes of the West. Yet it was the Santees who first massacred whites and terrorized pioneers in Minnesota, Dakota and adjacent states and territories.[42]

The war began when a hunting party of Santees, with little provocation, murdered several settlers at Acton, Minnesota, on August 17, 1862. Although not involved in this initial incident, the Sioux leader, Little Crow, and other chiefs realized that white reprisals were likely. In order to gain the advantage, they decided to initiate a preventive war against the whites. Estimates of the deaths of whites range from 300 to 800, yet the troops in Minnesota did the best they could, considering the diminished strength of the garrisons and the suddenness of the attack. Volunteer soldiers who had been stationed in Minnesota were aided by the state militia, which was commanded by Colonel Henry Hastings Sibley, a Minnesota politician who would distinguish himself in the Sioux uprisings. Sibley led a combination of volunteer troops, militia, and armed citizens who began inflicting heavy losses on the belligerent Indians, driving many from the state to join those who had left earlier.[43]

As the Sioux fled into neighboring territories and states, governmental officials began to call for aid in fighting the Indians. Authorities in Iowa, Nebraska Territory, and Dakota Territory telegraphed military officials, describing the vulnerability of the settlements of the area. Secretary of War Edwin M. Stanton quickly responded to the urgent requests of the leaders of the threatened area. In the first week of September, 1862, the War Department created the Department of the Northwest, including the states of Wisconsin, Iowa, Minnesota, and the territories of Nebraska and Dakota. Originally, the region had been under the jurisdiction of the Department of the West, but the new organization was designed to deal with the new situation. Major General John Pope, still embarrassed and confused about his recent defeat in the second battle of Bull Run, was brought from the East and designated as commander of the new department. By mid-September, Pope had taken command and began organizing and planning to defeat the Sioux and any other tribes that might happen to become belligerent.[44]

Pope was pleased with Colonel Sibley's actions. Sibley, by this time, had driven many Indians from the area and was in the process of collecting stragglers and peaceful Indians along the Minnesota River on the Sioux reservation. Little Crow, the major chief in the outbreak, was one of those who had fled with his followers. Other chiefs such as White Lodge, Sleepy Eyes, and Standing Buffalo, also left Minnesota and went into Dakota Territory. On September 23, 1862, about 500 Indians attacked Sibley's force of 1,400 infantrymen camped at Wood Lake in the northeastern end of the reservation. Sibley's men soundly defeated the unwise Sioux, killing approximately thirty and wounding many more, while four soldiers were killed and thirty-five to forty wounded. This victory split the

Sioux into two groups; those wanting war and those wanting peace. The majority of the hostile Santees, however, fled west to the plains of Dakota Territory. At this point, Sibley was made brigadier general, a reward for the dominance which he and his troops had obtained over the Indians in Minnesota.[45]

While Sibley was gaining control over the Sioux in Minnesota, the settlers of Dakota Territory were defending their homes from those Indian war parties that were coming from the east. There was general alarm in Dakota Territory over the Santee uprising in Minnesota, but this alarm changed to terror when a small party of belligerent Santees murdered Judge J. B. Amidon and his son a mile from Sioux Falls on August 25, 1862. Three days later a contingent of Company A of the Dakota Territorial Cavalry Regiment, stationed at the town, escorted its citizens to safety at Yankton. On August 30, after Governor Jayne heard of the murder at Sioux Falls, he issued a proclamation ordering the formation of citizens' militias throughout the various communities of the territory to be composed of every male from eighteen to fifty years of age. Then he organized a staff headed by Charles P. Booge, who was designated Adjutant-General. Many inhabitants of the major settlements responded and formed the necessary defense groups. Others fled from the area, leaving their crops in the fields, going to the more secure town of Sioux City, Iowa. Their fear was justified because renegade Sioux continued to commit depredations against whites. They waylaid and robbed a mail carrier on the Sioux Falls to Yankton road, killed a stage driver and took his horses near Fort Randall, and attacked farmers and burned their homes throughout the area.[46]

The belligerent activities of the Sioux kept the troops in Dakota on constant alert, and Company A of the Dakota Territorial Cavalry Regiment played a major role in protecting the settlers of the region. In early September, 1862, a small group of the cavalry led by Sergeant Abner M. English camped at the James River near Yankton. They encountered a small party of Sioux; and English, with seven men, pursued them as the Indians attacked a number of settlers along the way. Finally, catching the warriors near a slough, the soldiers killed one of them, yet sustained no casualties in the skirmish. The troopers returned to their friends in camp, gathered their gear, and moved to Yankton. There they alerted the citizens to the menace of marauding parties of Indians, for they had seen evidence of even more hostilities in the area. Captain Nelson Miner, having been informed of the problem, hurried from Vermillion with about forty members of Company A of the Dakota Territorial Cavalry Regiment and joined English at Yankton. It soon became apparent that the main forces of the Sioux were far to the north; the people gradually overcame their initial fright and many returned to their abandoned homes. In late November, 1862, Captain Miner escorted a group of former residents of Sioux Falls back to their homes.

They had buried some of their valuables and were returning to uncover them. As they retrieved their belongings, a small party of forty Sioux was seen in the area. Captain Miner chased and soundly defeated these Indians, who had earlier taken part in the Minnesota raids.[47]

Operations continued in Dakota Territory against the Sioux. Captain John Pattee unsuccessfully led members of the Fourteenth Iowa Volunteer Infantry Regiment and the Dakota Territorial Cavalry Regiment up the Missouri River in search of Santees. At Fort Pierre, Pattee learned that the Indians had moved to avoid his troops. Leaving a group of men at Fort Pierre, he returned to Fort Randall for winter quarters. The frontier remained relatively quiet through the winter except for the complaints raised by government officials who continually wrote to Washington warning that the Indians were planning a spring offensive. In December, 1862, Dakota authorities wrote Lincoln expressing concern that from 500 to 1,000 Sioux were on the Missouri River and would certainly be a threat in the spring. The citizens of Minnesota also believed that the Santees might return.[48]

Accordingly, Major General Pope began planning for a campaign against the belligerent Sioux in Dakota Territory. At first, he wanted to send three columns to intercept the Indians, but later decided that only two forces would be sent in an attempt to catch the Sioux between them. One contingent, headed by Brigadier General Sibley, would travel from a point near Fort Ridgely, Minnesota, northwest to Devil's Lake in Dakota Territory. The other force, ultimately led by Brigadier General Alfred Sully, would go from Sioux City and Fort Randall up the Missouri River to Fort Pierre and then across to Devil's Lake. The departure date for each column was to be July 1, 1863; however, both Sully and Sibley were more than two weeks late in leaving. Sully's tardiness was due to the low water level of the Missouri River, for he relied on steamboats to carry his supplies. Sibley had little or no excuse for being late.[49]

The strength of Sibley's column totaled approximately 2,800 men, whereas an equal number was left behind to protect the frontier settlements in Minnesota. The expedition traveled for more than a month before contacting the Indians. The dry summer heat on the dusty prairie baked the soldiers as they marched toward the northwest from Camp Pope on the Minnesota River, past Lake Traverse, and twice across the bending Cheyenne River. On July 17, 1863, the parched group stopped just southeast of Devil's Lake at a brackish pond. Establishing Camp Atchison here, the main column soon left on July 20, leaving behind the supply train and a group of 300 guards. The major force continued at a rapid pace, sending a substantial contingent which branched off to scour the area around Devil's Lake. However, few Indians were encountered for several days.[50]

On July 24, Sibley fought the first of three battles during the campaign. On that day some of his scouts reported a large body of Indians nearby. The soldiers immediately entrenched as Indians began arriving and circling the camp. These Sioux, numbering 1,000 to 1,500 evidently were confident they could fight Sibley's men. The hostiles included some of the bands from Minnesota as well as related Sioux from the immediate vicinity. Once the conflict began, the troops soon gained superior position because of a very useful six-pounder which quickly unleashed deadly shot at the surrounding hills, one of which was called Big Mound. By the end of the day, the Battle of Big Mound ended.[51]

This initial engagement was followed on July 26, 1863, by the Battle of Dead Buffalo Lake, which was not contested by the Indians because of the effectiveness of the cannon which kept them at a distance. The final battle occurred near Stony Lake on July 28. The expedition had followed the Sioux further west to Stony Lake, where the Indians attempted to attack the wagons. In this instance, 2,300 Sioux, according to Sibley, battled more desperately than before because their families were nearby. The troopers claimed they killed and wounded about 150 Sioux whereas Sibley's soldiers suffered only seven casualties. The next two days were spent chasing the Indians across the Missouri River. Sibley thought Sully should be in the area and tried to attract his attention, but to no avail. On August 1, Sibley began the return trip home, sending out small patrols along the way. The bulk of his forces arrived at Fort Snelling on September 12.[52]

While Sibley had hurried to meet the Indians, fought several skirmishes, and returned home, Brigadier General Sully slowly struggled northward along the Missouri River. Sully had left Sioux City, Iowa, with his initial force and gathered more men upriver at Fort Randall. His total expedition included about 1,900 men composed of the Sixth Iowa Volunteer Cavalry Regiment, eight companies of the Second Nebraska Cavalry Regiment, one company of the Seventh Iowa Cavalry Regiment, and a battery of four guns. Approximately 550 men from Iowa, Wisconsin, Nebraska, and Dakota, remained behind or dropped off along the route. The summer of 1863 was extremely dry, causing Sully to slow down along the way due to the scarcity of grass. Also, steamboats were carrying supplies for Sully at a very slow pace due to the extremely low level of the river. The column was so delayed that he only reached Fort Pierre on July 25, the date he was to have met Sibley and well over 200 miles away from the originally proposed destination of Devil's Lake.[53]

Sully soon ordered his men out of Fort Pierre and established Camp Peoria nearby. The soldiers waited patiently for the tardy steamboats to arrive, but General Pope became uneasy and irritated at the delay. As July became August, Pope's patience ended and he twice sent dispatches to Sully berating him for his dependence on the steamboats. With this pressure from his superior, on August 21, Sully finally broke camp and continued, almost a month after Sibley had completed his activities.[54]

As Sully's forces traveled northward, patrols scoured the surrounding terrain in search of hostile Sioux. These scouting parties brought in captive stragglers who informed the soldiers that Sibley had recently been through the area. Some of Sully's guides discovered the trail and ashes of the campfires of Sibley's expedition. They also recommended to Sully that he lead his column to an area near the tributaries of the James River where Indians customarily camped due to plentiful buffalo in the region. Sully followed this advice, and on September 3, an advance guard of 300 men led by Major Albert E. House stumbled across a huge village of over 400 Sioux lodges which included about 950 warriors. The alarmed Indians, not realizing that the main group of cavalry was nearby, surrounded House's men and waited patiently for an easy victory. A scout managed to escape to Sully and warn of the approaching calamity for House's soldiers. Sully responded quickly, arriving at the Indian village with four companies within an hour. In the ensuing hour-long Battle of White Stone Hill, 300 braves were killed; 250, mostly women and children, were captured, and over 400,000 pounds of dried buffalo meat destroyed. Sully's casualties were seventeen killed and thirty-eight wounded.[55]

Sully soon returned south with his forces, arriving at Camp Peoria on September 11. A short distance to the south his men constructed a new fort, beginning on September 14 and ending on October 13. Designed to deter Indian uprisings, the new post was immediately labeled "Fort Sully" to compliment the brigadier general. Sully also received another laurel from Pope, who praised him for his victory at White Stone Hill, saying, "I bear willing testimony to the distinguished conduct you have rendered to the Government....To yourself and your command, I tender my thanks and congratulations."[56] Such honors did Sully savor as he returned to Sioux City on November 14, 1863.

While the campaigns were being carried out in the north, the Dakota Territorial Cavalry Regiment remained behind, most of the men stationed at Fort Randall. The men shared quarters with soldiers from Iowa, Wisconsin, and Nebraska. These troops were on constant patrol chasing small groups of hostile Sioux who continued to raid on the fringe of frontier settlement. About forty men of Company A led by Captain Miner were stationed at newly erected Fort Thompson on the Crow Creek Reservation north of Fort Randall. The reservation eventually housed some 3,000 Sioux and Winnebagos who had been removed from Minnesota following the uprising. Captain Miner patrolled the region with much difficulty, for several hostile Sioux bands had surrounded the Crow Creek Reservation and continually harassed other Indians settled there. This difficult assignment would not end until October, when troops from Fort Sully would relieve Miner and his men. In the spring of 1864, Minor and the entire Dakota Territorial Cavalry Regiment would return to the Crow Creek Reservation to guard the discontented Indians.[57]

Although the Dakota Territorial Cavalry Regiment boldly defended the frontier and Sibley and Sully campaigned against the Indians in a ferocious manner, it was soon evident that more effort was needed to subdue the Sioux. As early as October, 1863, even civilians were claiming that the hostiles had not been totally defeated. The *Dakotian* claimed that harsh treatment was needed to subjugate the Sioux. ''The Sioux Nation is still hostile,'' the newspaper reported, ''and until every nose on each of its many heads is tweaked, and they bear the humiliation without a murmur, we shall not admit that the Indian war is ended.'' Because of sporadic Indian raids in both Minnesota and Dakota in the following winter and spring, many people agreed with this assessment. Accordingly, Major General Pope planned a new expedition which would have the dual purpose of routing the Indians and establishing military posts for future protection. The plan for this 1864 campaign was similar to the expeditions of the previous year. One contingent, ultimately led by Colonel Minor T. Thomas, would travel west from Minnesota and rendezvous with Sully's forces, which would have come up from Sioux City, Fort Randall, and Fort Sully. As it turned out, the meeting point would be Swan Lake Creek, about 100 miles north of Fort Sully.[58]

One June 6, Colonel Thomas proceeded from Camp Pope, Minnesota, with 1,600 men, including the Eighth Minnesota Volunteer Infantry Regiment, several companies of the Second Minnesota Volunteer Cavalry Regiment, part of the Third Minnesota Battery, and forty-five scouts. Also included with Thomas' group was an emigrant train of about 140 wagons headed for the gold fields of Montana. This column continued across the plains toward the Missouri River. Meanwhile, Sully hastily grouped his men at Fort Sully, a force consisting of troops from Iowa and Nebraska, and the Dakota Territorial Cavalry Regiment. Departing from Fort Sully on June 26, the men of the Dakota Territorial Cavalry Regiment were particularly anxious to see action because they had not previously been on a major campaign. On June 30, Sully's forces reached Swan Lake Creek, where Colonel Thomas' men joined them on the following day. From there the unified force went north to Fort Rice, which was newly erected. Surprisingly, the steamers accompanying Sully's troops did not lag behind, allowing the campaign to continue on schedule.[59]

After resting for several days, the expedition, along with the wagon train, left Fort Rice, ascending the Cannonball River in search of renegade Sioux. After futilely following that river, the entire force moved northward to the Heart River. On July 24, Sully learned that a large number of Sioux were encamped at Killdeer Mountain, several miles to the north of Heart River. Upon learning this, he left behind the emigrant train and the bulk of supplies to pursue the deceptive Indians. On July 28, the soldiers reached Killdeer Mountain, a system of high hills, ridges, and buttes cut by wooded ravines, where the Battle of Killdeer Mountain was fought. The Sioux warriors numbered approximately 1,600, of which about 100 were casualties. Sully listed five soldiers killed and ten wounded. By July 30, the troops had returned to the supply and emigrant wagons.[60]

After this battle, the expedition continued westward, etching its way across the treacherous Badlands, a task made necessary to reach supply steamers on the Yellowstone River. Struggling, the expedition met the boats on August 12 and resupplied. Then Sully led his men down the Yellowstone River and the Missouri River to Fort Rice. Originally, the plan was to seek out the Indians in the region, but the extremely dry conditions and scarcity of grass, due to a grasshopper plague, forced the expedition to curtail its activities.[61]

However, once back at Fort Rice on September 8, the disgruntled Sully learned that Captain James L. Fisk had led an emigrant train to the West en route to the gold fields of Montana and Idaho. This was the third of four trips that the stubborn Fisk would make. Against the advice of military officials, he continued his trek westward from Fort Rice, accompanied by a convoy of fifty men provided against orders by Colonel Daniel J. Dill. Fisk soon found himself surrounded by 300 Indians 160 miles west of Fort Rice. On September 10, Sully sent 900 men to the aid of the emigrants, and they were returned to safety on September 30.[62]

With the termination of this final major campaign, the Indians were generally ineffective except in small raiding groups. As the Civil War concluded, civilian pressure mounted to end the conflict by an official peace treaty. However, sporadic hostilities continued past the Civil War, and the treaties of peace in 1865 would prove futile. Major Sioux wars followed in quick succession.

During the Civil War, Indian activity in Wyoming and Montana was slight in comparison with other sections of Dakota Territory. Perhaps the activities of the Sioux incited the Shoshone, Bannock, and other warriors to continually attack wagon trains on such main emigrant roads as the Oregon Trail and the Bozeman Trail. Periodic raids and horse thievery caused alarm among the settlers of Montana, but these actions were limited when compared to the major hostilities to the east in the Missouri River Valley region of Dakota Territory. Nevertheless, in 1865 the Cheyenne, Arapaho, and Sioux tribes of the area were restless over the Sand Creek Massacre, and the Powder River expedition in Wyoming was being planned as the war ended.[63]

The nearby Indian uprisings and the distant Civil War had disastrous effects on the economy of Dakota

Territory and its offspring, Montana Territory. As the war progressed, the editor of the *Dakotian* recognized the difficulties encountered because of the Civil War: "In such a crisis, the territories were the first to suffer in as much as they are the children of the Government, fed and nurtured by Congress....Dakota above all others was left in a discouraging situation."[64] The territory was thus ignored and left to fend for itself. Later, in 1864, Governor Newton Edmunds of Dakota Territory would comment similarly about the Indian uprisings, indicating that it had retarded the development to an extent never before experienced by the other Northwestern territories. The attention diverted by the Civil War had caused the developing but harassed territory to be somewhat ignored.[65]

Perhaps the difficulties confronted by Dakota Territory farmers would have been less severe had Congress been more responsive. Agriculture in Dakota Territory seemed jinxed during the Civil War. Just before the war, prospects were favorable, however. In 1860, agricultural statistics indicated over 26,000 acres of farmland in the territory, producing corn, oats, potatoes, wheat, rye, peas, beans, and a variety of livestock. In 1861, even after the Civil War began, Dakotans were hopeful concerning growth and talked of the great opportunities for immigrants. Grain and livestock were particularly emphasized as being possible lucrative enterprises. The plentiful harvests being grown seemed to prove what the proud residents of Dakota Territory were saying, and the season of 1861 was marred only by prairie fires in the fall of the year.[66]

In the early summer of 1862, optimism grew in Dakota Territory. The mines in its extreme western reaches were proving prosperous; therefore, the gold bearing regions would provide customers for the crops grown in eastern Dakota Territory. Also, the Homestead Act had been passed in May, 1862, giving promise that the territory's population would grow. The *Dakotian* proclaimed, "We hail it as the forerunner of our prosperity."[67] In August, 1862, the hostile Sioux quickly annihilated the elated spirits of the Dakotans as well as some of their lives. The resulting depopulation of virtually all settlements except Yankton caused the harvest of that year to be much less than expected. Many persistent farmers who returned when the raids subsided found their farms plundered by Indians, ruined by neglect, or mutilated by roaming cattle.[68]

In the two years following 1862, nature became an ally of the Sioux, who continued periodic depredations on the frontier. The drought of 1863 became one of the most severe on record, and few crops survived. In 1864, the drought continued but was finally ended in late June, in time to revive the grains and vegetables. Yet, the Dakotans were to endure another hardship — a grasshopper invasion. Similar to other such occurrences, the grasshoppers, which came from the north in an army of millions, devoured virtually every living plant in their path. So complete was the devastation, the settlers had to depend on crops from Iowa and Minnesota for the winter. Only in 1865, after the Civil War had ended, did Dakota Territory see an end to its agricultural trials. In that year crops were abundant.[69]

Neither the devastation of agriculture in Dakota Territory nor the problems of the Civil War kept new settlers from entering its boundaries. In 1863, the newly organized Free Homestead Association of Central New York, located in Syracuse, determined to find a suitable area for its members to settle. The group, composed of farmers and mechanics, sent James S. Foster as their representative to find a suitable place in the West. He chose the Missouri River area of southeastern Dakota. By May, 1863, a caravan of about fifty families arrived in Dakota Territory, enheartening the older residents during this period of dejection.[70]

While the residents of eastern Dakota Territory were struggling to survive, the miners of the Montana area were struggling to find gold. The economy of this mining region was similar to other gold fields throughout the West. The boom-bust cycle of the communities was a prominent pattern. Probably the most vexing problems were the shortage of goods and inadequate transportation to the distant states in the East. One of the most important commodities which became alarmingly scarce during the war was flour. The roads throughout the mining region of the Montana area were blocked by severe weather during the winter of 1864-1865. The already precious and costly flour soared to over $40 a sack in the Alder Gulch mining area. This situation led to incidents in April, 1865, in which miners forced their way into stores at the towns of Nevada and Virginia City, taking the flour they needed.[71]

With transportation constantly a problem, those interested in traveling to the mining fields of the Dakota Territory region found new routes. Before the gold discoveries, a few roads had been opened into the area. After the development of the mines, new routes were mapped out, such as Captain James Fisk's route opened in 1862 through northern Dakota and Montana. Fisk led four wagon trains destined for Montana, three of which were sanctioned and protected by the United States government. Probably the most famous road was the Bozeman Trail, opened in 1863 and destined to be plagued by Indian attacks. Also, the residents of southeastern Dakota Territory continually memorialized and pressured Congress to open the Niobrara-Virginia City Trail, this being done in 1865. The road originated in the area of the counties along the Missouri River in Dakota Territory and was designed to attract customers for merchants in the region.[72]

Probably the most important means of transportation was by steamboat. The season for journeys up the Missouri River was extremely short, thus limiting severely the activities of the steamers. During the Indian uprising, several tribes attacked the boats from time to time, increasing the hazards of excursions up the river. Downstream both Confederate and Union soldiers commandeered boats for use. Nevertheless, navigation on the Missouri River was substantial during the Civil War years due to the lure of the gold fields. Between 1861 and 1865, over 100 steamers ascended the Missouri River into Dakota Territory.[73]

The Civil War affected Dakota Territory society much less than the economy. Various diversions and entertainments were typical of the frontier communities composing the area. In the settlements on the Missouri River in southeastern Dakota, the arrival of river boats often caused great excitement because they brought people and products from the outside world. In Yankton, the first social party was held on a steamer in 1860. With increasing numbers of settlers came the rudiments of society, as was customary in more populous centers. Various groups were formed to break the doldrums of frontier life. The Ladies Pioneer Sociable was such an organization, established in 1863, to provide suitable entertainment for women. Various dances held at special times of the year, such as the annual Christmas and New Year's balls, also aided the spirits of the early settlers. Of a scholarly nature were the local historical societies which eventually developed into the Dakota Territorial Historical Society, incorporated in December, 1863.[74]

The pioneers of Dakota Territory were also greatly concerned about education. The first primary school in Yankton opened in June of 1862. When this occurred, the *Dakotian* called for an awareness of education: "We trust our citizens and farmers living in this vicinity are sufficiently alive to the importance of educating their children." One of the first acts of the territorial assembly also illustrates a desire to provide education. On April 21, 1862, a bill was signed designating Vermillion as the site of the future territorial university.

The most prominent and active minister of these early years was Dr. Melancthon Hoyt. This Episcopalian pastor was originally in Sioux City, Iowa, before moving to Dakota Territory in 1862. From that point, he was the only religious leader for several communities and served as chaplain in the territorial assembly. He aided in establishing several Episcopal churches in the territory.[75]

The cultural and social life of the miners in the Montana area was very similar to that in Dakota Territory, the principal difference being the typical restlessness found in mining boom towns. Probably the most popular attractions were the fist fights between professionals who took advantage of the miners' hunger for such events. In January, 1865, the great fight between John C. Orem of Ohio and Hugh O'Neil of Ireland lasted 185 rounds and ended in a draw — all bets off. The coverage of this spectacle took up the entire front page of the *Montana Post*. Less violent activities and organizations were also found in the mining fields. The newly organized debating society at Biven's Gulch discussed a timely topic at its first meeting in December, 1864. It is not surprising that lonely miners would debate: "Resolved: That the Love of Woman has more influence on the mind of man than the love of gold."[76]

One effect of the Civil War on society in Dakota Territory was the suspicion aroused concerning loyalty to the Union. But such things were trivial. The war period proved to be a very crucial time for Dakota Territory and the related territory of Montana. The country as a whole gave much less attention to the activities and problems of the territories. This resulted in the intensification of major crises and the exaggeration of minor difficulties in the territories.

The political issues of Dakota Territory were influenced greatly by the relationships that Jayne and Todd had with President Lincoln, with each man claiming that his ties were the strongest. Yet the strong association with the chief executive was not peculiar to the Civil War. The officials and issues discussed and debated in all territories were always affected by the United States government which controlled them. Nevertheless, many of the basic political questions which arose during the Civil War period were also a part of political reality in Dakota Territory. The controversies over slavery in the legislature of Dakota Territory and the "Bloody Shirt" accusations in Montana Territory were microcosms of national Civil War issues. Along with these major facets of politics were campaigns with emphasis on personalities and the conflicts over the capitol location — both typical of the frontier.

The most devastating aspect of the Civil War in Dakota Territory was the indirect effect it had on the Indian uprisings. Initially, some of the major Indian leaders of the outbreaks had heard rumors that the Confederates were defeating Union forces. The instigators of the hostilites also must have been aware of the decreased number of troops stationed on the frontier. The Civil War had drawn these away to more crucial areas, leaving a large region virtually unprotected. Once the United States government responded to the situation, the number of soldiers in Dakota Territory and adjacent Minnesota Territory was much larger than ever before. Dakota Territory was not neglected except at the beginning of the Civil War. Perhaps because the war had already provided practice in recruiting and organizing troops, the soldiers who responded to the Sioux attacks may have been assembled more quickly than under other circumstances.

The Sully and Sibley campaigns did not complete their objectives of totally defeating the Sioux, yet neither would several larger expeditions attempting to bring them under control in subsequent years. In addition, the Sibley and Sully groups provided experience and lessons that were helpful later in fighting the Indians of the Northern plains. The Dakota Territorial Cavalry Regiment, an important part of the strategy in these campaigns, was small yet necessary. In 1863, the Dakotans constituted almost one fourth of the troops being used in the territory. The following year, Dakota territorial soldiers played significant roles as scouts and fighters in the Sully campaign. Thus, Dakotans supplied their share of manpower.

Economically, Dakota Territory was a catastrophe during the Civil War. The Indian uprisings caused a depopulation and slowed growth until after the Civil War. Indians and nature destroyed most of the crops, particularly during 1862, 1863, and 1864. Agriculture probably suffered more than during any other period.

Conversely, the economy in Montana Territory thrived much like any other mining area, with the main problem being inadequate transportation facilities. Despite all of the economic and political upheavals, the societies in both Montana Territory and Dakota Territory were typical of the frontier, showing little difference from peacetime.

NOTES

1. United States Department of War, *The War of the Rebellion: A Compilation of the Official Records of the Union and Confederate Armies* (70 vols., 128 books, Washington: Government Printing Office, 1880-1901), Ser. I, Vol. XIII, p. 613.
2. Moses K. Armstrong, "History and Resources of Dakota, Montana, and Idaho," *South Dakota Historical Collections,* Vol. XIV (1928), pp. 38, 44.
3. *Ibid.,* pp. 56-58; *Eighth Census of the United States, 1860* (4 vols., Washington: Government Printing Office, 1864-1865), Vol. I, p. 552; Armstrong, "History and Resources of Dakota, Montana, and Idaho," *South Dakota Historical Collections,* Vol. XIV, pp. 17, 62; *Ninth Census of the United States, 1870* (5 vols., Washington: Government Printing Office, 1872), Vol. I, p. 17.
4. Clement A. Lounsberry, *Early History of North Dakota* (Washington: F. H. Lounsberry, 1913), p. 40; Howard R. Lamar, *Dakota Territory, 1861-1889: A Study of Frontier Politics* (New Haven: Yale University Press, 1956), pp. 52-53.
5. Norman Thomas, "John Blair Smith Todd," *South Dakota Historical Collections,* Vol. XXIV (1949), pp. 178-181.
6. *Ibid.,* pp. 182-187; Herbert S. Schell, *Dakota Territory During the Eighteen Sixties* (Vermillion: Governmental Research Bureau, 1954), pp. 5-8.
7. Lamar, *op. cit.;* pp. 47-50, 55, 44, 65-66; Schell, *op. cit.,* pp. 10-15; *Congressional Globe,* 36th Congress, 2nd Session, p. 1362.
8. Lamar, *op. cit.,* pp. 67-71; Memorandum on Appointments to Territories, March 20, 1861, Roy P. Basler, ed., *The Collected Works of Abraham Lincoln* (9 vols., New Brunswick: Rutgers University Press, 1953-1955), Vol. IV, p. 294.
9. Thomas, *op. cit.,* p. 190; William Jayne to William Seward, May 30, 1861, Dakota Series, United States Department of State Territorial Papers, National Archives, Washington, D. C.; George W. Kingsbury, *The History of Dakota Territory* (2 vols., Chicago: S. J. Clarke Publishing Company, 1915), Vol. I, pp. 176-180; Proclamation by Governor William Jayne Announcing the Territorial Election, July 29, 1861, Dakota Series, United States Department of State Territorial Papers, National Archives.
10. Lamar, *op. cit.,* pp. 94-95, 97; *Dakotian* (Yankton, Dakota Territory), June 6, 1861, p. 2.
11. *Dakotian,* June 20, 1861, p. 2.
12. Kingsbury, *op. cit.,* pp. 184-185; Lamar, *op. cit.,* pp. 74-76; *Dakotian,* July 20, 1861, p. 2., June 27, 1861, p. 2.
13. Lamar, *op. cit.,* p. 75.
14. Thomas, *op. cit.,* pp. 193-194; *Congressional Globe,* 37th Congress, 2nd Session, pp. 32, 1042; *ibid.,* 3rd Session, p. 164.
15. Schell, *op. cit.,* pp. 62, 65, 71; Lamar, *op. cit.,* pp. 76-77, 84-86; Moses K. Armstrong, *The Early Empire Builders of the Great West* (St. Paul: E. W. Porter, 1901), p. 64.
16. Vincent G. Tegeder, "Lincoln and the Territorial Patronage: The Ascendancy of Radicals in the West," *Mississippi Valley Historical Review,* Vol. XXXV, No. 1 (June, 1948), pp. 79-80; Address of Governor William Jayne to the First Legislature, March 17, 1862, Dakota Series, United States Department of State Territorial Papers, National Archives; Armstrong, *The Early Empire Builders of the Great West,* p. 69.
17. Lamar, *op. cit.,* pp. 86-87.
18. Kingsbury, *op. cit.,* pp. 268, 328-329; Schell, *op. cit.,* p. 65; Lamar, *op. cit.,* p. 93.
19. *Ibid.,* p. 90
20. Thomas, *op cit.,* pp. 196-199; *Dakotian,* July 22, 1862, p. 2; Kingsbury, *op. cit.,* p. 217.
21. *Ibid.,* pp. 230-232; Schell, *op. cit.,* pp. 77-78; *Senate Document No. 27,* 38th Congress, 1st Session, pp. 1-3; *Congressional Globe,* 38th Congress, 1st Session, pp. 2893-2894.
22. Lamar, *op. cit.,* pp. 92-93.
23. Tegeder, *op. cit.,* pp. 80-81; Kingsbury, *op. cit.,* pp. 368-379.
24. *Dakotian,* September 29, 1863, p. 2
25. Armstrong, *The Early Empire Builders of the Great West,* pp. 71-72.
26. James McClellan Hamilton, *From Wilderness to Statehood: A History of Montana, 1805-1900* (Portland: Binfords and Mort, 1957), pp. 214-219, 273.
27. *Ibid.,* pp. 275-277; Sidney Edgerton to William H. Hunt, May 23, 1892, *Montana Magazine of History,* Vol. I, No. 4 (October, 1951), pp. 43-45.
28. *Congressional Globe,* 38th Congress, 1st Session, p. 2510; Hamilton, *op. cit.,* p. 279.
29. Merrill G. Burlingame and K. Ross Toole, *A History of Montana* (3 vols., New York: Lewis Historical Publishing Company, 1957), Vol. I, p. 219; Stanley R. Davison and Dale Tash, "Confederate Backwash in Montana Territory," *Montana: The Magazine of Western History,* Vol. XVII, No. 4 (October, 1967), p. 52; Joseph Kinsey Howard, *Montana: High, Wide, and Handsome* (New Haven: Yale University Press, 1943), pp. 38-39; Francis Meager to William Seward, December 11, 1865, Montana Series, United States Department of State Territorial Papers, National Archives.
30. Francis Meager to William Seward, February 20, 1866, Montana Series, United States Department of State Territorial Papers, National Archives; Robert G. Athearn, "Civil War Days in Montana," *Pacific Historical Review,* Vol. XXIX, No. 1 (February, 1960), p. 21; *Montana Post* (Virginia City, Montana Territory), September 24, 1864, p. 4, October 8, 1864, p. 2.
31. Athearn, *op. cit.,* p. 21.
32. *Ibid.,* p. 22; *Montana Post,* November 6, 1864, p. 2, November 19, 1864, p. 2.
33. Athearn, *op. cit.,* pp. 22-23; *Montana Post,* December 24, 1864, p. 2, January 7, 1865, p. 3.
34. Robert L. Housman, "The First Territorial Legislature in Montana," *Pacific Historical Review,* Vol. IV, No. 4 (December, 1935), pp. 377-378; Hamilton, *op. cit.,* pp. 281-282, 285; Athearn, *op. cit.,* pp. 23-24.
35. Robert H. Jones, *The Civil War in the Northwest: Nebraska, Wisconsin, Iowa, Minnesota, and the Dakotas* (Norman: University of Oklahoma Press, 1960), pp. 24, 25, 27; Proclamation of Acting-Governor John Hutchinson, December 7, 1861, Montana Series, United States Department of State Territorial Papers, National Archives.
36. Abner M. English, "Dakota's First Soldiers," *South Dakota Historical Collections,* Vol. IX (1918), pp. 242-245; William Jayne to Moses K. Armstrong, John McBride, and Bligh E. Wood, April 11, 1862, Dakota Series, United States Department of State Territorial Papers, National Archives.
37. English, *op. cit.,* p. 243; Jones, *op. cit.,* p. 25; *Senate Miscellaneous Document No. 241,* 58th Congress, 2nd Session, p. 10
38. Jones, *op. cit.,* pp. 16-21.
39. *House Executive Document No. 68,* 37th Congress, 3rd Session, p. 29.
40. *Ibid.*
41. Stephen R. Riggs, *The Gospel Among the Dakotas* (New York: Arno Press, 1972), pp. 330-331.
42. Jones, *op. cit.,* pp. 22-23.
43. *Ibid.* p. 23-24, 28, 34.
44. *Official Records,* Ser. I, Vol. XIII, p. 618; Jones, *op. cit.,* pp. 30, 12, 45.
45. *Ibid.,* pp. 51-52, 46-48; *Official Records,* Ser. I, Vol. XII, p. 234.
46. Schell, *op. cit.,* pp. 47-48; *Dakotian,* September 15, 1862, p. 1; *Senate Miscellaneous Document No. 241,* 58th Congress, 2nd Session, pp. 1, 82.
47. English, *op. cit.,* pp. 245-249; *Dakotian,* September 15, 1862, p. 1; English, *op. cit.,* pp. 253-255.
48. *Ibid.,* pp. 260-263; *Official Records,* Ser. I, Vol. XXII, Pt. I, p. 867.
49. *Official Records,* Ser. I, Vol. XXII, Pt. 2, pp. 116-117, 186; Jones, *op. cit.,* pp. 60-63.
50. *Official Records,* Ser. I, Vol. XXII, Pt. 2, pp. 352-353, 358-360; Jones, *op. cit.,* pp. 63-64.

51. *Official Records*, Ser. I, Vol. XXII, Pt. 1, pp. 353-354; Doane Robinson, *A History of the Dakota or Sioux Indians* (Minneapolis: Ross and Haines, 1956), pp. 318-322.

52. *Official Records*, Ser. I, Vol. XXII, Pt. 1, pp. 354-356; Robinson, *op. cit.*, pp. 322-325.

53. *Official Records*, Ser. I, Vol. XXII, Pt. 2, p. 349; *ibid.*, Ser. I, Vol. XXII, Pt. 1, pp. 555-568; Geraldine Bean, "General Alfred Sully and the Northwest Indian Expedition," *North Dakota History*, Vol. XXXIII, No. 2 (Summer, 1966), pp. 250-252.

54. *Ibid.*, p. 251-252; *Official Records*, Ser. I, Vol. XXII, Pt. 2, pp. 484, 496-497; Jones, *op. cit.*, p. 68.

55. *Official Records*, Ser. I, Vol. XXII, Pt. 1, pp. 555-561; Robinson, *op. cit.*, pp. 326-328; Bean, *op. cit.*, pp. 253-254.

56. Jones, *op. cit.*, p. 69; Steven Hoekman, "The History of Fort Sully," *South Dakota Historical Collections*, Vol. XXVI (1952), pp. 230-231; *Official Records*, Ser. I, Vol. XXII, Pt. 1, p. 608.

57. English, *op. cit.*, pp. 264-279; Edmund J. Danziger, "The Crow Creek Experiment: An Aftermath of the Sioux War of 1862," *North Dakota History*, Vol. XXXVII, No. 1 (Spring, 1970), pp. 106, 113; English, *op. cit.*, p. 270.

58. *Dakotian*, October 13, 1863, p. 2; Jones, *op. cit.*, pp. 79-80, 82, 85.

59. *Official Records*, Ser. I, Vol. XXXIV, Pt. 4, p. 288; English, *op. cit.*, pp. 273, 279; Jones, *op. cit.*, pp. 83-85.

60. *Official Records*, Ser. I, Vol. XLI, Pt. 1, pp. 141-144; Robinson, *op. cit.*, pp. 331-334; Jones, *op. cit.* pp. 85-87.

61. *Ibid.*, pp. 87-90.

62. "Expeditions of Captain James L. Fisk to the Gold Mines of Idaho and Montana, 1864-1866," *Collections of the Historical Society of North Dakota*, Vol. II (1907, pp. 424-429; Jones, *op. cit.*, pp. 90-91.

63. *Montana Post*, September 10, 1864, p. 1, October 1, 1864, p. 1.

64. *Dakotian*, July 7, 1863, p. 2.

65. Second Annual Message of Governor Newton Edmunds, December, 1864, Dakota Series, United States Department of State Territorial Papers, National Archives.

66. *Eighth Census of the United States, 1860*, Vol. II, p. 170; *Dakotian*, June 20, 1861, p. 2, July 6, 1861, p. 2; Schell, *op. cit.*, p. 32.

67. *Dakotian*, June 10, 1862, pp. 1-2, June 24, 1862, p. 2.

68. Schell, *op. cit.*, p. 32.

69. *Ibid.* p. 33; *Dakota Union* (Yankton, Dakota Territory), July 5, 1864, p. 2; Harold E. Briggs, "Grasshopper Plagues and Early Dakota Agriculture, 1864-1876," *Agricultural History*, Vol. VIII, No. 1 (April, 1934), pp. 51-53; *Dakota Union*,

August 2, 1864, p. 2.

70. James S. Foster, "Outline of History of the Territory of Dakota and Emigrant's Guide," *South Dakota Historical Collections*, Vol. XIV (1928), pp. 89-92; Kingsbury, *op. cit.*, 331-335; *Dakotian*, May 31, 1864, p. 1.

71. Hamilton, *op. cit.*, pp. 211-225; Dorothy M. Johnson, "Flour Famine in Alder Gulch, 1864," *Montana: The Magazine of Western History*, Vol. VII, No. 1 (January, 1957), pp. 18-27; *Montana Post*, April 22, 1865, pp. 1-2.

72. Hamilton, *op. cit.*, pp. 131-176; *House Executive Document No. 58*, 39th Congress, 1st Session, pp. 1-30.

73. Hamilton, *op. cit.*, pp. 144-148; Armstrong, "History and Resources of Dakota, Montana and Idaho," *South Dakota Historical Collections*, Vol. XIV, p. 59.

74. Schell, *op. cit.*, p. 30; *Dakotian*, December 22, 1863, p. 3. January 12, 1864, p. 3; Kingsbury, *op. cit.*, pp. 348-349.

75. *Dakotian*, June 3, 1862, p. 3; Cedric Cummings, "The University of Dakota: Higher Learning on the Plains," *North Dakota History*, Vol. XXXIV, No. 3 (Summer, 1967), p. 245; Kingsbury, *op. cit.*, pp. 214-215.

76. *Montana Post*, January 7, 1865, pp. 1-2.

SELECTED READINGS

Moses K. Armstrong, *Early Empire Builders of the Great West* (St. Paul: E. W. Porter, 1901).

Robert G. Athearn, "Civil War Days in Montana," *Pacific Historical Review*, Vol. XXIX. No. 1 (February, 1960), pp. 19-33.

Abner M. English, "Dakota's First Soldiers," *South Dakota Historical Collections*, Vol. IX (1918), pp. 241-307.

James McClellan Hamilton, *From Wilderness to Statehood: A History of Montana, 1805-1900*

(Portland: Binfords and Mort, 1957), pp. 131-176; 211-412.

Robert H. Jones, *The Civil War in the Northwest: Nebraska, Wisconsin, Iowa, Minnesota, and the Dakotas* (Norman: University of Oklahoma Press, 1960).

George W. Kingsbury, *The History of Dakota Territory* (2 vols., Chicago: S. V. Clarke Publishing Company, 1915), Vol. I, pp. 175-396.

Howard R. Lamar, *Dakota Territory, 1861-1869: A Study of Frontier Politics* (New

Haven: Yale University Press, 1956), pp. 28-99.

Doane Robinson, *A History of the Dakota or Sioux Indians* (Minneapolis: Ross and Haines, Inc., 1956), pp. 245-340.

Herbert S. Schell, *Dakota Territory During the Eighteen Sixties* (Vermillion: University of South Dakota, 1954).

Norman Thomas, "John Blair Smith Todd," *South Dakota Historical Collections, XXIV (1949)*, pp. 178-219.

Washington And Idaho Territories

By Sara Jane Richter

In the mining town of Florence, Idaho, a part of Washington Territory during the beginning of the Civil War, Southerners and Northerners did not get along. Main Street divided the two factions. In 1861 and 1862, several arguments, brawls, and murders occurred due to differences of opinion over war issues. Both sides of Florence's Mason-Dixon Line — Main Street — dreaded the approaching Fourth of July celebration of 1862.

People realized that trouble was brewing, and the holiday began arousing the residents of Florence to more than just hostile words. A few of the more reasonable citizens of the community decided to devise a symbol that would unite the factions. Charles Ostner was burdened with the task of creating a tribute to the United States of America — a united nation. Committees from each side instructed gold miners to bring snow from the mountains and deposit it in the middle of Main Street. The snow, drenched with water each evening, formed a huge block of ice in the high altitude. Ostner began to work on the ice shrouded by a veil of canvas. The nation's birthday dawned, threatened by violence, but when the people were invited to celebrate their country's birth, everyone flocked to the scene of the mystery project. At the appointed time, Ostner's diligent work was unveiled — George Washington astride a horse. This roughly hewn ice sculpture melted the hostile attitudes and momentarily avoided trouble.[1]

The single most important event of the territorial years (1853-1889) of Washington was likely the Civil War. Most inhabitants of Washington Territory claimed to be strong supporters of the United States, although a few sympathized with the Confederate States. The reason for the imbalance lay in the fact that no one north of the Columbia River advocated slavery. Even though the military action of the Civil War occurred many miles distant in the Mississippi River valley and in the East, the people of Washington Territory watched the developments of the war with keen interest.

Prior to the war, several military men, who subsequently became leaders in the conflict, had left their mark on the Pacific Northwest region, and their actions were followed closely by the populace of Washington Territory. Union General Philip H. Sheridan served in the army as a lieutenant in the territory in 1855. George B. McClellan, for a time the commander of the Union Troops, spent the winter of 1853-1854 in the Puget Sound area selecting military road routes. Union General Ulysses S. Grant served at Fort Vancouver in 1853. Washington Territory's first governor, Isaac I. Stevens, who also had been a territorial delegate to Congress, died at the Battle of Chantilly, wearing the

U. S. Grant, who became a lieutenant-general in command of all United States armies during the Civil War, served at Fort Vancouver in Washington Territory in 1853.

Union blue. The first United States marshal in the territory, J. Patton Anderson, fought in the Confederate Army. The third territorial governor, Richard Gholson, who resigned when Abraham Lincoln became President, also served the Confederacy. George E. Pickett, the American commander of the San Juan Islands (located near Washington Territory's northwest coast) in 1861, joined the Confederate cause and led the Gettysburg charge that bears his name. Events dealing with these men lent a definite connection between the Civil War and Washington Territory and generally prompted a pro-Union attitude.[2]

Unstable politics existed in Washington Territory in the early 1860s. Near the outbreak of the Civil War, President Lincoln appointed William H. Wallace from Ohio to the executive office of Washington Territory, thus naming the first Republican governor of the territory. Soon afterward, Wallace ran for territorial delegate to Congress, won the election, resigned the governor's post, and went to Washington, D. C. Until Lincoln assigned another person to fill the vacancy, Wallace's secretary, L. J. S. Turney, acted as governor. Lincoln's first choice, due to pressure applied by the Methodist Church, was John Evans of Illinois. Evans refused the

position on the grounds of Washington's remoteness. The President's second choice and favorite man for the job was William Pickering.[3]

British born, Oxford educated, and from Illinois, Pickering chose the governorship of Washington Territory over becoming the United States minister to Great Britain. He took office in 1862 and remained until 1866. During his administration, the legislature of Washington Territory asked the United States to consider acquiring Alaska, for the residents of the Northwest believed Alaska to hold incredible riches. Pickering, at his own expense, had 300 single women from Boston, Massachusetts, transported to the territory to provide appropriate wives for the decidedly male population. He strongly favored the construction of wagon roads through the Cascade Mountains to better transportation, communications and troop transport needs. During his term, the statehouse in Olympia was constructed in 1863. Pickering sent the first telegram from Washington Territory on September 7, 1864, to President Lincoln, in which the governor assured the President of the territory's prayers and blessings for the nation.[4]

In Washington Territory, the news of South

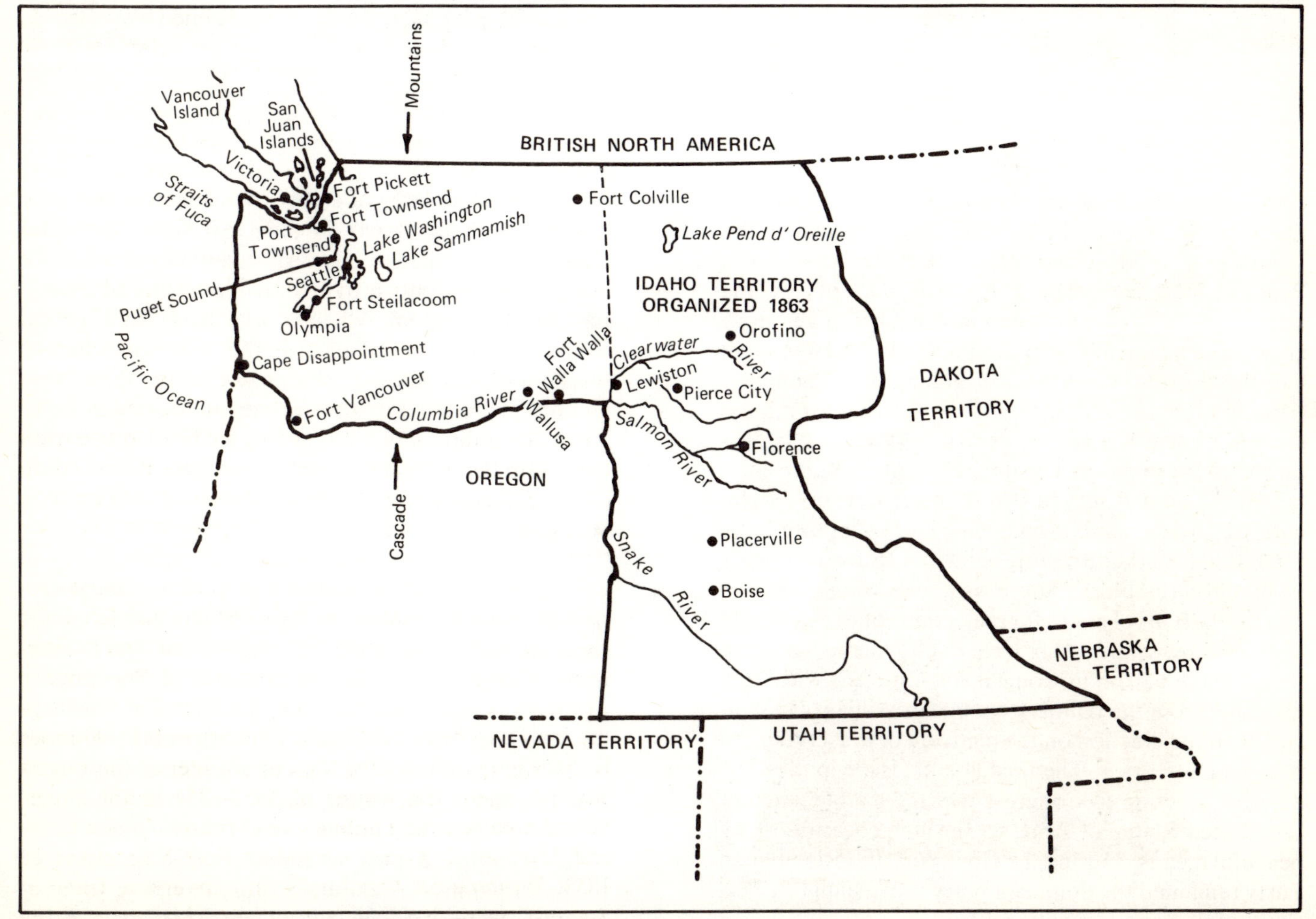

Washington and Idaho Territories During the Civil War

Map Drafted by Georganne T. Bartow

William H. Wallace of Ohio was appointed by President Abraham Lincoln as governor of Washington Territory, but soon was elected territorial delegate to Congress.

William Pickering, President Abraham Lincoln's second appointment as governor of Washington Territory, served from 1862 to 1866 and promoted many noteworthy developments.

Carolina's denial of the Union in 1860 caused the Democrats to turn to the Republicans, who wanted the Union preserved at any cost. After the Washington Peace Conference met in 1861, and the hope of patching up the Union faded, politicians in Washington Territory grew more adamant on this point of view. Newspapers like the *Washington Standard* voiced this opinion.

Soon after the outbreak of the war, handsome ex-governor Isaac I. Stevens, a proslavery Democrat, returned to Washington Territory from the nation's capital, where he had served two terms as territorial delegate to Congress. He had, however, supported the Union and worked to stop secession. Stevens' larger position on the North-South issue was widely known, and this hurt his chances for reelection. The Democrats decided they would rather have a solid Union advocate than a slave patron in Congress, so Stevens withdrew his name from the ballot. Republican William H. Wallace won the election on the platform of preserving the Union at any price. The fundamental issue in the 1861 delegate election to Congress was the maintenance of the United States of America through coercion or by peaceful means. During the Civil War, the Republican Party remained the dominant party in Washington Territory, following the national lead.[5]

To add to the confusing politics in Washington Territory, the Idaho area of eastern Washington Territory posed a problem. Early in the Civil War, the Idaho country was divided into several counties with separate county governments provided by the territorial legislature of Washington. All territorial lands west of the Rocky Mountains and east of the 115th meridian of west longitude became Missoula County. Shoshone County included territory south of the Clearwater River. In addition, Nez Percé and Idaho counties soon came into being. Idaho County consisted of land south of the Salmon River divide and some of present-day Wyoming.[6]

Between 1860 and 1862, because of the discovery of gold, 20,000 to 25,000 people moved to the Idaho section of eastern Washington Territory, and agitation for separate territorial status began. "Eastsiders" harbored ill feelings against "Westsiders." Idaho County residents resented the fact that the capital of Washington Territory was so distant; approximately 700 miles separated them from the seat of government in Olympia. The fact that Seattle received the territorial university also fomented hard feelings.[7]

In 1861, this discontent climaxed. People clamored for the creation of a distinct territory composed of eastern Oregon and eastern Washington Territory. A bill proposing the formation of Walla Walla Territory came before the legislature of Washington Territory. Naturally, the western part of Washington Territory did not want to relinquish the eastern part, and the bill was defeated. Not giving up, the Eastsiders presented another bill calling for a constitution for a new state, Idaho. This passed the Washington Territory Council, but the territorial House of Representatives substituted the word "Washington" for "Idaho" and set the bill aside for future consideration.

Those who wanted separate territorial status for Idaho refused to bow to the western controlled legislature and appealed directly to the United States Congress. Congress acted readily, and on March 4, 1863, President Lincoln officially approved the bill creating Idaho Territory. This new territory included the land of Washington Territory east of Oregon and the 117th meridian of west longitude. The fact that Idaho received territorial status scarcely caused much excitement throughout the region, because most of the population, scattered about the goldfields and isolated settlements, did not have the benefits of a telegraph or regular mails even to hear about the event. The laws of Washington Territory remained in force in Idaho Territory until 1864.[8]

All men in the regular military service stationed in Washington Territory at the beginning of the Civil War quickly received orders of transfer to Eastern military installations for duty. To fill the gap left by the departed forces, the Volunteer Employment Bill was passed by Congress in July, 1861. This legislation called for men to militarily serve the United States as volunteers for no less than six months, but no more than three years, and to receive the same treatment as soldiers in the regular army ranks. Acting Governor Henry McGill encouraged "all the citizens of this territory capable of bearing arms and liable to militia duty" to join the army.[9]

Nevertheless, not many men filled the military ranks. In the twenty-two counties of Washington Territory, only 6,000 men between the ages of sixteen and sixty were capable of bearing arms. All of these men did not enlist, however, for many men used their energies to repair damages done by rampaging Indians or rambunctious miners. Enlistment lagged especially in the Puget Sound area. Many men mined for gold, because mining was much more profitable than shouldering a rifle. Brigadier General George Wright, the third commander of the Department of the Pacific, complained that "the newly discovered gold mines naturally draw off a large portion of the able-bodied men."[10]

For those who did enlist, luxuries were scarce and supply costs astounding. Twenty dollars bought a barrel of flour, beef sold for 15 cents a pound and usually spoiled, a cord of wood cost $30, and potatoes, when available, brought $1 a bushel. Log barracks, hay mattresses, beans, pork, and some sugar became the staple items. Bourbon whiskey at $17.60 a gallon was the chief medicinal cure-all. A number of men enlisted, usually receiving a bounty for joining the army, oftentimes

deserted, and then reenlisted when the initial bounty money ran low.[11]

Northwest volunteers served their country with little recognition. Much of the area, unmapped and wild, confronted soldiers unaccustomed to military service. The volunteers had to contend with neglect by citizens and government alike. They suffered from less than effective medical service, short pay, inadequate provisions and supplies, and dull duty. Military service in Washington Territory was not desirable. The most exciting activities of soldiers were to start fights with each other or chase disobedient Indians. Climate and terrain did not increase the morale of the soldiers, since they had to combat fog, snow, rain, forests, mountains, rivers, and the Pacific Ocean. They became forgotten men who did their duty in silence and simply endured their service.

Colonel Justus Steinberger, at the time in California, received orders on October 18, 1861, from Brigadier General Wright to raise one regiment of infantry volunteers in Washington Territory. By early 1862, Steinberger had raised only four infantry companies, one each at Port Townsend, Walla Walla, Whatcom, and Port Madison. Returning to California, Colonel Steinberger raised four more companies, and in May, accompanied by these soldiers, returned to Washington Territory. These California volunteers did not like living in Washington Territory and emphatically insisted on keeping their California relationship. By summer, enlistment had almost come to a halt in Washington Territory. Altogether, Washington Territory during the Civil War furnished only 964 men as militia volunteers, creating ten companies, which served until 1866.[12]

In early January, 1862, Governor Pickering of Washington Territory informed the United States government that the Washington regiments had been filled and asked that they be used as part of the regular United States Army or be assigned to Washington Territory as a militia body. The troops remained in the territory and served at several military installations: Fort Pickett, Fort Walla Walla, Fort Steilacoom, and Fort Vancouver. The primary duty, as always, was to garrison these military posts, but on occasion the forces found themselves accompanying some of the Oregon cavalry units in pursuing restless Indians, usually Shoshones. The winter of 1861-1862 proved to be detrimental to the training and movements of the Washington Territory soldiers. Harsh weather also hampered the mobility of the Indians, however, so the first winter of the Civil War passed in relative quiet.[13]

In June, 1862, two companies of Washington Territory militia relieved the Californians who had been stationed at Fort Colville since November, 1861. They had a lot of ground to cover and patrolled the well-traveled roads from Walla Walla to Lapwai, Boise, Salmon Falls, Bruneau Valley, and the Utah border. Because of the size of this region and the severe weather of the following winter, a post to protect a company of Washington infantry and a company of Oregon cavalry was established in late 1862. This base, named Fort Lapwai, served as a supply camp for the area to the east and as a calming agent for the Nez Percé Indians in the vicinity. From this base, a relatively stable peace between the Snakes, Nez Percé , and the whites ensued for the next three years. [14]

Washington Territory soldiers had to contend with frequent Indian problems during the Civil War. One such expedition to round up some Indians who had strayed from the Siletz Reservation originated at the Siletz Blockhouse and involved ten California volunteers under the leadership of Lieutenant Louis Herzer of the First Washington Volunteer Infantry Regiment. In twenty-one days, these men traveled 262 miles, paralleling present United States Highway 101. The journey required much energy, for nature did not cooperate: rivers needed to be forded, high tides had to be waded, brush and fallen trees needed to be cleared, and the roads, what there were of them, had to be repaired. Thirty-one Indians, most of whom had never set foot on a reservation, were captured and brought to the Siletz Reservation. Seventeen additional Indians returned voluntarily to the reservation rather than suffer the long, harsh, wet winter near Coos Bay. [15]

In August, 1862, Colonel Steinberger received a request for troops in the Grande Ronde Valley. William Barnhart, the Indian agent on the Umatilla Reservation, maintained that Cayuse Indians in the area had not lived up to treaty expectations and were creating disturbances by not allowing whites to settle in the valley. Barnhart believed that the army ought to arrest the Indian troublemakers and station at least twenty cavalrymen at the reservation. Twenty-three men of the valley petitioned Steinberger for protection also, claiming that the weak defenses of the valley endangered its inhabitants. Barnhart's request for troops probably stemmed from fear, for on June 12, he had killed an Indian while trying to quiet a riot on the reservation. [16]

In response to Barnhart's request, fifteen men, each provisioned for seven days and with forty rounds of ammunition, under Lieutenant J. T. Apperson of Company E, First Oregon Cavalry Regiment, left Fort Walla Walla for the Umatilla Reservation on August 17, 1862. Their orders were to protect government property, help Barnhart in the performance of his duties, and remain until relieved by Captain George B. Currey and twenty men of the First Oregon Cavalry Regiment. When Currey arrived, he proceeded to arrest the allegedly guilty Indians. As a result, four of the resisting Indians were killed, including the Indian leader, Dreamer. Hostilities then ceased, and Currey returned to Fort Walla Walla on August 22. [17]

Many Indian problems had white sources. Unscrupulous white men sold Indians whiskey, stole their horses, and raped their women. Whites, without realizing the consequences, killed innocent Indians because they happened to be Indians. The *Seattle Weekly Gazette* commented that "if the whites would...respect what rights belong to the Indians[,]there would be...fewer tragedies, [b]ut this they will not do."[18] Naturally, the red men retaliated, which prompted reprisals by oftentimes drunken white men. Both whites and Indians had reason to fear the other, and these fears sometimes erupted into serious altercations which necessitated military intervention. [19]

The Washington Territory Nez Percé Reservation became an example of this type of activity. J. W. Anderson, the reservation's sub-Indian agent, asked Brigadier General Benjamin Alvord, the commanding officer of the Military District of Oregon and Washington, on October 12, 1862, to send "two or three companies of troops... [to] be stationed...on the reservation [to] overawe the disaffected...Indians, and thus maintain peace."[20] Several whites had been killed near the reservation, and Anderson felt the soldiers already there could not handle the situation. Governor Pickering heard of the trouble with the Nez Percé through a petition signed by 151 concerned citizens of nearby Lewiston. He urged Alvord to take immediate action to forestall any further depredations by the Indians. The Nez Percé had always been known for their friendliness toward the whites, and this crime greatly upset both whites and Indians. At Fort Lapwai, Chief Lawyer of the Nez Percé tribe turned the guilty Indians over to military officials. Then a meeting between the militia and the Indians to discuss this agitation convened. Indian grievances stemmed from the thousands of miners trying to find their fortunes on reservation lands which violated a United States treaty made in 1855. A new treaty was then negotiated which allowed whites to prospect on land purchased from the Indians. [21]

Often whites and Indians joined forces to attack immigrant wagon trains making their way to new homes in Washington Territory between the Missouri River and the Columbia River. These men were seldom caught and proved to be examples for other misfits and criminals who added to the wave of murder and theft in the territory. On January 16, 1862, the United States Senate appropriated $25,000 to be used by the War Department to protect immigrants traveling overland to Washington Territory and the West Coast. Soldiers tried to prevent raids by whites and Indians. In November, 1864, soldiers arrested three white men in connection with an Indian murder and on charges of selling whiskey to the Indians. [22]

Not all Indians in Washington Territory were hostile. The Yakima Indian agent, A. A. Bancroft, was extremely proud of his farming Indians. In August, 1863, he reported to Calvin H. Hale, the superintendent of Indian affairs in Washington Territory, that his charges favored whites and the government. To Bancroft, farming seemed the only way to civilize the Indians and prevent them from returning to their nomadic past. Fourteen houses had been built for the Yakimas and their farm plots ranged in size from five to twenty-five

Asa Mercer, a prosperous Washington Territory businessman during the Civil War, transported marriageable women from the East to provide wives for the decidedly male population of the territory.

acres. School attendance had been good, with boys outnumbering girls in the classroom. Both the Indians and their agent were encouraged and happy due to the progress of the tribe and the peaceful nature of their lives.[23]

The Northwest Pacific area had to cope not only with internal Indian problems, but also with the fear of a Confederate invasion from the Pacific Ocean. Only San Francisco, California, was fortified, and the loss of that city could mean the loss of the entire coast. Fearing this, Congress passed a Northwest Coastal Defense Plan in July, 1862. In all, $300,000 was allotted for these fortifications. At Cape Disappointment, Washington Territory, which became Fort Cape Disappointment in 1864, a part of the coastal defense system was built.[24]

People in Washington Territory had reason to fear an invasion. Treasure ships left California, bound for the East Coast and Europe, carrying rich cargoes which were tempting targets for the Confederacy. Captain James I. Wadell of the Confederate Navy left London, England, on October 8, 1864, flying the British flag over the ship *Sea King*. Wadell, ostensibly headed for Madeira Island near the northwest coast of Africa, actually was sent to capture treasure ships on the Pacific Coast. Soon out of London, Wadell lowered the Union Jack, unfurled the Confederate banner, and changed the name of his ship to the *Shenandoah*. She cruised the Pacific Northwest during the latter part of the war and captured thirty-eight merchant vessels. Wadell allowed eight of the ships to go free, carrying the crews of all thirty-eight. The other ships he burned or scuttled. Washington Territory reacted to the threat of the *Shenandoah* with apprehension. Many steamers traveled from Puget Sound to Oregon and San Francisco, and no one knew what ship Wadell would strike next. This possibility frightened many sea travelers and added to the pro-Union attitude of Washington Territory.[25]

Civilians and troops in Washington Territory did not always live in fear of Confederate invasion or attacks by hostile Indians. The San Juan Islands, located off the northwest coast of Washington Territory and jointly occupied by American and English forces, enjoyed a rather carefree existence. The Pig War between Great Britain and the United States over the ownership of the San Juan Islands began and ended in 1859, but it never really settled the ownership question. Due to the preoccupation of the two nations during the Civil War, the islands lay unmolested, for they were the least of anyone's problems. The only difficulties encountered on the islands occurred between bored male civilians spoiling for activity, but the military personnel of England and the United States stationed there had cordial relations. On July 4, 1863, as the dust and bugle calls of Gettysburg faded, the English and American garrisons on San Juan Island engaged in a track meet and a grand banquet to celebrate the day. Another example of San Juan's unconcerned attitude occurred later in the summer when 100 men and women from nearby Victoria Island made a social call on both posts and a huge picnic ensued. The gaiety of these social events transcended the agony and destruction of the Civil War found elsewhere in the nation. Distance created a vacuum and largely removed from visibility in the Washington Territory area even a dispute the size of the Civil War.[26]

During the Civil War, Washington Territory's population was somewhat lopsided, for the ratio of men to women was nine to one. To follow in Pickering's footsteps in providing wives for the territory, Cupid chose Asa Mercer, a Washington Territory businessman. He saw the many mateless males of Washington Territory and the many young widows and unwed girls in the East due to the Civil War. Mercer hoped to play matchmaker and went East and returned with eleven young women, who married within the year. Upon hearing news of the imminent arrival of the girls, the *Seattle Gazette* entreated all bachelors to ''bring out your boiled shirts'' for the occasion.[27] Success nurtured another similar plan of Mercer's; why not ask his friend, President Lincoln, to assist him in finding women without husbands to bring to Washington Territory? On Mercer's arrival in New York City, he was shocked to hear of Lincoln's assassination. Nevertheless, he gathered about 100 women, and through the generosity of others purchased passage on a ship to take them around Cape Horn and north to Washington Territory. One year later, out of money, Mercer and the women were stranded in San Francisco without the means for transporting them to Washington Territory. Eventually, he raised enough money to place the women, by then known as the Mercer Girls, on lumber vessels heading north to Seattle. The girl importation effort proved to be a success, and Mercer was asked, if not begged, to bring more females to the territory, but his last trip spoiled his enthusiasm for the task.[28]

Divorces posed a social problem in Washington Territory throughout the Civil War years. Divorces were granted by the legislature, but Governor Pickering did not like the way it bestowed divorces so quickly and in such numbers. He "called attention to the sad and immoral effects" stemming from the many divorces.[29] In 1862, Pickering appealed to the legislature to "refuse all applications for divorces and . . .refer the parties to the courts of the Territory."[30] During the legislative year of 1862-1863, sixteen marriages ended, and in 1863, the governor again asked for the courts to assume this type of proceedings. Finally, in 1866, the territorial courts started handling divorce cases.[31]

Women in Washington Territory actively participated in the Civil War. They realized the need for medical supplies and, although their numbers were small, they organized themselves into groups that provided clothing, bandages, and other hospital supplies. Far away from the death and destruction of the war, these hardy, willing women gave of their time in an attempt to alleviate some of the suffering caused by the Civil War. Actually, based on population, women did more of this type of work than the women of most other Union states or territories.[32]

Despite the beginning of the Civil War, collegiate education expanded in Washington Territory in 1861. On a tract of ten donated acres of land in Seattle, the University of Washington Territory opened in September, with thirty-one students attending, and Asa Mercer, of Mercer Girl note, as president. Congress, in 1862, passed the Morrill Act, which designated sites on federal land in each territory and state to be used for land-grant universities emphasizing the mechanical and agricultural arts. In 1864, the territorial legislature accepted the provisions of the Morrill Act and decided to locate the school at Vancouver, but at the time of statehood in 1889, the college had not opened. It was finally relocated at Pullman and organized in 1890.

In Washington Territory, it was difficult to raise taxes or levies for the erection and support of public schools. Since the territory lacked abundant numbers of children, the population could not be readily induced to provide adequate funds for schools. The inhabitants of Walla Walla, the largest town in the territory, in 1864, finally consented to a two and one-half mill tax to furnish the city with a public school. Schools in the terri-

tory enrolled all ages, for the literacy rate among miners and children alike was not very high.

Men of the cloth saw in Washington Territory's Indians and miners a veritable harvest of souls. During the Civil War, Methodists established numerous churches in Washington Territory, as did Roman Catholics. The *Seattle Gazette* complained that the first Methodist Church completed in town needed a choir "to add interest to the services."[33] The number of churches almost tripled between 1860 and 1870. Among the Indians, Protestant missionaries continued the work started by Marcus Whitman some years earlier and Jesuit Catholic priests established three missions along the Mullan Road.[34]

Journalism also played an important role during the Civil War. Most of the newspapers had a Republican bent echoing national views. The majority of the newspapers commenced with the influx of miners, for in them the proprietors saw potential sources for news items and editorials. Seattle's first newspaper, the weekly *Puget Sound Gazette,* appeared in 1863, but was short lived. Washington Territory boasted the first journalistic enterprise in the interior of the Pacific Northwest, for Lewiston, Idaho, nurtured the *Golden Age*, issued first on August 2, 1862. The periodical was aptly titled, for during the Civil War the Idaho country produced great quantities of gold.[35]

In spite of the turbulence of the 1860s, the population of Washington Territory doubled — 11,594 to 23,955 — during the decade. This increase can be credited to many people escaping the traumas and pressures of the war in the East, plus promises of new horizons and quick fortunes. Draft evaders from North and South added to the immigrants. Many Chinese-born laborers were imported during the early 1860s for use as inexpensive labor in the gold mining districts. The influx of settlers and miners came by overland trails, and by sailboats or steamboats, because the war had interrupted the construction of the transcontinental railroad.[36]

The many miners in Washington Territory prompted more and better methods of transportation. By 1865, the Oregon Steam Navigation Company, which held a monopoly on Columbia River travel, owned and operated thirteen schooners, four barges, and twenty-nine passenger boats on the river alone. The company enhanced overland travel when it opened a stage line between Wallula, in Washington Territory, and Lake Pend Orulle, in Idaho Territory, to transport miners to inland diggings and into Montana. This run covered 1,730 miles, but did not last long.

To facilitate overland immigration in Washington Territory, the Mullan Road was built by Washington Territory soldiers under the direction of First Lieutenant John Mullan of the Second Artillery. This road stretched from Fort Benton on the Missouri River to Walla Walla and took four years, 1861-1865, to complete. The Department of War foresaw the road as an easy route for troop transportation in the Northwest. Over this rustic highway, material for the transcontinental railroad could travel also. The only consistent use of the road in the long run was for immigrant passage. Only one group of soldiers used the road in the 1860s, and very little railroad construction goods reached their destinations over it.[37]

Washington Territory had a stable economy during the Civil War era, with several items for exportation. Since 1851, the staple export had been lumber. Three annual shipments left Seattle bound for the East Coast of the United States or more exotic destinations, such as Spanish naval stations. In the early 1860s, plentiful schools of codfish swam in the Strait of Juan de Fuca, and fishermen caught thousands of pounds of fish per voyage. Dogfish, procured in the Northwest waters, provided the standard lubricant for the area. The lumber industry used the oil as a lubricant for saws and other machinery in its mills. This substance also found its way into the medicine of the day as a cod-liver oil substitute.[38]

The exportation of coal closely followed that of lumber as a source of revenue for Washington Territory. In the years between 1860 and 1879, the coal yield equaled approximately 13,000 tons each year. A coal fever, akin to gold fever, struck the territory. A major coal field was found in 1863 in King County along what became known as Coal Creek. This discovery prompted a more concentrated push for railroads in the territory. Coal proved to be a very necessary commodity for the steamships that puffed about Puget Sound and the Northwestern waters. At the time, the transportation of coal was expensive, a fact which hindered the early development of the industry. In Squak Valley, more appropriately known as Issquawh Valley, in King County, coal had to be hauled in wagons to Lake Sammamish, transferred to boats to be transported to Lake Washington, and then by wagons to Seattle. Experts considered coal from the Squak Valley to be the finest on the Pacific Coast for smelting purposes.[39]

In the Yakima and Nile River valleys of eastern Washington Territory, the climate and indigenous lush grasses made the cattle industry very profitable. Two-thirds of Washington Territory was excellent grazing pasture and settlers did not hesitate to make the most of it. Horses and cattle multiplied fast in the superb environment. Corn and fruit trees also grew well in this section of the territory.[40]

The first gold discovery of the 1860s in Washington Territory brought an immense influx of miners and adventurers to the area around Harvey and Keethley creeks by August, 1861. Gold was discovered there in 1860, but winter delayed the spread of the news and the migration of fortune seekers to the promised land. Soon after the initial gold rush, farms in the territory suffered from neglect as the farmers flocked to the diggings. Secessionists as well as Unionists dug side by side in the Northwest for gold. People of different political persuasions were urged by dreams of wealth to swallow their pride and try their hand at panning for the precious metal.

At the Harvey and Keethley diggings, miners extracted an amount of metal equal from $8 to $50 a day. E. D. Pierce added another find near the Clearwater branch of the Snake River. To handle the hundreds of men rushing to the area, two steamboats were built to transport miners on the Snake and Columbia rivers. The army attempted to dissuade miners from going to the Clearwater diggings because the route meandered through the Nez Percé Reservation. Nevertheless, gold seekers made their way to the strike, while a hurriedly negotiated treaty in April, 1861, pacified the Indians by promising them military protection. In this matter, the Indians had no choice, for the white man preferred the gold over the friendship of the Indians.[41]

Ambitious fortune hunters sought to find gold diggings even more lucrative than those in the Clearwater district. North of the Salmon River in September, 1861, several men accidentally found rich deposits on Miller Creek. Most of these men have faded into history, but John H. Bostwick, B. B. Rogers and John J. Healey were among the discoverers. By October, Millersburg had been born. The first pan taken from the creek yielded the panner $25; thus, 1,000 men sought claims in the area by November. These men needed supplies to winter at the camp, but not enough provisions were available, which caused many to return to Oro Fino, about 100 miles distant, to endure the cold weather and gold fever.[42]

The winter was hard and the men were extremely anxious to return to the gold fields. Some even started going back in February, 1862. Many farmers and settlers had lost their means of livelihood during the winter floods and envisioned the strike areas as a quick way to recapture their lost fortunes. The *Golden Age* of Lewiston, Washington Territory, lamented that these people had no recourse "except to repair their broken fortunes by resorting to the mines."[43] Some brave, hardy women even tried their hands.

At Salmon River, the diggings produced rich ore and many miners took $30 to $80 of gold per pan. One pan totalled $151. This same claim produced $1,800 in three hours for two men operating a rocker. Men stored gold in every conceivable type of container — pickle jars to tin cans to leather pouches. Most miners could well afford the dollar-per-pound provisions, with high-priced beef the cheapest food to be had.[44]

Mining communities were constructed hastily and with whatever building materials were available. Saloons were the first to be built, usually made of rough-hewn boards and blankets. By July, 1861, 5,000 men lived in the Pierce City region, with only three families in residence. The absence of female companionship was felt, prompting many men to take Indian wives and often more than one. Pierce City grew in response to the growing population of the gold mines in the vicinity. The Pierce strike was the biggest find north of the Columbia River, and thousands of people migrated to the district. Merchants with inflated prices, miners with dreams of gold, and gamblers with stacked decks flooded to the new city and all other communities spawned by diggings throughout Washington Territory. The typical route followed by miners heading for the fields began by taking a steamboat to old Fort Walla Walla, then by stage to the town of Walla Walla, and from there horses carried the miners to their final destinations, or they simply walked.[45]

In combining quantities of men and gold, Washington Territory attracted lawless elements. Liquor and thieves mixed with gold added to the color and confusion of the mining districts. Horse thieves struck in organized parties; claims were disputed and often stolen from the original claimant; tempers flared, arguments ensued and, consequently, men died. The *Golden Age* complained against this "indiscriminate use of knives and pistols, for the settlement of any and all difficulties."[46] Washington Territory encompassed a fast-paced, dangerous environment for all of its inhabitants.

A group of miners on their way to the Florence gold fields in 1862 did not see eye to eye over the Civil War question. In a short while, all 150 men in the camp were lined up facing one another — Northerners on one side, Southerners on the other. Armed with an array of butcher knives, picks, and pistols, they were ready to fight their own Bull Run until the more levelheaded of their number dissuaded them from assaulting each other.[47]

The majority of those in the mining camps held Confederate sympathies. When in the company of United States soldiers, fights occurred regularly. Mining roughs taunted the soldiers with cries of "Lincoln's Hirelings" and claimed that they were paid to slaughter innocent Southerners. If soldiers refused to drink to the health of Confederate President Jefferson Davis, or the Confederacy's highest ranking general, Robert E. Lee, as ordered by the desperadoes, a fight was sure to follow. Often these roughhouse incidents led to deaths; some towns reported several murders each night. In the early 1860s, the United States government realized that federal law could not be enforced in the mining regions, and allowed local laws to suffice. The local laws did not seem to be adhered too closely, and the enforcement of them turned out to be lax.[48]

Politically, the gold fields had considerable impact. Miners could vote and were entitled to acknowledgement and representation, being citizens of Washington Territory. Needing more legislative seats and counties, more counties were created, but with the emergence of more counties, more courts and judges were needed. Before the creation of Nez Percé and Idaho counties, three judges served all of Washington Territory. Afterward, at least three more could have been used. To remedy this situation, the territorial legislature allowed each county a district court to have jurisdiction within that county, except in instances where the United States was involved.[49]

Washington and Idaho territories during the Civil War were distracted and preoccupied. Since the agonies of the war occurred far from the area, its residents never fully felt the heavy hand of wartime despair and loss. Gold fever gripped the territories, and not much else was important to those involved in finding wealth; through mining development, however, the population of the territories increased rapidly. The changes of the Civil War era in Washington and Idaho territories revolved around men bound to develop the area into a viable part of the Pacific Coast. As a relatively undeveloped area, the inhabitants of the two territories needed to grapple first with the environment to survive and to make a living.

Because the Civil War developments removed the regular army from Washington and Idaho territories, militia volunteers had to suffice. These men were unaccustomed to being soldiers, keeping the peace on the frontier and pacifying the Indians. With no formal military training, they faced a large responsibility, but they learned as they performed and functioned satisfactorily. Controlling friction between Indians and whites in Washington and Idaho territories proved to be the only military work for the soldiers, just as it had been for professional soldiers before the Civil War.

The Civil War played a secondary role in the lives of the people of Washington and Idaho territories. Their daily existence was not altered or influenced to any significant degree by the conflict. Thus, they appeared to be casual about the war, as if to put it out of mind because it was out of sight. The use of 964 militia men of Washington and Idaho territories to perform duties formerly carried out by the regular United States Army within the two territories was the only basic impact of the war on them. The war was not a current, realistic issue because of the slow communications of the day, the lack of troop involvement outside of the territory, and the geographical remoteness of the large battles in the South and in the East. Washington and Idaho territories, therefore, absorbed the tragedy of the Civil War without feeling it.

NOTES

1. Sister M. Alfreda Elsensohn, *Pioneer Days in Idaho County* (2 vols., Caldwell, Idaho: The Caxton Printers, 1947), Vol. I, pp. 67-68.

2. Richard O'Connor, *Sheridan the Inevitable* (Indianapolis: Bobbs-Merrill Company, 1953), p. 43; Bryan Conrad and A. J. Eckenrode, *George B. McClellan: The Man Who Saved the Union* (Chapel Hill: University of North Carolina Press, 1941), p. 13; Frank L. Green to Author, Tacoma, Washington, September 3, 1975; Louis A. Magrini, *Meet the Governors of the State of Washington* (Tacoma: the Author, 1946), p. 16; Keith Murray, *The Pig War* (Tacoma: Washing-

ton State Historical Society, 1968), p. 69.

3. Belle Reeves, *Historical Highlights: State of Washington* (Olympia: the Author, 1941), p. 4; Earl Coe, *Historical Highlights of Washington State* (n. p.: the Author, n. d.), p. 16; *The Collected Works of Abraham Lincoln* (9 vols., New Brunswick: Rutgers University Press, 1953-1955), Vol IV, p. 550.

4. Coe, *op. cit.*, p. 16; Hubert Howe Bancroft, *History of Washington, Idaho, and Montana, 1854-1889* (San Francisco: History Company, 1890), p. 215; United States Department of War, *War of the Rebellion: A Compilation of the Official Records of the Union and Confederate Armies* (70 vols., 128 books, Washington: Government Printing Office, 1880-1901), Ser. I, Vol. L, Pt. 1, p. 972.

5. Robert W. Johannsen, *Frontier Politics and the Sectional Conflict: The Pacific Northwest on the Eve of the Civil War* (Seattle: University of Washington Press, 1955), p. 215.

6. Elsensohn, *op. cit.*, p. 21.

7. *Ibid.*; Coe, *op. cit.*, p. 15.

8. Bancroft, *op. cit.*, p. 262; Elsensohn, *op. cit.*, p. 22.

9. Aurora Hunt, "The Far West Volunteers," *Montana: The Magazine of Western History*, Vol. XII, No. 2 (Spring, 1962), p. 49; *Official Records*, Ser. I, Vol. L., Pt. 1, p. 489.

10. Bancroft, *op cit.*, p. 228; *Official Records*, Ser. I., Vol L, Pt. 1, p. 850.

11. Aurora Hunt, *The Army of the Pacific: Its Operations in California, Texas, Arizona, New Mexico, Utah, Nevada, Oregon, Washington, plains region, Mexico, etc., 1860-1866* (Glendale: Arthur H. Clark Company, 1951), p. 227- Doyce B. Nunis, Jr., ed., *The Golden Frontier: The Recollections of Herman Francis Reinhart, 1851-1869* (Austin: University of Texas Press, 1962), p. 262.

12. *Official Records*, Ser. I, Vol. L, Pt. 1, p. 850; Hunt, "The Far West Volunteers, " *Montana: The Magazine of Western History*, Vol. XII, p. 51; Bancroft, *op. cit.*,

pp. 228-230; Green to Author, September 3, 1975.

13. Bancroft, *op. cit.*, pp. 228-230.

14. Hunt, *The Army of the Pacific*, pp. 231-232.

15. *Ibid.*, pp. 229-230.

16. *Official Records*, Ser. I, Vol. L, Pt. 1, p. 1149.

17. *Ibid.*, pp. 158-166.

18. *Seattle Weekly Gazette*, November 28, 1864, p. 2.

19. *Official Records*, Ser. I, Vol. L, Pt. 2, pp. 1076-1077.

20. *Ibid.*, p. 166.

21. *Ibid.*, pp. 166, 191, 208, 477, 482-486.

22. *Ibid.*, p. 182; *Congressional Globe*, 37th Congress, 2nd Session, p. 358, *Seattle Weekly Gazette*, November 21, 1864, p. 2.

23. United States House of Representatives, 38th Congress, 1st Session, *Executive Document No. 240* (Washington: Government Printing Office, 1864), pp. 517-518.

24. Aurora Hunt, "The Civil War on the Western Seaboard," *Civil War History*, Vol. IX, No. 2, (June, 1963), p. 178.

25. Murray Morgan, *Dixie Raider: The Saga of the C.S.S. Shenandoah* (New York: E. P. Dutton and Company, 1948), pp. 13, 17; Hunt, *The Army of the Pacific*, p. 319; Brainerd Dyer, "Confederate Naval and Privateering Activities in the Pacific," *Pacific Historical Review*, Vol. III, No. 4 (Winter, 1934), p. 433.

26. *Official Records*, Ser. I, Vol L, Pt. 1, p. 445; Murray, *op. cit.*, p. 71.

27. *Seattle Gazette*, May 3, 1864, p. 2.

28. Coe, *op. cit.*, p. 17; Archie Binns, *Sea in the Forest* (Garden City: Doubleday and Company, 1953), p. 135; *Harper's Weekly*, January 6, 1866, pp. 8-9.

29. Charles M. Gates, ed., *Messages of the Governors of the Territory of Washington to the Legislative Assembly, 1854-1889* (Seattle: University of Washington Press, 1940), p. 113.

30. *Ibid.*

31. Coe, *op. cit.*, p. 16; Bancroft, *op. cit.*, pp. 274-275.

32. Green to Author, September 3, 1975.

33. *Seattle Gazette*, March 22, 1864, p. 2.

34. *Ninth Census of the United States, 1870* (4

vols., Washington: Government Printing Office, 1872), Vol I, pp. 558, 506-508; United States Senate, 37th Congress, 3rd Session, *Executive Document No. 43* (Washington: Government Printing Office, 1863), p. 51.

35. Elsensohn, *op cit.*, p. 21.

36. *Eighth Census of the United State, 1860* (Washington: Government Printing Office, 1862), p. 2; *Ninth Census of the United States, 1870*, Vol. I, p. 3.

37. A. C. McGregor, "The Economic Impact of the Mullan Road on Walla Walla, 1860-1883," *Pacific Northwest Quarterly*, Vol. LXV, No. 3 (July, 1974), pp. 118-119; *Official Records*, Ser. I, Vol. L, Pt. 1, pp. 434, 462-463, 1043; *Seattle Weekly Gazette*, September 3, 1864, p. 2.

38. Bancroft, *op. cit.*, pp. 338, 345, 348; Thomas F. Gedosch, "A Note on the Dogfish Oil Industry of Washington Territory," *Pacific Northwest Quarterly* LIX, No. 2. (April 1968) pp. 100-101.

39. Bancroft, *op. cit.*, p. 340; *Seattle Gazette*, January 26, 1864, p. 2; December 17, 1863, p. 2; December 19, 1863, p. 2.

40. Gretta Gossett, "Stock Grazing in Washington's Nile Valley: Receding Ranges in the Cascades," *Pacific Northwest Quarterly*, Vol. LV, No. 3 (July, 1964), p. 119.

41. Bancroft, *op. cit.*, pp. 233-236; *Official Records*, Ser. I, Vol. L, Pt. 1, pp. 468-469.

42. Bancroft, *op. cit.*, p. 245.

43. *Golden Age*, (Lewiston, Washington Territory), August 2, 1862, p. 1.

44. Bancroft, *op. cit.*, p. 247.

45. *Ibid.*. p. 236-237.

46. *Golden Age*, August 2, 1862, p. 2.

47. Elsensohn, *op. cit.*, p. 52.

48. Kenneth Owens, "Judge Lynch in Washington Territory," *Pacific Northwest Quarterly*, Vol. LV, No. 4 (October, 1964), pp. 177-178; Nunis, *op. cit.*, p. 205; Roy M. Robbins, "The Federal Land System in an Embryo State," *Pacific Historical Review*, Vol. IV, No. 4, (Winter, 1935), p. 372; Elsensohn, *op. cit.*, p. 56.

49. Bancroft, *op. cit.*, p. 251.

SELECTED READINGS

Hubert Howe Bancroft, *History of Washington, Idaho, and Montana, 1845-1889* (San Francisco: History Company, 1890), pp. 201-301.

Sister M. Alfreda Elsensohn, *Pioneer Days in Idaho County* (2 vols., Caldwell, Idaho: The Caxton Printers, 1947), Vol. I, pp. 20-23, 27-77.

Aurora Hunt, *The Army of the Pacific: Its Operations in California, Texas, Arizona, New Mexico, Utah, Nevada, Oregon, Washington, plains region, Mexico, etc., 1860-1866* (Glendale: Arthur H. Clark Company, 1951).

Aurora Hunt, "The Civil War on the Western Seaboard," *Civil War History*, Vol. IX, No. 2 (June, 1963), pp. 178-186.

Aurora Hunt, "The Far West Volunteers," *Montana: The Magazine of Western History*, Vol. XII, No. 1 (Spring, 1962), pp. 49-61.

Robert W. Johannsen, *Frontier Politics and the Sectional Conflict: The Pacific Northwest on the Eve of the Civil War* (Seattle: University of Washington Press, 1955).

A. C. McGregor, "The Economic Impact of the Mullan Road on Walla Walla, 1860-1883," *Pacific Northwest Quarterly*, Vol. LXV, No. 3 (July, 1974), pp. 118-129.

Doyce B. Nunis, Jr., ed., *The Golden Frontier: The Recollections of Herman Francis Reinhart, 1851-1869* (Austin: University of Texas Press, 1962), pp. 204-207, 242-243, 262.

Kenneth Owens, "Judge Lynch in Washington Territory," *Pacific Northwest Quarterly*, Vol. LV, No. 4 (October, 1964), pp. 177-178.

United States Senate, 37th Congress, 3rd Session, *Executive Document No. 43* (Washington: Government Printing Office, 1863), p. 51.

James W. Nye, Civil War governor of Nevada Territory and a leading advocate of statehood, achieved in 1864.

Nevada Territory

By James Thomas

On July 7, 1861, Governor James W. Nye entered Carson City, and for the first time the territory of Nevada welcomed its chief executive. Horsemen and carriages, decorated with Union flags, met his stage five miles outside of town. His entry into the city was announced by a twelve pound cannon and was greeted by a cheering and enthusiastic crowd that provided an audience for the governor's first speech. Nye's reputation as a gifted orator was not damaged by his short but forceful comments. He asked the people of Nevada not only to support the laws of the Federal government but also those that would be made by the territorial legislature in order to protect personal and property rights. Then he expressed his loyalty to the Union and warned secessionists against any attempt to oppose his authority: "Allow me to assure you that not one star shall be permitted to be removed from the old [flag]." Then he waited for the loud applause to die, and added, "twenty-five million freemen will not permit it. And I have come here to this distant country with the hope of adding one more — a bright and glorious star — Nevada!"[1]

The arrival of Governor Nye ended a long struggle by the citizens of western Utah to form a new territory. After the gold and silver rush of 1859 had changed the sparsely populated agriculture settlements into booming mining camps, the authorities were not able to control the lawless elements that followed the mineral strikes. The Unionists were fearful that Southern sympathizers might capture the area for the Confederacy. Congress, cognizant of the economic importance of the mines and responding to the citizens' plea, on March 2, 1861, passed the Organic Act which set up the political framework necessary for Nevada to become a territory.

Courtesy of Nevada State Historical Society

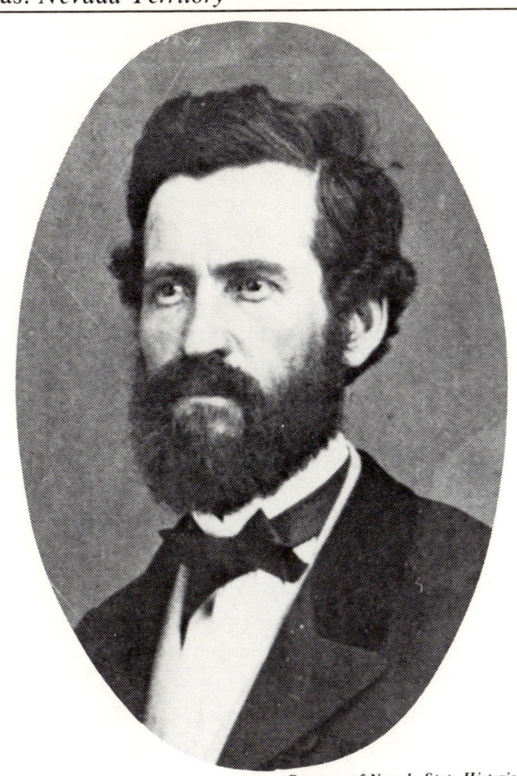

Orion Clemens, first secretary of Nevada Territory and brother of Samuel L. Clemens (Mark Twain).

Governor Nye, a prominent New York politician, rewarded for his campaign activities for Abraham Lincoln in the presidential election of 1860, was given the executive appointment. Nye's loyalty to the Republican Party, and his appointment of many of his Republican friends from New York to minor positions in the territorial government, assured Nevada's allegiance to the Union cause during the Civil War.[2]

The second most powerful position in the Nevada government, Secretary of the Territory, was given to Orion Clemens. By virtue of his friendship with high ranking Republicans, Orion had received his appointment, but he was unable to pay for his transportation to Nevada. Broke and unable to obtain a loan, he persuaded his brother Samuel, Mark Twain, to accompany him to Nevada and pay both fares. In return, Samuel was to be appointed personal secretary to his brother. Samuel had lost his job as a pilot on the Mississippi River when Civil War hostilities had stopped traffic, but he saved enough money to provide funds for their trip. However, the territorial budget did not have allo-

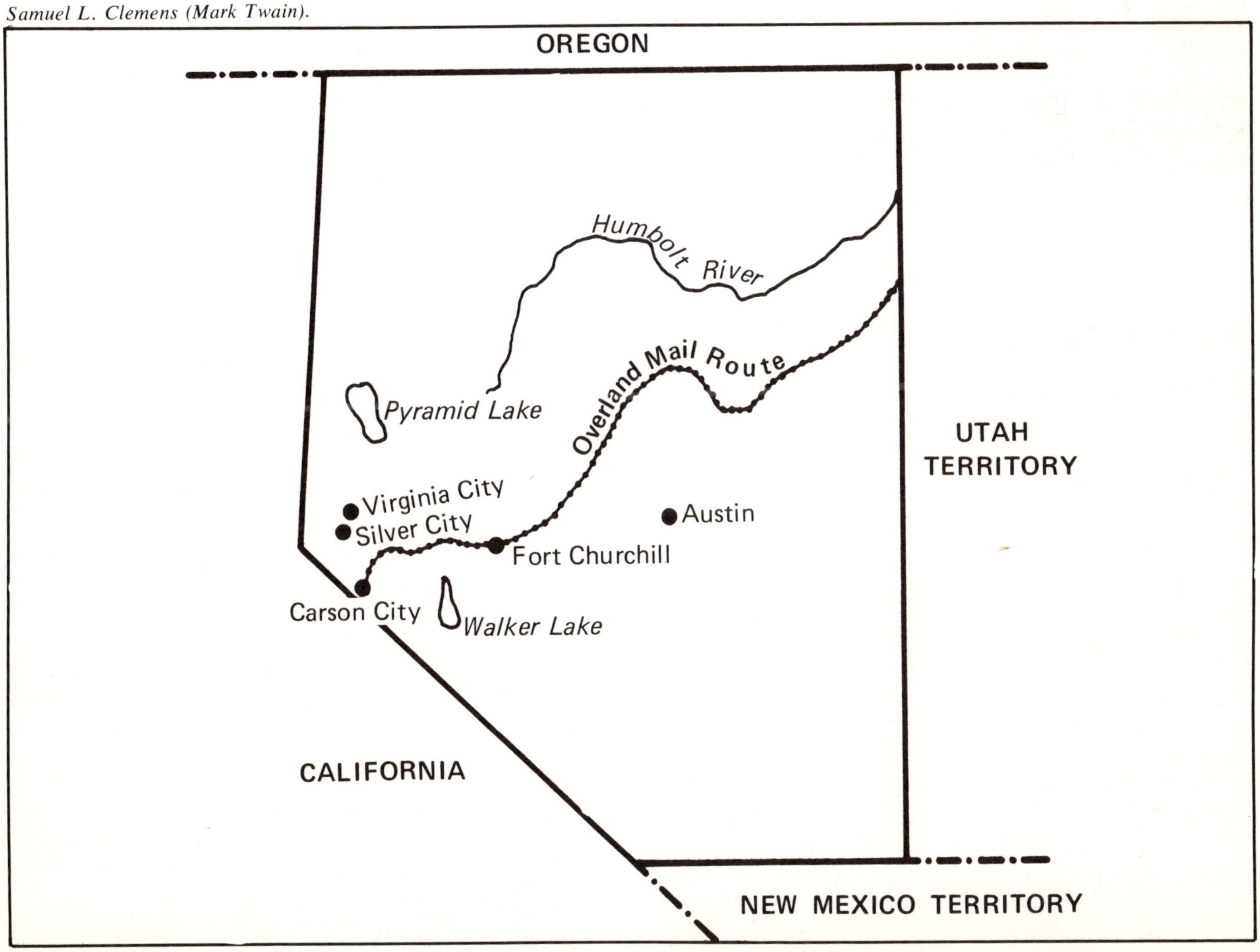

Nevada Territory During the Civil War

Map Drafted by Georganne T. Bartow

cations for the secretarial post, and Samuel accepted a job with Carson City's *Territorial Enterprise*.[3]

The newly appointed governor, eager to establish law and order, declared on July 11, 1861, that the government had been legally established. Within two weeks he set up a judiciary, appointed judges to the lower courts, and ordered a territorial census to be taken. Arrangements were made for dividing the territory into voting districts, for the election of delegates to the territorial legislature, and for the election of a territorial representative to the United States Congress.[4]

The election for delegates to the territorial legislature took place on August 31, 1861, and the nine members of the upper chamber and the fifteen members of the House of Representatives were to meet on October 1 in Carson City. Of the 16,374 residents in Nevada Territory, 4,306 voted for Unionists and 985 voted for pro-slavery candidates. The election not only showed the secessionist strength in the territory, but also reflected the rough element in the mining camps. At one polling station the ballot box and all of the ballots were destroyed; fist fights, assaults, and even one death were attributed to the high-spirited election.[5]

Governor Nye asked the two houses of the legislature to show their loyalty to the Union in their law making, to support the war effort by collecting the national war tax as soon as possible, and to pass civil and criminal codes which would give order to the chaos that existed. The lawmakers responded to the governor's suggestions by passing resolutions that declared their loyalty to the Union, the Federal Constitution, and the war effort. Moreover, an order was issued to make Carson City a Federal government record depository, so that the records could be protected from secessionists.[6]

Even though the majority of the lawmakers were abolitionists, ethnic bias appeared throughout their civil and criminal codes. In a court of law a Black, Mulatto, Indian, or Chinese could not testify in a trial involving a white. Moreover, whites were prohibited from marrying Blacks, Mulattoes, Indians or Chinese. The guilty parties were subject to imprisonment for up to six months and fines were not to exceed $100.[7]

To provide funds for governmental operations, a property tax of ten percent was to be paid on all taxable property; the territorial government would receive sixty percent of this revenue while the country's government would be given the remaining forty percent. A two dollar poll tax was to be collected from all males between the ages of twenty-one and fifty years. Licenses had to be obtained by businesses that provided entertainment for the citizens of Nevada: theaters paid five dollars per day, circuses paid twenty dollars per day, and bowling alleys paid twenty dollars per quarter. Pawnbrokers and agents for freight lines, mining companies, and ore mills had to purchase a license each quarter for $100.[8]

The lawless element that had arrived in the territory after the gold rush received much attention from the delegates of the territorial legislature. Provisions were made for establishing a territorial prison system, for providing security for Federal prisoners, and for the building of a new prison for the territory. The houses of prostitution, gambling, claim disputes, and the frequency of armed robberies made it necessary for the criminal codes to be defined in exacting detail. Judicial squabbles had been common before the establishment of Federal authority; therefore, the jurisdictions of the courts were carefully outlined to avoid future problems.[9]

After most of the laws had been passed and all of the territorial offices were functioning, a general election was called to elect county officers on January 14, 1862. As the government sought to establish order in the territory, it found that most of its laws and governing policies were inadequate to cope with active and hostile communities. The mining codes had not settled disputes, and criminal laws had not stopped illegal activity, and the citizens were not happy with conditions in the territory. With the birth of the territory came the call for statehood. The governor made an urgent plea to the Federal government for aid in settling the problems besieging the territory, but Washington was busy fighting the Civil War. As long as Nevada remained loyal and the Federal treasury received gold and silver from its mines, Nevada was to be neglected.[10]

The loyalty of Nevada was not in question, but the absence of a mining code threatened to close the mines, stop the flow of precious metals needed to carry on the war effort, and destroy the territorial government. The prominent men of the state, knowing that the future of the state was in mining, and that the mining codes had to be changed, clamored for a national mining code and statehood. Most of the judges, not trained to make technical and legal decisions that involved millions of dollars, and in some cases corrupt, compounded the problem. The judges were not only unqualified and corrupt, but they were not responsible to the citizens of Nevada. Statehood was necessary so that qualified judges could be elected and representatives could be sent to Congress to lobby for the development of a national mining code.[11]

The statehood movement was aided on the national level by the passage of a bill in Congress in February, 1863, providing for Nevada, Montana, Nebraska, and Colorado to frame constitutions and submit them to the Federal government for statehood approval. Legally, Nevada did not have sufficient population to become a state, but Senator William Latham of California argued that the territory was increasing in population each day and with statehood more settlers would be attracted. He assured Congress that the Republican Party in Nevada was in full control of the territory and would guarantee support of the Union both politically and economically. Moreover, statehood should increase the bullion production to $36 million per year. The

United States Senate passed an enabling act for the state of Nevada on March 3, 1863, However, the House of Representatives refused to vote on the measure, thus postponing the passage of the act until the next year.[12]

When news of the Federal government's interest in transforming the territory into a state reached Nevada, a new and stronger call for statehood echoed across the territory. In September, 1863, the territorial legislature called for an election to decide if statehood should be sought. Thirty-nine delegates were elected to frame a constitution and present it to the voters for approval. A majority of the young active delegates that met in Carson City during the first week of November, 1863, were from California and represented mining interests, lawyers, and merchants. The month long session produced minor objections from secessionists over a strong statement against states' rights, disfranchisement of Confederates who bore arms against the Union, and the pledge to uphold the Federal Constitution. However, minor conflicts were compromised or, in the case of the secessionists, outvoted; but the major controversy, taxing the mines, destroyed the chances for the adoption of the constitution by the voting public. William M. Stewart, the most powerful opponent of the tax clause and the most prominent lawyer in Nevada, led the fight against taxing mine property. Stewart believed that taxing the equipment, shafts, and lands of an unproductive mine would create an unfair advantage for the rich miner and cause the poor miner to go bankrupt. Even though he used his power as chairman of the judiciary committee to influence the delegates, the tax clause remained in the constitution.[13]

Through mine litigations and the subsequent legal fees, Stewart became very wealthy and sought to protect the mining interest and his livelihood by defeating the constitution. After closing his law office, Stewart traveled to the mining camps, gaining support from a majority of the mining industries and many merchants. While his efforts alone did not defeat the constitution, they contributed significantly. In addition, the Union Party's nominating convention held in Story County, the most populated county in the territory, split over personal quarrels. The candidates who did not receive nominations for state offices broke from the party, complained of unfair backroom dealings, and formed a new nominating convention. They not only campaigned against their old party's candidates, but also against the proposed constitution, which they believed to be secessionist inspired. The constitution was overwhelmingly defeated on the following day, but the governor responded to the defeat by calling for a new constitutional convention.[14]

Again the statehood movement dominated territorial politics during the election of delegates in February, 1864. Mine litigations had all but stopped productive work in the shafts. Judges, paid a meager sum of $1,500 per year, were open to bribe, and those who were not corrupt were incompetent. Moreover, there was a movement in Congress to sell or lease the mining areas, which were on public domain, to help pay for the war. Nevada would have to achieve statehood in order to protect its mining interests. The territory's position was aided by President Lincoln and in his 1863 annual message to Congress he showed his concern for the admission of Nevada and its importance to the war effort by encouraging immigration. Moreover, in anticipation of a close vote on the adoption of the Thirteenth Amendment, Lincoln wanted another Republican state represented in Congress to guarantee its passage.[15]

The major opposition to Nevada's admission to the Union was based on insufficient population. In spite of the objections, Congress passed a bill admitting Nevada on March 21, 1864, and Lincoln, determined to gain a new Republican state, signed the bill on the same day. In order to qualify for statehood, the territorial government had to submit a state constitution that could not be "repugnant" to the United States Constitution, could not allow slavery, and could not deny religious freedom. When the news reached Nevada, the constitutional delegates, with renewed vigor, started framing a new document. Within a month they completed their task. The constitution resembled the first document, but the odious tax on mines was omitted. William Stewart again took to the stump, only this time he campaigned for the adoption of the constitution; again he was victorious.[16]

William Stewart, prominent Civil War era lawyer in Nevada Territory and the first United States senator of the state of Nevada, admitted in 1864.

The governor, knowing that the constitution sent by regular mail would not reach Washington in time for Nevada to participate in the national election in November, 1864, decided to send the entire document by telegraph. The message not only established a record for the longest telegram, but also the cost, $3,000, was the highest price that had ever been paid for a single transmission. On October 31, 1864, according to law, Lincoln approved the constitution without action from Congress, and Nevada became the thirty-fifth state admitted to the Union.[17]

The first state legislature of Nevada met during the second week of December, 1864. Stewart was elected on the first ballot for a senatorial appointment, but the other seat was hotly contested, and the voting ended in a deadlock. The following day, Stewart used his influence in favor of James Nye, and he became the second senator. The two senators then drew lots to determine which one would have the longer term. Stewart won, and Nye was to serve for two years. On the first day that Stewart assumed his duties in Washington, he called on President Lincoln. Traveling down Pennsylvania Avenue, deeply rutted and muddy, Stewart was forced to leave his hack and "wade ashore." At the White House the president cheerfully received the newly appointed senator and welcomed the new Republican state. "We need as many loyal states as we can get," Lincoln said, and then he added, "the gold and silver in the region you represent has made it possible for the government to maintain sufficient credit to continue this terrible war for the Union."[18]

It was not an accident that Nevada was a loyal state. Union and Confederate sentiment seemed evenly divided in the territory at the outbreak of the Civil War, but President Lincoln had appointed Republicans to the territorial offices, and through their activities the Unionists prevailed. However, before Governor Nye established the territorial government, rumors of secessionist activities in Nevada reached army headquarters in San Francisco, and a contingent of California militia was sent to Fort Churchill to stop the secessionists' threat. On June 6, 1861, Captain Tredwell Moore, with twenty men, was dispatched from Fort Churchill to check the rumor that agents from the Confederacy were active in some mining camps.[19]

Moore collected arms from the citizens in Carson City, marched to Silver City to collect more arms, and then to Virginia City to investigate the flying of a Confederate banner. The raising of the flag was considered a joke by the owner of the building from which the flag was flown. Moore, however, believing that there was a secret secessionist organization in Virginia City, formed two companies of volunteers, gave them the confiscated arms, and made them swear an oath to protect the Union and to suppress any rebellion that might occur.[20]

The next year, Colonel P. Edward Connor, commander of the Third Regiment of California Volunteers and of Fort Churchill, responded to yet another secessionist rumor. On August 6, 1862, he issued an order making it a crime to express sentiment against the government. Persons found guilty would be confined until they swore an oath of allegiance to the Federal government. If the crime were repeated, the person would be confined until Connor was notified so that he might prescribe further punishment.[21]

At the beginning of the war, regular United States army troops garrisoned in Nevada were ordered east to take an active part in the war. Without federal troops or law enforcement in the territory, the Overland Mail Route was open to attacks by Indians and robberies by highwaymen. The suspension of the combined water-land route from New York across Panama to San Francisco made the Nevada route extremely important. The trail became the only route that people, goods, and mail could travel from the East Coast to the West Coast. Recruited with a promise of seeing action in the Eastern war zone, the Nevada state militia reluctantly guarded the route.[22]

The Indians had killed a few cattle and attacked some wagons on the Overland Mail Route. Governor Nye was aware of the Indian problem, but thought that it could be avoided with food and clothing, for the white population had destroyed many of the Indians' food sources. Major streams and lakes made favorable sites to build communities and mills; and the Indian was driven to more arid regions. Also, chemical residue from washing ore, sawdust from the lumber mill, and diverting water from stream beds to mills, combined to destroy the fish habitat. The game that had been plentiful before the coming of the white man was killed or chased from the area. The pine nut groves, a major source of food for the Indian, were cut to be used for building houses, shoring mine shafts, and heating. An Indian agent thus reported the condition of the native population: "Their chief food in the short summer which we have is a large bug or cricket and a weed called tuley which disappears when snow or frost appears."[23] Governor Nye read the report, relayed the information to the military Department of the Pacific, and suggested that food be passed out along the Overland Mail Route to pacify the Indians. Headquarters agreed with Nye's plan, and he was given 60,000 rations of flour and 40,000 rations of meat to distribute among the Indians.[24]

Nye's pacification program did not stop all Indian hostilities. Isolated cases of stealing cattle, killing prospectors, and attacking stages continued throughout the Civil War. During the spring of 1862 an east bound stage was attacked at Eight Mile Station. A band of Indians had killed the station master and then ambushed the approaching stage. The driver, although mortally wounded, managed to drive the coach until a "film gathering in his eyes" blurred his vision and he called to his passengers for help. One of the occupants of the stage "made his way by clinging to the sides of the stage'' and gained control of the horses as ''Happy Harry sank dying under the seat.''[25] The stage was able to elude the Indians, and all of the passengers' lives were spared. Many other such incidents, although not as dramatic, occurred along the Overland Mail Route until the end of the Civil War.

With continued outbreaks of minor Indian hostilities and with an insufficient number of troops to protect the citizens of Nevada, the military Department of the Pacific ordered Governor Nye to raise one full regiment of infantry and one full regiment of cavalry. Four companies, one infantry and three cavalry, guarded the Overland Mail Route. The remaining men were garrisoned in the forts throughout the territory. The horse troops were easily recruited, but infantry duty was less glamorous, and many men balked at volunteering. However, by the end of the war, 1,180 men had served in Nevada's military forces.[26]

Although the Nevada volunteers did not engage the Confederate Army, they proved their fighting ability against the Indians. Most military action against the Indians was confined to small skirmishes, and often the military showed restraint by arresting the Indians that had broken the law rather than waging war against a whole tribe.[27]

In March, 1865, the First Nevada Cavalry Regiment had to take more drastic actions against a band of Smoke Creek Indians. Farmers and ranchmen in the Pyramid Lake area complained that a band of Indians had been stealing a large number of their cattle. Captain Almond B. Wells left Fort Churchill on March 12 with fifty men to arrest the guilty Indians. After a two day march, the troop reached Pyramid Lake and received news of the Indian encampment. Captain Wells divided his command into three squads and approached the Indians. Before the cavalry was within 100 yards, the Indians opened fire, and Wells ordered a sabre charge. The Indians scattered, and as they retreated the horsemen followed for ten miles, killing twenty-nine Indians while suffering only one wounded. Captain Wells, relating the incident, wrote that ''The Indians fought like veterans,'' but in ''Hand-to-hand conflicts...my men behaved with a valor and fortitude rarely equaled.''[28]

The engagement involving the Smoke Creek Indians was the bloodiest single conflict in Nevada during the Civil War. Most of the Indians were peaceful, but some had to steal food in order to elude starvation. Old Winnemucca, chief of the Paiutes, talked with Captain Wells after the Pyramid Lake skirmish, and said he was highly pleased with the outcome. All through the winter Winnemucca had warned the Smoke Creek Indians not to steal the white man's cattle; he believed the punishment they received was the justice they deserved.[29]

The military, busy protecting against Indian raids, was not able to protect the citizenry against the lawless elements of the mining camps. Wells Fargo bullion shipments traveling from the Comstock Lode to San Francisco were robbed regularly. Many of the highwaymen were men of position and high standing in their communities. However, most juries hated Wells Fargo for their unethical business practices more than they cherished justice, and few highwaymen were punished. The thieves of the road avoided harming the passengers, for in some cases they were first gentlemen and second thieves. In one such case a stage was stopped by highwaymen, and as the express box was being removed, some champagne was discovered. Rugs were spread on the ground for the lady passengers, and the robbers mingled among their guests, drinking and entertaining.[30]

However, many of the lawbreakers were thugs and murders who came to the mining camps because there was little law enforcement. Prostitution, gambling, and saloons provided a breeding ground for the many crimes committed in the mining camps. Seldom, however, did any crime result in punishment. Juries were subject to bribes, citizens were afraid to testify, and in some cases judges and marshals were the greatest offenders against the law.

John L. Blackburn, a deputy United States marshal who was elected sheriff of Ormsby County, provides a typical example of a corrupt official. Blackburn had been considered one of the best lawmen in Nevada, but by the spring of 1861 he was known as one of the most ruthless lawbreakers. He not only assaulted or killed criminals that he came in contact with, but also prominent citizens. After arresting a drunk on a minor offense, Blackburn stopped at a saloon to have a drink before taking his prisoner to jail. The drunk, singing very loudly, was asked several times to be silent. After he refused to comply with the repeated warnings, Blackburn drew his pistol and killed him. With the corpse lying at his feet, the sheriff and his friends continued to drink. Blackburn was later stabbed to death in front of witnesses, but the murderer was allowed to escape because of the service he had rendered the public.[31]

The gold rush brought other illegal trades to Nevada, including the legal profession. After the Comstock Lode was discovered, a controversy arose over the many overlapping claims, and the problem was compounded by the appointment of territorial judges. John Cradlebaugh had been appointed as territorial judge by Utah Territory, but the miners, opposed to Mormons, would not accept him as a legal authority. President James Buchanan replaced Cradlebaugh with R. P. Flenniken, but again the miners did not approve of the newly appointed judge. Also, Cradlebaugh argued that Buchanan did not have the authority to replace him and refused to resign his post. When Buchanan's appointee arrived, Judge Cradlebaugh agreed to resign his post only if the Utah Supreme Court decided against him or if the Lincoln administration failed to pay him his salary. When the Pony Express brought the Utah Supreme Court's decision in favor of Cradlebaugh, Flenniken refused to comply.[32]

William Stewart, the outstanding lawyer in the Comstock Lode area, became involved in the struggle. Stewart had received many favorable decisions from Cradlebaugh and wanted to retain the territorial judge. To arm himself with some legal authority, Stewart had Sheriff Blackburn deputize him, and then Stewart strapped on his pistols and looked for Flenniken. When he found the judge, Stewart recalled, "I grabbed him by the collar and jerked him on to his knees, and drawing my pistol" told him he should resign. The judge was then marched to the telegraph office, and forced to sign and send several dispatches "that he was not judge, that Cradlebaugh was, and his orders must be obeyed."[33] The Nevada judiciary failed to hold court until President Lincoln appointed three territorial judges in July, 1861, to handle the large backlog of cases.

The judiciary floundered for the next three years while litigation and counter litigation filled the courts' dockets. Without a detailed mining code, each claim on the Comstock Lode was in question. Some mining companies based their claims on eye witnesses who were often on the company's payroll, or deeds that were often fraudulent, and still others laid claims without any legal grounds, hoping to gain a settlement out of court. The district court, whose jurisdiction included the Comstock Lode, tried 247 cases involving mining claims.[34] Investors would sue a mine, get an injunction to stop mining operations, and when the price of stock would drop, the investor would buy the cheaper stock, withdraw the litigation, and wait for a return on his investment.[35]

Lawyers, hearing of the huge profits to be made defending mining interests, flocked to Nevada. In 1863, Virginia City could boast a total population of almost 10,000 people, including a total of 215 resident lawyers. The single most important problem facing the legal fraternity was the ledge theory. At first, the claims that were staked out in the Comstock Lode were mined according to the surface area described in the claim. However, as the shafts descended, many shafts intersected, giving rise to the single-ledge theory. One group of miners and their legal council believed, to their own advantage, that a claim was not made for a specified area but for a ledge; a company should be able to mine a ledge, even if it crossed into another claim. The other faction disagreed, and proposed that a claim was for a specified area and could contain many ledges.[36]

Each faction fought, in and out of court, to achieve favorable decisions. By bribes, threats, and blackmail, William Stewart became the most sought after lawyer in Nevada. He handled most of the cases involving the richer mines, and through legal fees he earned $500,000. Stewart's ability to gain favorable decisions for his clients was not from extensive legal training, but from his ability to control the judiciary. Judge George Turner tried all of the Comstock Lode cases, and gave decisions favorable to the single-ledge theory, to the major mining companies and to Stewart, their lawyer. In his

memoirs, Stewart admitted giving the judge $5,000 to receive an injunction, and in 1863 the same judge resigned when accused of receiving $25,000 from a company that Stewart represented.[37]

In 1863, James A. North replaced Turner, and became the district judge presiding over the Comstock Lode area. North had been appointed surveyor general for the territorial government, was prepared to invest in a quartz mill, and to enter law practice to supplement his meager income. Serious minded, hard working, and not very diplomatic, North was considered honest and upright, but not a qualified judge. In 1864, his downfall came when he supported the multi-ledge theory and rendered a decision against Stewart's client. The case was appealed to the territorial supreme court that consisted of North and the two other territorial judges. Turner, now the chief justice, favored the one-ledge theory and was considered a Stewart man, but the third judge, Powhattan B. Locke, was not partial to either theory. Both parties involved in the litigation tried to sway Locke's judgment, and the result was favorable to Judge North.[38]

Failing to win in court, Stewart decided upon a new plan; he attempted to force all the judges to resign. After a long newspaper campaign accusing Judge North of accepting bribes, Stewart involved the other judges and published a petition in the *Territorial Enterprise* demanding the resignation of all three judges. Judge North was the first to resign, and then Stewart concentrated his attack on the other judges. Chief Justice Turner had either been loaned or given $2,000 by a banker who owned an interest in one of the major mines, and Stewart presented the receipt and claimed it was a bribe paid for an injunction. Turner succumbed to the pressure and resigned.[39]

Powhattan B. Locke, the only remaining judge, did not have the strength or the intelligence to stop Stewart. When Stewart had denounced North as dishonest and Turner as corrupt, he said Locke was "too ignorant for denunciation."[40] Instead of bringing charges against Locke to prove that he had not fulfilled his duties as a judge, Stewart resorted to his own brand of frontier justice. All of Stewart's friends were invited to celebrate the resignation of North and Turner. After a large quantity of champagne was consumed, Stewart asked two young lawyers "physically strong and endowed with a reaonable amount of courage," to bring Locke to the party. When Stewart was told that the judge was in his room, he replied, "if he is locked in his room, locks can be broken." Frightened by the hostile crowd and confused at the request for his resignation, Locke returned to Stewart for advice. Stewart replied, "resign and do it quick." Locke intimidated by the crowd and fearful for his life, signed a resignation statement. The backlog of cases had to wait for state elected judges to take charge of the courts, and even then settlement of many claims did not take place until the adoption of the national mining code in 1866.[41]

Illegal activities in the mining camps were offset by a stable population. Blue laws designed to regulate Sunday activities were passed but proved ineffective; churches were built, school districts were organized, and theater flourished. An example of generosity and patriotism of the law-abiding citizens of Nevada was their contribution to the United States Sanitary Commission. During the city election for mayor of Austin in the spring of 1864, a wager was made between Ruel Colt Gridley, a Democrat, and Dr. H. S. Herrick, a Republican, on the outcome of the election. The loser would have to carry a fifty pound sack of flour across Austin. If Herrick lost he would have to march to the tune of "Dixie," and if Gridley lost the tune would be "John Brown's Body." The day after the election, Gridley, the loser, shouldered his burden that had been garnished with Union flags, marched behind a brass band, and passed the cheering crowd that gathered to watch a Southerner pay tribute to the Union. After the march had been completed, the sack of flour was auctioned off to provide funds for the United States Sanitary Commission. The Democrats vied against the Republicans in the spirited bidding that followed. When the flour was finally sold, the proud owner returned his prize to be auctioned off again. When the day ended, $4,549 in gold had been collected, and Gridley volunteered to travel to other cities to auction off the flour and donate the money to the United States Sanitary Commission. Austin, proud of its contributions, adopted the sack of flour as its city seal. Gridley did not stop his efforts at raising money until he had visited all the major cities in Nevada and California, and even some cities in the East. After one year of volunteer work, Gridley's sack of flour had provided $275,000. This amount, along with other funds, raised Nevada's total contribution to the United States Sanitary Commission to over $338,000.[42]

The small population of Nevada and the necessity for its militia to quell Indian hostilities, kept her from taking an active part in the war. However, the militia provided a valuable service to the Union effort by securing the Overland Mail Route, thus allowing communications and merchandise to flow from the East to the West. Moreover, Nevada's loyalty guaranteed that her resources would be used for the Union cause. The $45 million of bullion produced within her borders during the Civil War enabled the Union to maintain its credit and finance the war. The Civil War indirectly brought about Nevada's premature admission to the Union, but with statehood Nevada was able to bring order to its mining area and increase production. After the Civil War, Nevada's resources were again called upon to provide financing to reconstruct the war-torn nation.

NOTES

1. *Daily Alta California*, July 22, 1861.
2. *Ibid.*, June 18, 1861; United States Department of War, *The War of the Rebellion: A Compilation of the Official Records of the Union and Confederate Armies* (70 vols., 128 books, Washington: Government Printing Office, 1880-1901), Ser. I, Vol. L, Pt. 1, pp. 490-500.
3. Mark Twain, *Roughing It* (New York: Harper and Brothers, 1877), p. 180.
4. Myron Angel, ed., *History of Nevada* (Oakland: Thompson and West, 1881), pp. 77-78.
5. *Ibid.*
6. Effie Mona Mack, *Nevada: A History of the State From the Earliest Times Through the Civil War* (Glendale: Arthur H. Clark Company, 1936), pp. 230-231.
7. Angel, ed., *op. cit.*, pp. 77-79.
8. Edward S. Dodson, "A History of Nevada During the Civil War" (Master of Arts Thesis, Eugene: University of Oregon, 1947), pp. 28-29.
9. *Congressional Globe*, 37th Congress, 1st Session, p. 1022.
10. United States Congress, *Journal of the House of Representatives*, 37th Congress, 2nd Session, p. 486.
11. Eleanore Bushnell, *The Nevada Constitution: Origin and Growth* (Reno: University of Nevada Press, 1968), p. 34.
12. *Congressional Globe*, 37th Congress, 2nd Session, pp. 1510-1512, 1543, 1549.
13. *Virginia Evening Bulletin*, December 1 and 12, 1863.
14. Dodson, *op. cit.*, p. 91; Angel, ed., *op. cit.*, pp. 84-85.
15. Frederick L. Bullard, "Abraham Lincoln and the Statehood of Nevada," *American Bar Association Journal*, Vol. XXIV, Nos. 3 and 4 (March and April, 1940), p. 236.
16. *Congressional Globe*, 38th Congress, 1st Session, pp. 521, 693.
17. Mack, *op. cit.*, p. 264.
18. George Rothwell Brown, ed., *Reminiscences of Senator William M. Stewart of Nevada* (New York: Neale Publishing Comapny, 1908), pp. 168-169.
19. *Official Records*, Ser. I, Vol. L, Pt. 1, pp. 499-505.
20. *Ibid.*, pp. 510-511.
21. Angel, ed., *op. cit.*, p. 266.
22. *Official Records*, Ser. I, Vol. L, Pt. 2, p. 379.
23. Sam P. Davis, ed., *The History of Nevada* (2 vols., Reno: Elms Publishing Company, 1913), p. 35; *Official Records*, Ser. I, Vol. L, Pt. 1, p. 667.
24. *Ibid.*, p. 745.
25. Davis, ed., *op. cit.*, p. 321
26. *Official Records*, Ser. I, Vol. L, Pt. 2, pp. 379, 413, 499.
27. *Ibid.*, Pt. 1, pp. 405-408.
28. *Ibid.*, p. 405.
29. *Ibid.*
30. Davis, ed., *op. cit.*, pp. 243-244.
31. *Ibid.*, pp. 252-256; William R. Gillis, *Gold Rush Days With Mark Twain* (New York: AMS Press, 1969), p. 83.
32. Gilman M. Ostrander, *Nevada: The Great Rotten Borough, 1859-1864* (New York; Alfred A. Knopf, 1966), pp. 25-26.
33. Brown, ed., *op. cit.*, pp. 137-138.
34. Ostrander, *op. cit.*, pp. 17-30.
35. Merlin Stonehouse, *John Wesley North and the Reform Frontier* (Minneapolis: University of Minnesota Press, 1965), p. 160.
36. Ostrander, *op. cit.*, pp. 17-30.
37. Brown, ed., *op. cit.*, p. 161.
38. Stonehouse, *op. cit.*, pp. 164-171.
39. Brown, ed., *op. cit.*, p. 161.
40. *Ibid.*, p. 160.
41. *Ibid*, p. 162.
42. Angel, ed., *op. cit.*, pp. 268-270.

SELECTED READINGS

George Rothwell Brown, ed., *Reminiscences of Senator William M. Stewart of Nevada* (New York: Neale Publishing Company, 1908), pp. 129-169.

Frederick L. Bullard, "Abraham Lincoln and the Statehood of Nevada," *American Bar Association Journal*, Vol. XXIV, Nos. 3 and 4 (March and April, 1940), pp. 210-213, 236, 313-317.

Eleanore Bushnell, *The Nevada Constitution, Origin and Growth* (Reno: University of Nevada Press, 1968).

Edward S. Dodson, "A History of Nevada During the Civil War" (Master of Arts Thesis, Eugene: University of Oregon, 1947).

George M. Ostrander, *Nevada: The Great Rotten Borough, 1859-1864* (New York: Alfred A. Knopf, 1966).

Merlin Stonehouse, *John Wesley North and the Reform Frontier* (Minneapolis: University of Minnesota Press, 1965).

Mark Twain, *Roughing It* (New York: Harper and Brothers, 1877).

Courtesy of Utah State Historical Society

The parade grounds and headquarters of Camp Douglas, a 2,560 acre military reservation established by the United States Army during the Civil War overlooking Salt Lake City, Utah Territory.

Utah Territory
By Gary L. Watters

When the Civil War began, most everyone in Utah Territory viewed it as the fulfillment of divine prophecy, for on Christmas day, 1832, the Mormon leader Joseph Smith received a revelation concerning the sectional war which soon would disrupt the whole of American society. Smith not only predicted the outbreak of the Civil War some twenty-eight years before its occurrence, but also prophesied that the rebellion would begin in South Carolina and eventually would lead to death and destruction on a scale not yet experienced by the people of the United States. Northern states would take up arms against Southern states, Smith said, brother would fight brother, and the slaves would rise up against their masters and be marshalled

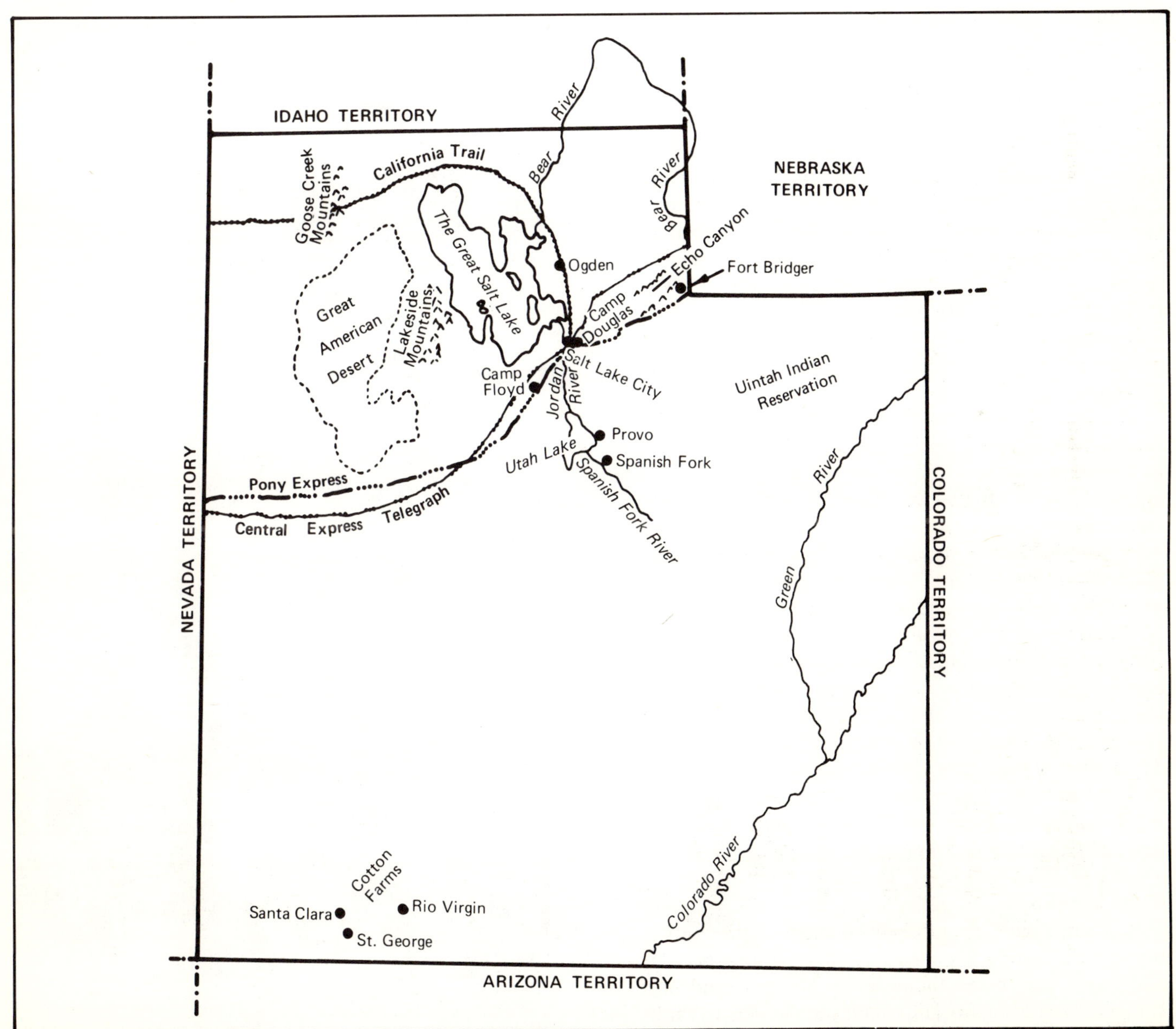

Utah Territory During the Civil War

into the military service of the Northern states.[1]

The years between 1832 and the outbreak of the Civil War were marked not only by the unfolding tragedy in the United States, but also by the personal trauma of the Mormon people. The Mormons, known formally as the Church of Jesus Christ of Latter-day Saints, were first organized in New York state in 1830, and the early followers came from the central and North Atlantic states. The intense persecution suffered by the Latter-day Saints in New York encouraged Smith, on whose religious revelations the movement was based, to begin a journey westward in hopes of finding a New Jerusalem. The search for this holy spot would lead them to Ohio, Missouri, Illinois, and finally to the basin of the Great Salt Lake Valley in Utah.

The trek westward led first to Kirtland, Ohio. By 1831, this location was the central Mormon community and remained so until 1838. During this time, church government became highly developed, and with it patterns of a theocratic state. The guidance of Joseph Smith also strengthened and expanded the doctrines of the church. By 1838, the movement had enlarged greatly, due to increased missionary vigor by the Latter-day Saints, but this also had induced hostility from the Gentile community. The final blow came unexpectedly from the national level. In a time of plenty, the Mormons had wisely organized the Kirtland Safety Society Bank, but the Panic of 1837 resulted in a great financial loss to the Mormon bank, and Smith received much of the blame. His enemies attempted to replace him as head of the Latter-day Saints, after which Smith gathered those who remained faithful and migrated to Missouri.[2]

The immediate Mormon goal still remained that of establishing a permanent residence. Missouri seemed to be a good location. Located on the Western frontier, it was centrally situated and would be advantageous in furthering the spread of Mormonism. The Mormons established a community at Far West, near Independence. Scarcely had the Mormons become acquainted with their new surroundings, when the governor of Missouri issued an order demanding that they leave the state or face extermination. Attacks upon Mormon communities became increasingly violent. In the Haun's Mill massacre of 1838, Gentile partisans killed seventeen Mormon men, women, and children. Within days, some 2,000 state militia under the direction of General Sam D. Lucas arrived at Far West and demanded that the Mormons leave Missouri. Smith refused. Missouri courts bound over for trial Smith and a number of his followers. The Mormons had not yet found the promised land.

Brigham Young, an influential member of the church, became the temporary leader of the Mormon people, and safely conducted them out of Missouri and into Illinois. After escaping jail, Smith soon joined his faithful followers at Quincy, Illinois. Some fifty miles up the Mississippi River from Quincy, Smith established the

city of Nauvoo, and with it the practical workings of a theocratic state. Nauvoo had a population of 15,000, the largest in Illinois. As the Mormons became further alienated from American society, they began a campaign to make their community self-sufficient. They established their own educational system and their own military force called the Nauvoo Legion, and in every way attempted to maintain complete independence and sovereignty over their affairs.[3]

Prospects at Nauvoo seemed bright until fateful events in 1844 altered the face of Mormon life. The problem centered around a disloyal believer named William Law. Under the guidance of Law, a newspaper entitled the *Nauvoo Expositor* discredited and defamed the character of Smith. Consequently, Smith had the paper suppressed and removed from circulation. This allowed the Illinois government formally to press charges against the prophet for violating freedom of the press. Illinois Governor Thomas Ford ordered Smith bound over for trial at Carthage, Illinois. It was in the Carthage Jail on June 27, 1844, that an angry mob rushed the jail and shot Joseph Smith and his brother

Courtesy of Utah State Historical Society

Brigham Young, although removed from the governorship of Utah Territory by President James Buchanan, retained leadership of the Mormon community throughout the Civil War era.

Stephen S. Harding, governor of Utah Territory in 1862-1863, severely criticized polygamy and declared the territory unprepared for statehood.

wired the territorial delegate to Congress, William Hooper, that the Nauvoo Legion was ready and willing to protect the mail line if called upon to do so. This was the only military service involving Mormons during the Civil War.[20]

Utah Territory's geographical location made it an important part of the Union's war strategy. With the outbreak of hostilities, Congress had rerouted the Overland Mail from a southern to a central route through Utah Territory so that it would not fall into secessionist hands. With the completion of the transcontinental telegraph in October, 1861, two of the Union's most vital lines of communication with the West Coast ran through Utah Territory. Consequently, the United States government decided that assets this valuable should not be left in the hands of people who might prove to be disloyal.

The man given the responsibility of protecting these assets was Colonel P. Edward Connor, the commanding officer of the Third California Volunteer Infantry Regiment. Connor had distinguished himself during the Mexican War and quickly quit his business and volunteered for service in the Union forces upon hearing about the outbreak of the Civil War. Connor assumed command of the Military District of Utah on August 6,

1862, an area that comprised the territories of Utah and Nevada.[21]

In mid-August, the new district commander left Fort Churchill bound for the plains of the Great Salt Lake. On September 9, while his troops waited at Fort Ruby, Nevada Territory, Connor journeyed on to Salt Lake City to select a proper site for a military post. Union troops had occupied old Camp Floyd located near Salt Lake City before the war, but by 1862 it had fallen into disrepair. Furthermore, the army had sold it to private interests who now were asking $15,000 as the price of reclamation. The Overland Mail Company had purchased what usable buildings were present at the campsite, and the establishment of a permanent post would require a good deal of time and money. The final assessment made by Connor was that the old government reserve was poorly located, in desperate need of many repairs, and an unsuitable position in which to establish a new outpost.

Colonel Connor recommended a location about three miles from Salt Lake City. High on a plateau overlooking the city, the soldiers would be strategically located to maintain a watchful eye on the Mormons and also to control hostile Indian outbreaks. The site was close also to good timber and saw mills; hay, grain, and other produce could likewise be obtained much more easily. Connor's first contact with the Mormon people convinced him that this was indeed a community of "traitors, murderers, fanatics, and whores" who were openly rebellious to the Union government. From the very beginning of his command of the Military District of Utah, Connor interpreted his orders twofold: to maintain peace with the Indians along the overland trails and to quell the treasonous activities of the Mormon population.[22]

Connor fully expected trouble from the Mormon people in his attempt to establish the new military post, but with 700 troops he marched across the Jordan River and through the streets of Salt Lake City. This display of force caused a great deal of discontent and irritation, but no incidents occurred. The troops occupied their new campsite and quickly constructed temporary winter shelters. On October 26, 1862, Connor officially established the military post as Camp Douglas, a 2,560 acre military reservation overlooking Salt Lake City. The installation was named in honor of Stephen A. Douglas, the late senator from Illinois who had once called the Mormons a "pestiferous, disgusting cancer."[23]

The resentment that accompanied Colonel Connor's entry into Utah Territory was only the beginning of a conflict which led both political and military officials to the brink of disaster in Utah. The hostility displayed by Colonel Connor and Governor Harding toward the Mormon people encouraged rebellion to develop among the Latter-day Saints. A daily barrage of abusive condemnations concerning the nature of Mormonism, coupled with administrative decisions which ran contrary to the will of the Mormons, only heightened tension which already existed.

Within months after his arrival, Colonel Connor began an effort to undermine deliberately the goodwill of the Mormon people. In letters sent to United States authorities both in San Francisco, California, and in Washington, D.C., Connor complained excessively regarding alleged bitter and unrelenting hostility of the Mormon Church toward the government. In particular, he accused Young of oppressing the people in the name of religion, and constantly denouncing the missions of the Union so as to create a treasonous attitude among the people. Connor prided himself on the selection of Camp Douglas, because of its commanding position to oversee alleged Mormon mischief. Furthermore, Connor insinuated that Mormon leaders often provoked the Indians into hostilities so as to take advantage of the smaller number of Union troops located in the territory, and that in case of a foreign war the Mormons represented a far greater danger than the Indians. Connor also accused Young of usurping the power of the government and making military preparations for open rebellion against the United States government. [24]

These blistering verbal attacks by Connor coincided with the equally harmful administrative and judicial policies of Governor Harding, and Judges Waite and Drake. On December 8, 1862, Harding approached the legislature with his first territorial message. After gestures of friendship, he began a scathing attack concerning the state of affairs in Utah Territory, and clearly insinuated that the people were not ready for the responsibilities of statehood. Furthermore, he made a point of bringing up the controversial subject of polygamy and emphasized that it was an illegal practice that went on daily in the territory. The mockery polygamy made of marriage, he continued, and the consequences it might have upon civilized society made it intolerable; he advised the Mormon faithful to forsake high church authorities and obey United States law. [25]

Two months earlier, Harding had written a letter to Secretary of State William H. Seward concerning the Mormon question. He told Seward that the Mormon people were disloyal to the United States government and delighted in the fact that peace had not been restored. In addition, proper administration in a territory which had no reverence for the United States government and its laws was impossible without adequate military authority to give the law credence. Similar communications resulted in complete alienation between Harding and the Mormons. [26]

In the early part of 1863, Judge Waite attempted to amend the Organic Act of Utah Territory. The proposed revisions called for the selection of juries by the United States marshal, and authorized the governor to appoint all militia officers. Furthermore, the amendment restricted the powers of the probate court to limited criminal jurisdiction. This was an attempt on the part of the territorial government to deprive the Mormons of local judiciary and military powers. Governor Harding approved the amendment and forwarded it to Congress. The campaign of anti-Mormonism begun under Harding's administration had brought troops into the territory, accused the population of disloyalty, questioned the moral implications of the practice of polygamy, and now threatened to limit the civil liberties of the people. Consequently, Young and his followers reacted vigorously against the territorial administration of Harding. [27]

The Mormon population gathered in the Mormon Tabernacle in Salt Lake City on March 3, 1863, to examine the actions of territorial officials. In an address before the congregation, Young demanded that Governor Harding, and judges Drake and Waite leave the territory, and said if they did not go willingly, they would be forcefully removed. In closing, Young remarked that Harding was governor in name only, and that the actual authority was in his hands. The governor replied that he would remain in his position, though his life be threatened. When the news reached Judge Drake through Young's emissary, John Taylor, the judge told Taylor to "Go back to Brigham Young, your master, that embodiment of sin and shame and disgust, and tell him that I neither fear him, nor love him, nor hate him, but that I utterly despise [him]." [28]

The result of the meeting was a signed petition from the Mormon congregation to President Lincoln. In summary, the resolution accused the governor and his two judges of not only attempting to create strife between the people and the troops at Camp Douglas, but also between the people and the United States government. The petition then requested the removal of these officials. The *Deseret News* attacked the three territorial officials as subversive individuals who were attempting to establish military despotism and violate the civil liberties of the Mormon people. [29]

Colonel Connor circulated a counter-petition among the military forces at Camp Douglas, urging Lincoln to retain Harding, Waite, and Drake and dismiss such Mormon sympathizers as Secretary Frank Fuller and Chief Justice John F. Kinney. President Lincoln did not personally want to be involved in the Mormon question. In an interview granted to T.B.H. Stenhouse, a special emissary from Young, Lincoln compared the Mormon question to a log that was "too hard to split, too wet to burn and too heavy to move, so we plowed around it." [30] Thus, in an act of reconciliation, Lincoln made concessions to both sides. He removed Harding from office but retained Waite and Drake. Lincoln also removed Secretary Fuller and Chief Justice Kinney from office. A new slate of territorial officials included the popular James Duane Doty as governor, Amos Reed as secretary, and John Titus as chief justice. As an epilogue, Judges Waite and Drake in disgust told President Lincoln that it would take at least a 5,000-man military force to make the United States courts in Utah Territory effective. [31]

At the same time that this political drama unfolded, a strange anomaly within the Mormon church developed. This involved a new self-named prophet, Joseph Morris, who claimed to have received a revelation from God concerning Young and alleged sins committed by him. Orthodox Saints drove Morris from the Mormon Church, but with a few followers he established his own "Kingdom" at Kinkton Fort, some thirty-five miles north of Salt Lake City. The new prophet revealed that Christ soon would descend to earth, and in fact fixed the time of the Lord's return. Subsequently, his followers did no farming, and when Christ failed to return at the expected time, provisions began to run out. Furthermore, Morris had demanded the communization of property, and when several disgruntled followers requested the return of their property, Morris imprisoned three of them.

Dissident Morrisites appealed to Young and Judge Kinney, and Kinney responded by issuing warrants for the arrest of the Morrisite leaders and a writ of habeas corpus to the three imprisoned men. Morris reacted to the court order by saying that he was not subject to the orders of the United States or Judge Kinney. Colonel R.T. Burton, the sheriff of Salt Lake City, was ordered with over 300 troops of the Nauvoo Legion to go to Kinkton Fort and enforce the writs. Morris refused to surrender, believing that God would continue to protect him and his followers. This resulted in a three-day siege and a blood bath which left six of the Morrisites dead, as well as two members of Burton's posse. Later testimony revealed that Colonel Burton personally killed Morris and declared, "There's your prophet, what do you think of him now?"[32]

In March of 1863, the remaining Morrisites came to trial. Seven were convicted of second degree murder while sixty-six others were fined $100. Governor Harding viewed this as a violation of the law and felt that Young merely had wanted to silence the voice of dissent. The partiality shown by Harding toward the Morrisites was yet another reason for the Utah Territory governmental shakeup in the spring of 1863.[33]

Colonel Connor had been so obsessed with controlling the Mormons and bolstering the administration of Governor Harding that he had given inadequate attention to Indian problems. Throughout the year 1862, the sporadic raiding practices of the Indian tribes menaced the overland trails. It was the Indian threat which had justified the sending of Union troops to Utah Territory

The Mormon Tabernacle in Salt Lake City, Utah Territory, nearing completion at the close of the Civil War.

at such a critical period of the Civil War. Until the arrival of Connor, a regiment of the Nauvoo Legion under the leadership of Captain Lot Smith had guarded the 200 mile route from Salt Lake City to the Green River. Not only did these volunteers guard against Indian attack, but they also rebuilt many stations and bridges, and escorted emigrant trains across Utah Territory. [34]

Upon assuming command, Connor promised to deal forcefully with the Indian problem and bring it under complete control. Between 1857 and 1862, Indian outbreaks had occurred frequently, with very little success in effectively curbing the menace. Particularly troublesome were the depredations of the Shoshone and Bannack tribes who had joined forces under the leadership of Chief Pashego and Chief Bear Hunter. Reports of the kidnapping of a ten-year-old boy by a group of Shoshones and Bannacks prompted Connor to take action. On January 22, 1863, Connor sent Captain Samuel N. Hoyt with Company K of the Third California Volunteer Infantry Regiment to find the Shoshone and Bannack camp. Under forced march in the dead of winter, the troops reached the Indian camp on Bear River at daylight on January 29. By this time, Connor and 230 cavalry had joined Hoyt. Shortly after dawn the

engagement began; for more than four hours Connor relentlessly attacked the Indians, until they were nearly annihilated. Chief Bear Hunter was killed, along with 300 men, women, and children. Only sixteen soldiers were killed, although fifty were wounded. The Mormon people viewed the Bear River incident as a massacre, but it won a promotion to brigadier general for Colonel Connor, and put an end to Indian hostilities in northern Utah Territory. [35]

The Southern Utes had caused Brigadier General Connor some concern, but in the spring of 1863 a further expedition successfully routed this Indian tribe at Spanish Fork and left them desiring peace. Connor arranged a treaty with Little Soldier, the chief of the Southern Utes, which moved them to West Mountain Valley, twenty-five miles west of Salt Lake City. The treaty with Little Soldier led to similar agreements with other Indians, including the Snake, Shoshone, and Goshute tribes. By the fall of 1863, Connor reported that the Indian situation was under control and that the overland routes were completely safe. James Doty, the commissioner of Indian Affairs, emphasized that the Indians "now realize the fact that Americans are the masters of this country, and it is my purpose to make them continue to feel and acknowledge it." Doty also stressed the importance of maintaining troops in Utah Territory if the situation were to remain stable. [36]

With the Indian situation under control, Connor again turned his attention to the Mormons. He reaffirmed his opinion that they continued to violate the anti-polygamy law of Congress and displayed both covert and overt hostility toward the United States government. He urged that troop strength in Utah Territory be increased and that the Mormon question be boldly confronted, or that the troops be withdrawn to California. This was the only way, he emphasized, in which unlawful actions of the Mormons could be suppressed and the laws of the United States rightfully fulfilled. [37]

The Indian problem had contributed to this bellicose attitude of Brigadier General Connor toward the Mormon people. He believed that Young willfully had incited the Indians into hostile actions against government troops in order to weaken the position of United States military forces in Utah Territory. Connor felt that the Mormons not only were giving the Indians provisions such as food and clothing, but were also furnishing them with guns and ammunition. For much of this reasoning, he alluded to the fact that Mormon communities in Utah Territory were comparatively safe from Indian hostilities. Thus, Connor logically concluded that it was necessary to alleviate the Mormon problems to obtain peace in Utah Territory. [38]

But open hostilities between the Mormons and United States Army forces were inadvisable at so critical a juncture in the Civil War, and Connor, therefore, resorted to a more subtle approach. He believed that the ultimate means of shattering Mormon control in Utah

Courtesy of Utah State Historical Society
Brigadier General Patrick Edward Connor, commander of United States Army forces in Utah Territory during the Civil War.

Territory would be through the migration into its boundaries of non-Mormon elements. To encourage this, he constructed a plan to develop the mineral wealth of the territory. Thus, Connor ordered all commanders of posts and detachments to allow their forces to prospect the entire countryside; the troopers, turned miners, were furnished with all necessary provisions. Throughout the remainder of 1863 and during most of 1864, the troopers searched for elusive veins of gold, silver, and other minerals. During this period, the army miners explored the whole of Utah Territory.

The results of their labor encouraged Brigadier General Connor, who reported to his army superiors the discovery of valuable mineral deposits throughout the territory. Gold, quartz, and silver had been discovered at Egan Canyon, about 200 miles west of Salt Lake City. Connor believed other areas, such as the Ruby Valley and the Goose Creek Mountains to the northwest of Salt Lake City, contained a wealth of minerals. He reported extensive deposits of salt, sulphur, and coal north of Salt Lake City. This encouraged him to incorporate the Jordan Mining Company, which erected its first smelting furnaces at Stockton, Utah, in 1864.

To bring his plan to fruition, Connor wrote several letters to encourage migration into Utah Territory. He freely and openly extended an invitation to the general public of the United States to come to Utah Territory and enrich themselves upon its mineral wealth. He promised these new migrants safety and security from the menace of either ''Indian or white''. Though the stories told by him concerning the abundance of mineral wealth throughout the entire territory may have encouraged some migration into the area, it failed in its purpose of shattering Mormon control.[39]

Connor's hatred of Young and all that he stood for encouraged him to establish a daily newspaper, the *Union Vedette*, in an attempt to dismantle the religious authority that controlled Utah Territory. The *Union Vedette* not only waged a fierce campaign against the Mormons, but also became the mouthpiece of Gentile views. Through this outlet, Connor hoped to encourage the further development of the Gentile population in Utah Territory and bolster its officials in their struggle against Mormon Church authority.[40]

In the end, however, Brigadier General Connor's intentions of undermining Mormon control through the press and through mining activity failed completely. Young's influence and power never wavered. Not only did Connor fear the political power of Young, but also the military prowess of the Mormons. Governor James A. Doty shared these sentiments. Connor was impressed with the strength of the Nauvoo Legion and the fact that Young easily could assemble 5,000 men to fight against United States troops. Connor emphasized that not only the numbers but also the artillery and discipline which the Mormon militia possessed were formidable. The Mormon armed forces assembled daily at Young's residence to conduct artillery and infantry drills.[41]

The fear expressed by Governor Doty and Brigadier General Connor led to a confrontation in 1864 that nearly resulted in open warfare. The situation which sparked this tense incident concerned recent issues of United States paper money. Connor interpreted the actions of a few Salt Lake City merchants in refusing to accept the paper money as an attempt to undermine the national currency and initiate a forced change in the currency of Utah Territory to a gold standard. Thus, Connor appointed Captain Charles Hempstead as provost marshal of Salt Lake City on July 9, 1864. Hempstead was then ordered, along with a company of the Second California Volunteer Cavalry Regiment, to assume a military position on South Temple Street, a location directly across the street from the Mormon Tabernacle. The response of the Mormons was deep resentment and outrage.

Young, who was touring Provo at the time, quickly returned to Salt Lake City, escorted by 200 men. By the time Young reached Salt Lake City, an additional 300 men were guarding the Mormon leader, and by nightfall a force of over 5,000 men had assembled for possible defensive action. Major General Irvin McDowell, the commander of the Department of the Pacific, alleviated the tense situation by demanding that Connor avoid combat with the Mormons at all costs. McDowell reminded Connor that the main objective of United States troops in Utah Territory was to protect the Overland Mail Company route and not the settlement of the government's problems with the Mormons. Furthermore, a Mormon war would likely be an important opportunity for the secessionists in the Southwest to strengthen their position and would prove to be a major mistake for the Union cause.[42]

Upon receiving these orders, Connor recalled the provost guard from Salt Lake City and improved relations with the Mormons. This incident marked the climax of Mormon-Gentile hostility during the Civil War. As the outcome of the Civil War became more apparent, relations between the religious, political, and military greatly improved. All sides made concessions and tensions lessened considerably after the summer of 1864.

Perhaps the most significant impact of the Civil War in Utah Territory was economic. The outbreak of hostilities deepened the belief of Young that the Mormons should work toward a totally self-sufficient economy. This became an official policy of the church, and the Civil War years were keynoted by progress in this direction. However, the economy also was strengthened by windfalls directly attributed to the Civil War.[43]

After the removal of troops from Camp Floyd upon the outbreak of the Civil War, the United States government dispensed with its property through a large auction. It was estimated that four million dollars of property was sold for approximately $100,000 at this auction. This included not only equipment and tools, but livestock, feed, and large supplies of food. Most of this the army originally had purchased from the Mormons for high prices and now was reselling it to them at ridiculously reduced rates. An example of this trading system was flour, which Mormon merchants had sold to the military post for $28.40 per hundred pounds and bought back for fifty cents per hundred pounds.[44]

Though Utah Territory merchants sorely missed the military business during the year of 1861, the arrival of Connor and the Third California Volunteer Infantry Regiment again stimulated local finances. The Mormons furnished the troops with most provisions needed. An unexpected economic boom also resulted when Connor initiated his plan to encourage mining. The mining activities in neighboring territories also opened a large market for Mormon produce. Located in the center of the mining region, Utah was the most practical and economical place to purchase supplies. The Pike's Peak discoveries in Colorado and further discoveries in Idaho and Montana between 1859 and 1864 resulted in enormous profits for Mormon merchants.[45]

Another economic windfall resulting from the Civil War was rerouting of the Overland Mail Company road and the hurried completion of the transcontinental telegraph through Utah Territory. Threatening secessionist activity throughout the Southwest made rerouting imperative. Salt Lake City became the junction between the Pacific Telegraph Company and the Overland Telegraph Company. The companies, therefore, granted contracts to the Mormons to supply material needs and subsistence to the workers in the construction of the lines. Young alone received $11,000 in gold for his participation in the project. The Overland Mail Company also ran through Salt Lake City. This operation carried more than 100 million pounds of freight in 1864 alone, and this resulted in more than $200,000 annually in sales of supplies to this company.[46]

These windfalls of the Civil War provided the capital to allow the Mormons to further experiment and implement their plan of self-sufficiency. One of the most important aspects of this planned economy was an increase in agricultural production and diversification. Many of the sermons delivered in the Mormon Tabernacle dealt with the problems of agriculture and emphasized the importance of agriculture to the overall well-being of the economy. In particular, the proper use of water, management of crops and livestock, and colonization of all parts of the territory received attention.

The construction of canals and irrigation works was necessary if agriculture was to develop in Utah. The alkaline soil and blistering summer heat seemed insurmountable to many, but direct planning and financial assistance by the Mormon Church achieved some progress. The territorial legislature granted a charter to the Deseret Irrigation and Navigation Canal Company, and work began using the Jordan River. The territorial governor vetoed the measure, but the company began

construction of the Jordan Dam in July of 1861. Utah residents built further irrigation and flood control developments throughout Utah Territory.[47]

The Deseret Agricultural and Manufacturing Society was responsible for a great deal of experimentation during the Civil War era. As an educational instrument of the Mormon Church, the society held monthly meetings and lectures, published pamphlets, and maintained a library for the furtherance of agricultural progress. It established an experimental farm in 1861 to improve seed and grain productions, and also experimented with improving the quality of livestock with Utah Territory. The society also was responsible for the introduction and development of commodities not previously produced in the territory. Under this plan, residents of Utah Territory began to produce and refine such items as cane sugar, molasses, tobacco, flax, hemp, and silk.[48]

Young felt that colonization of all parts of Utah Territory was necessary to keep its economy strong. In establishing these new settlements, he gave careful consideration to the contributions that each would make toward the economic concept of self-sufficiency. An example of this plan as it relates to the Civil War was the decision of the Mormon Church to grow cotton in southern Utah Territory. Due to the scarcity of cotton in northern territories and the relatively high price of the product, Young ordered over 300 families to go to southern Utah Territory as a part of the Cotton Mission. Young told these colonizers that their particular job was as important as preaching the gospel, and they established settlements at St. George, Rio Virgin, and Santa Clara. Though the Cotton Mission never proved profitable, it enhanced the settling of southern Utah Territory, as the Mormon Church commissioned nearly 3,000 persons to settle in this area of the territory.[49]

Another stimulus to the economy of Utah Territory at the outbreak of the Civil War was an influx of population. In 1860, the population of Utah Territory was only 40,000, but a remarkable growth during the decade that followed pushed the total population to over 85,000 by 1870. Much of this population growth was the result of organized emigrant wagon trains sponsored by the Mormon Church. Groups were dispatched yearly to the East to bring back Mormon faithful that had been left behind in Missouri, Illinois, and Ohio. The wagon trains carried adequate provisions for the emigrants, and the "down and back trips" could be completed in a season. Groups chosen for the journey were selected from each ward; such service was considered an obligation to the Mormon Church. Each wagon carried from ten to twenty immigrants, depending on whether orders had been sent along to purchase freight for the Mormon Church. The success of this effort was noticeable, as over 11,000 immigrants came into Utah Territory during the Civil War by way of the Mormon Church wagon trains.[50]

The population influx had social as well as economic implications. This was particularly evident in a massive building and public works program. In 1861 and 1862, immigrant labor employed by the church completed the Salt Lake Theater at a cost of nearly $100,000. With a seating capacity of 3,000, it was the finest theater west of the Mississippi River, and attracted the best actors and actresses available in the nation. Construction of the Mormon Tabernacle also began during the Civil War, though it was not dedicated finally until 1875. Mormon leaders planned this immense structure to seat 10,000 people and cost $300,000. Likewise, the construction of many other buildings was a great boon to the economy and allowed immigrants to earn a living once they arrived in Utah Territory.[51]

All social activity centered around the Mormon Church. Educational training was excellent, gatherings at church fellowships a common occurrence, and communication between the various communities complete. Young annually visited all Mormon communities to insure that affairs were operating smoothly. Furthermore, the Mormons took advantage of their transcontinental mail and telegraph connections by establishing regular mail routes between the major cities of Utah Territory and constructing a network of telegraph lines to over 100 Mormon communities.

By 1865, the Mormon people had become increasingly loyal to the United States. In particular, the toleration and policy of non-interference that characterized the policies of President Lincoln made him a revered hero. Mormons greeted news of Lincoln's reelection and subsequent inauguration with jubilation. In fact, the occasion of Lincoln's inauguration inspired a proclamation from the Salt Lake City Council that all civil, military, and religious elements should unite in honor of Lincoln. A month later the Mormon people mourned Lincoln's death; thousands gathered in the tabernacle for funeral services. For the first time since the beginning of the Civil War, civil, military, and religious leaders in Utah Territory united in a common cause, the mourning of Lincoln's death.[52]

The Mormons made the situation of Utah distinctly different from the other Western territories. Though an organized territorial government existed, the actual authority rested with the Mormon Church and its leader, Brigham Young. The persecution received by the Mormons led them to the Great Salt Lake Valley, all in an effort to free themselves from further restrictions and regulations of a sometimes unfriendly government. Viewing the Civil War as a fulfillment of a divine prophecy, the Mormons labored strenuously to perfect a theocratic state and prepare themselves for economic self-sufficiency.

No military combat related to the Civil War occurred in Utah Territory and no Confederate troops entered its boundaries, but the impact of the war had numerous repercussions on its development. The removal of United States troops from Utah Territory at the outbreak of the Civil War allowed the Mormon Church more freedom and caused the territorial officials some concern. This was manifested in the decision of the United States to reassign troops to Utah Territory in 1862 and the passage of an Anti-Bigamy Act in Congress in the same year. This reassignment brought Colonel P. Edward Connor to Utah Territory, a man obsessed with breaking Mormon theocratic control. The tensions between civil, military, and religious authority in Utah Territory which highlights the Civil War years usually were a product of Connor's efforts.

The most important impact of the Civil War years on Utah Territory was economic. The Southern rebellion and secessionist activities in the Southwest brought a decision to remove mail and telegraph routes to friendlier soil, and Utah Territory offered a desirable alternative. The desire of the Mormons for self-sufficiency also made Utah Territory an agricultural center for the mining activity of surrounding territories. Undoubtedly, military combat in the East influenced the decision of many Mormons to migrate to Utah Territory. This resulted in not only an increased population, but also in social and economic changes in Utah Territory that would be felt during the Civil War and in years to come.

NOTES

1. *The Doctrines and Covenants of the Church of Jesus Christ of Latter-day Saints* (Salt Lake City. Utah: Church of Jesus Christ of Latter-day Saints, 1953), pp. 144-145.
2. Wain Sutton, ed., *Utah: A Centennial History* (2 vols., New York: Lewis Historical Publishing Company, 1949), Vol. I, pp. 343-373.
3. *Ibid.*, pp. 375-388.
4. *Ibid.*, pp. 403-418; Brigham H. Roberts, *A Comprehensive History of the Church of Jesus Christ of Latter-day Saints* (6 vols., Salt Lake City, Utah; Deseret News Press, 1930), Vol. II, pp. 221-231.
5. *Ibid.*, Vol. III, throughout; Otis G. Hamond, ed., *The Utah Expedition (1857-1858): Letters of Captain Jesse S.* Grove (Concord, New Hampshire: New Hampshire Historical Society, 1928). For biographies of Brigham Young, see Stanley P. Hirshon, *The Lion of the Lord* (New York: Alfred A. Knopf, 1969), Milton R. Hunter, *Brigham Young the Colonizer* (Independence, Missouri: Zion's Printing and Publishing Company, 1945), Preston Nibley, *Brigham Young: The Man and His Work* (Salt Lake City, Utah: Deseret News Press, 1936), and M.R. Werner, *Brigham Young* (New York: Harcourt, Brace, and Company, 1925). For a complete account of the Westward trek, see *William Clayton's Journal: A Daily Record of the Journey of the Original Company of Mormon Pioneers from Nauvoo, Illinois to the Valley of the* Great Salt Lake (Salt Lake City, Utah: Deseret News, 1921).
6. *Eighth Census of the United States, 1860* (3 vols., Washington: Government Printing Office, 1862), Vol. I, p. 575; Gustive O. Larson, "Utah and the Civil War," *Utah Historical Quarterly*, Vol. XXXIII, No. 1 (Winter, 1965), pp. 64-66.
7. *Ibid.*
8. *Deseret News*, January 2, 1861, p. 1.
9. William A. Linn, *The Story of the Mormons: From the Date of Their Origin to the Year 1901* (New York: Russell and Russell, 1963), p. 544.
10. *Eighth Census of the United States, 1860*, Vol. I, pp. 575-577.
11. *Deseret News*, July 10, 1861, p. 1.

12. George U. Hubbard, "Abraham Lincoln as Seen By the Mormons", *Utah Historical Quarterly*, Vol. XXXI, No. 2 (Spring, 1963), p. 95; Roberts, *op. cit.*, Vol. II, pp. 148-158.

13. Larson, *op. cit.*, pp. 60-61.

14. *New York Times*, June 25, 1862, p. 2. For a treatment of this subject, see Dale L. Morgan, "The State of Deseret", *Utah Historical Quarterly*, Vol. VIII, Numbers 2, 3, 4 (April, July, October, 1940), pp. 132-150.

15. Ray C. Colton, *The Civil War In The Western Territories: Arizona, Colorado, New Mexico, and Utah* (Norman, Oklahoma: University of Oklahoma Press, 1959), p. 183.

16. *Deseret News*, January 29, 1862, p. 1.

17. *Congressional Globe*, 37th Congress, 2nd Session, pp. 2906, 3023, 3082.

18. Clarence Edwin Carter, ed., *Territorial Papers of the United States* (2 vols., Washington: Government Printing Office, 1934), Vol. I, pp. 29-30; Larson, *op. cit.*, p. 67.

19. United States Department of War, *War of the Rebellion: A Compilation of the Official Records of the Union and Confederate Armies* (70 vols., 128 books, Washington: Government Printing Office, 1880-1901), Ser. III, Vol. II, p. 27.

20. Larson, *op. cit.*, p. 59.

21. *Official Records*, Ser. I, Vol. L, Pt. 2, p. 55.

22. *Ibid.*, p. 19; Aurora Hunt, *The Army of the Pacific: Its Operations in California, Texas, Arizona, New Mexico, Utah, Nevada, Oregon, Washington, Plains Region, Mexico, etc., 1860-1866* (Glendale, California: Arthur H. Clark Company, 1951), pp. 190-191.

23. *Official Records*, Ser. I, Vol. L, Pt. 2, p. 195.

24. *Ibid.*, pp. 748-749, 917.

25. Linn, *op. cit.*, pp. 546-547.

26. Letter from Stephen S. Harding to William Seward, United States Department of State, (Washington: National Archives), Vol. II, pp. 553-554.

27. Larson, *op. cit.*, p. 72.

28. *Official Records*, Ser. I, Vol. L, Pt. 2, p. 55.

29. Hubbard, *op. cit.*, p. 102; *Deseret News*, March 4, 1863, p. 1.

30. Hubbard, *op. cit.*, p. 550.

31. Linn, *op. cit.*, p. 550.

32. T.B.H. Stenhouse, *The Rocky Mountain Saints* (Salt Lake City, Utah: Shepard Book Company, 1904), p. 599.

33. *Ibid.*, pp. 593-598; *New York Times*, July 7, 1862, p. 5.

34. Colton, *op. cit.*, p. 162.

35. *New York Times*, August 24, 1862, p. 3; Hunt, *op. cit.*, pp. 194-196.

36. *Official Records*, Ser. I, Vol. L, Pt. 2, pp. 583, 527-530.

37. *Ibid.*, pp. 887, 529.

38. *Ibid.*, p. 415.

39. *Ibid.*, pp. 656-657, 774-775; Colton, *op. cit.*, pp. 187-188.

40. *Ibid.*, p. 1185; Larson, *op. cit.*, p. 74.

41. *Official Records*, Ser. I, Vol. L, Pt. 2, pp. 584, 904.

42. *Ibid.*, p. 909.

43. Leonard J. Arrington, *Great Basin Kingdom: An Economic History of the Latter Day Saints, 1830-1900* (Cambridge, Massachusetts: Harvard University Press, 1958), p. 195.

44. *Ibid.*, p. 199.

45. *Ibid.*, pp. 201-204.

46. *Ibid.*, pp. 199-200.

47. *Ibid.*, pp. 223-224.

48. *Ibid.*, pp. 226-227.

49. *Ibid.*, pp. 216-219; Gustive O. Larson, *Prelude to the Kingdom: Mormon Desert Conquest* (Francestown, New Hampshire: Marshall Jones Company, 1947), pp. 181-193.

50. *Ninth Census of the United States, 1870* (3 vols., Washington: Government Printing Office, 1872), Vol. I, p. 67; Arrington, *op. cit.*, pp. 204-208.

51. *Ibid.*, pp. 211-213.

52. Hubbard, *op. cit.*, pp. 104-107.

SELECTED READINGS

Leonard T. Arrington, *Great Basin Kingdom: An Economic History of the Latter-day Saints* (Cambridge, Massachusetts: Harvard University Press, 1958), pp. 191-249.

Ray C. Colton, *The Civil War in the Western Territories: Arizona, Colorado, New Mexico, and Utah* (Norman, Oklahoma: University of Oklahoma Press, 1959), pp. 171-190.

William Clayton's Journal: A Daily Record of the Journey of the Original Company of Mormon Pioneers from Nauvoo, Illinois to the Valley of the Great Salt Lake (Salt Lake City, Utah: Deseret News, 1921).

George U. Hubbard, "Abraham Lincoln as Seen By the Mormons", *Utah Historical Quarterly*, Vol. XXXI, No. 2, (Spring, 1963), pp. 91-108.

Aurora Hunt, *The Army of the Pacific: Its Operations in California, Texas, Arizona, New Mexico, Utah, Nevada, Oregon, Washington, Plains Region, Mexico, etc., 1860-1866* (Glendale, California: Arthur H. Clark Company, 1951), pp. 185-215.

Milton R. Hunter, *Brigham Young the Colonizer* (Independence, Missouri: Zion's Printing and Publishing Company, 1945), pp. 150-245.

Gustive O. Larson, *Prelude to the Kingdom: Mormon Desert Conquest* (Francestown, New Hampshire: Marshall Jones Company, 1947), pp. 181-276.

Gustive O. Larson, "Utah and the Civil War", *Utah Historical Quarterly*, Vol. XXXIII, No. 1 (Winter, 1965), pp. 55-77.

William A. Linn, *The Story of the Mormons: From the Date of Their Origin to the Year 1901* (New York: Russell and Russell, Inc., 1963), pp. 543-551.

T.B.H. Stenhouse, *The Rocky Mountain Saints* (Salt Lake City, Utah: Shepard Book Company, 1904), pp. 584-614.

Fort Union, N.M. from the Southwest as it was in the Civil War with the Star Trace Bastion in the foreground.

Colorado Territory

By Thomas D. Isern

In early November, 1862, a score of men and a few children rolled east across the Texas panhandle. Six lay sick with smallpox, and the rest saw ahead of them several hundred Comanche Indians, mounted and prepared for war. Three men riding ahead of the train reined in to wait for their friends before approaching the Indians, when suddenly from a nearby ravine a voice commanded: "Halt. Surrender or you are dead men." The three turned and saw a Union Army officer and twenty-eight men with leveled muskets, and inquired only to whom they were surrendering. "To Lieutenant Shoup, commanding United States Cavalry," answered the officer.[1]

Second Lieutenant George L. Shoup of the First Colorado Volunteer Infantry Regiment took the caravan into custody, thinking he had captured a party of Confederate guerrillas. He had expected a stiff fight and had engaged the Indians as allies. Shoup soon discovered that his prisoners were not guerrillas, but Georgians bound for home from strongly Unionist Colorado Territory. Shoup immediately recognized the names of several of the prisoners — William Green Russell, James O. Russell, Dr. Levi J. Russell, J. H. Pierce, and Samuel Bates. These men in 1858 had made the original discovery of gold that had sparked the Pike's Peak gold rush. Nevertheless, Shoup placed them under arrest, confiscated $20,000 in gold dust, and escorted them to Fort Union, New Mexico. Fort Union authorities later released the prisoners and restored to them their gold, but their arrest indicated that the Civil War had affected Colorado Territory deeply. Even former heroes were suspect. These and more profound changes taking place in Colorado made the Civil War a severe testing time for the young territory.[2]

Settlement had come to the area only two years earlier with the Pike's Peak gold rush of 1859-1860. The year 1858 had been a time of economic hardship in the western United States because of a depression which had followed the Panic of 1857. Consequently, in the spring of 1859, sixty to eighty thousand "Pike's Peakers" embarked for alleged new mines along the upper South Platte River. The mines were unproven, but most of the gold-seekers went because economic opportunity at home was nonexistent. The prospectors who arrived first discovered that the gold mines were a mirage created by real estate speculators who had come out in 1858. The would-be miners turned homeward, announcing that they had been humbugged. As a result, settlement in the area would then have evaporated, but two rich gold strikes by prospectors George A. Jackson and John H. Gregory restored faith in the gold fields. Immigration to the mines in 1859 and 1860 gave Colorado Territory a population of around 30,000 when the Civil War began.

The economic causes of the gold rush determined the character and the place of origin of the early population of the mining region; this had great implications for the Civil War period. During the gold rush, the greatest number of immigrants came from those areas most affected by the depression — the Ohio, Missouri, and upper Mississippi River valleys. At least seventy percent came from northern states or territories, about twenty percent from border states, chiefly Missouri, and only about ten percent from southern states. Consequently, the great majority of the residents of Colorado Territory were loyal to the Union.[3]

At the outbreak of the Civil War, Colorado Territory had a hardy but fluid population, mostly unmarried male gold miners. Denver, with 2,600 to 4,000 citizens, was the largest city, while the remainder of the population sprawled through mining camps in the mountains and settlements along the Arkansas River valley. The Arkansas and Rio Grande River valleys contained a sizeable number of Mexicans, but less than 100 Negroes were in the territory. East of the mountains lives Cheyenne, Arapaho, Kiowa and Comanche Indians, while the principal mountain tribe was the Ute.[4]

When the Civil War began, the region had no effec-

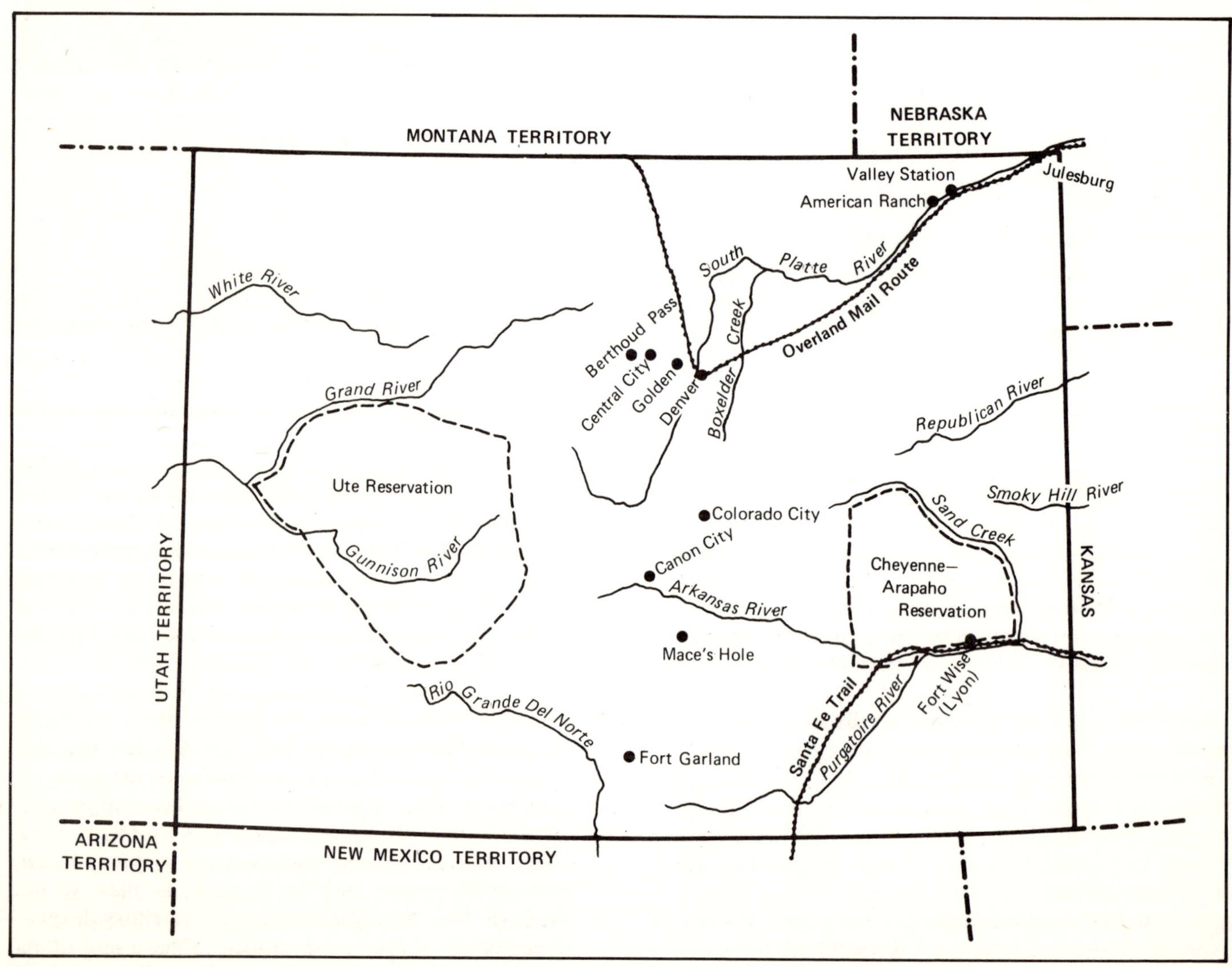

Colorado Territory During the Civil War

Map Drafted by Georganne T. Bartow

tive government except miners' laws and impromptu municipal organizations, though early residents repeatedly had sought recognition from Congress. The gold fields originally lay within the boundaries of Kansas, Nebraska, New Mexico and Utah Territories, but none of them successfully extended authority over the area. Early efforts to organize the region as part of Kansas or as a separate territory were practical failures. However, in August of 1859 a convention in Denver drafted both a constitution for a proposed state of "Jefferson" and a memorial for territorial organization, the people to decide by special election which instrument would be presented to Congress. On September 7, the voters chose territorial organization, but Congress was stalled by sectional issues and withheld action until February of 1861. With many representatives from seceded states gone, Congress created Colorado Territory. Meanwhile a provisional government of Jefferson Territory had lost all but a facade of authority. When the war began in April of 1861, territorial officers for Colorado had not yet arrived.[5]

In early 1861, reaction in Colorado Territory to Southern secessionism was just as disorganized as governmental affairs. Some spokesmen favored the Union unreservedly; others opposed coercion to preserve it; a few favored the Southern cause. Still others talked of alignment with a proposed "Western power" formed of confederated states and territories of the mountain and Pacific West, or even of organization alone as a separate entity. Many residents of Colorado Territory refused to take secession seriously, such as a correspondent for the Denver *Rocky Mountain News* in the mining camp of Bortonsburg. He burlesqued a fictitious Bortonsburg secession movement in which conspirators enlisted as "hour men" militia, ate banquets of ravens, sent emissaries to surrounding camps and to Coney Island, and communicated by "Donkey Xpress."[6]

Nevertheless, powerful Union sentiments arose. On Washington's birthday, 1861, citizens of Denver assembled to salute the Stars and Stripes with an artillery salvo. Then they adjourned to the home of prominent citizen Hiram P. Bennett, where they heard patriotic speeches and music and gave rousing cheers for the Union. After consuming four and one-half gallons of Bennett's whiskey, the crowd formed a noisy street procession.[7]

Unionism in Colorado Territory intensified following the firing on Fort Sumter. On April 23, residents of Golden tramped boisterously through the streets and demanded that the local postmaster and a prominent citizen display their colors. They complied. More sober citizens of Central City on April 25 trooped into the courthouse to sing anthems and pass Union resolutions. On the same day, seventy prominent Denver residents signed notices asking "Who Will Keep Step to the Music of the Union?" and calling for an evening meeting in front of the Tremont House hotel. Over

Courtesy of State Historical Society of Colorado

William Gilpin, always colorful and flamboyant, served briefly as the first governor of Colorado Territory.

1,000 enthusiasts answered the call and built a blazing bonfire. Patriotic speeches invoking the founding fathers moved the crowd to three loud cheers for the Union. Next they resolved that Colorado Territory would "follow the flag and keep step to the music of the Union" and that "the flag of Colorado Territory is the STAR SPANGLED BANNER."[8] Communities throughout the territory had similar meetings. In two instances in the Denver area, maverick Southerners raised "secess" flags, but Unionists soon pulled them to earth. The *Rocky Mountain News,* the principal paper of the territory, declared: "There is a spirit of patriotism everywhere prevalent....We stand by the Constitution framed by our forefathers."[9]

In the midst of these events, the first governor of Colorado Territory arrived in Denver. He was William Gilpin, whom President Abraham Lincoln had appointed at the insistence of Francis P. Blair, Jr., a prominent Missouri politician and confidant of Lincoln. Gilpin was a well-known writer and explorer of the West who had crossed the continent to Oregon with Second Lieutenant John C. Fremont in 1843. In the Mexican War, he served valiantly with Colonel Alexander W. Doniphan's detachment of the Army of the West. Finally, Gilpin settled in Independence, Missouri, and during the 1850s wrote extensively on the topic of Western expansionism, culminating in 1860 with *The Central Gold Region.* Gilpin, the Westerner, entered Denver to assume his duties on May 27, 1861.[10]

Gilpin's Denver reception was apparently enthusiastic: crowds of citizens, bands playing, flags flying, cannon booming, and a grand speech by Gilpin. Newspapers lauded the new governor's intellectual capacity and distinguished career. But many people had wary opinions of Gilpin, for they were familiar with his outlandish geopolitical and geological theories. In 1858, Gilpin publicly predicted that miners in the Pike's Peak region soon would discover literally a mountain of gold — "gold in mass and in position and infinite in quantity."[11] He had made a similar prediction in regard to California during the gold rush there. The enthusiastic reception for Governor Gilpin was more likely for the office than for the man.[12]

The erratic but energetic Gilpin soon erected a full-blown territorial government. He ordered a territorial census, toured the mining region, created three judicial districts and assigned judges to them, and called an election for August 19 to elect a two-house legislature and a delegate to Congress. A hotly-contested race for delegate ensued between Republican candidate Hiram P. Bennett and B. D. Williams, nominee of a "People's Convention." Republicans cast doubts on the loyalty of Williams, a former Kentuckian, and thereby won the victory, 6,703 votes to 2,892. The first territorial legislature convened on September 9, and the next day Gilpin urged its members to establish county governments, adopt a code of civil law, and organize a militia. The legislature demonstrated its loyalty with a joint resolution denouncing "rebel traitors...among us and around us" and expressing confidence in Governor Gilpin. In an efficient session lasting just two months, the legislators put the machinery of territorial government into operation. They created seventeen counties, fixed the mill levy for territorial taxation, incorporated the city of Denver, and outlined a code of criminal law that soon brought a measure of order in the young territory.[13]

Gilpin also organized the territory militarily. He at first found the territory "at peace, devoted to the Union, and full of energy;" so he harnessed that energy by organizing two companies of three-year volunteer troops.[14] This followed a request on June 6, 1861, from Lietuenant Colonel E. R. S. Canby, commanding the Department of New Mexico, to send two companies to Fort Garland in southern Colorado to relieve Canby's troops there for use against Indians in New Mexico. Gilpin commissioned John P. Slough, a Denver attorney, and Samuel F. Tappan, a Denver journalist, as captains. Slough recruited his company of volunteers in Denver and Tappan his in Central City, after which Tappan joined Slough in quarters in Denver on August 21. Gilpin never dispatched the companies to Fort Garland, though he wrote Canby he would. At the same time, a former associate of Kansas politician James

Colonel John P. Slough, the commander of the First Colorado Volunteer Infantry Regiment and the victor at the Battle of Glorieta Pass, New Mexico Territory.

Lane, Samuel H. Cook, also recruited an independent company with himself as captain. This effort by Cook had no governmental authorization. However, on August 20 Cook brought eighty-eight men recruited in mountain camps to Denver to seek transportation to eastern Kansas to join Lane.[15]

Cook's company never got to Kansas, for in the last week of August Gilpin decided to form the First Colorado Volunteer Infantry Regiment with Slough as colonel and Tappan as lieutenant colonel. Their existing companies became Companies A and B of the new regiment. Gilpin persuaded Cook to enlist his men as Company F by promising to mount them within forty-eight hours, though the rest of the regiment was to be infantry. Seven other First Colorado Volunteer Infantry Regiment companies began recruiting, while the governor also commissioned several companies of home guards.[16]

Gilpin justified his recruiting activities not only with warnings of an invasion from Texas, but also with references to Confederate insurgency within Colorado

Territory. Charley Harrison, owner of the Criterion Saloon, held Southern sympathies and bore a personal grudge against First Lieutenant Samuel Logan of Company B, First Colorado Volunteer Infantry Regiment. In late August, Harrison's saloon crowd and Logan's soldiers clashed in a brawl in a Denver bordello. A few nights later Company B tried to force entry into the Criterion itself. A scuffle began and, as gunfire crackled from the saloon windows, two soldiers received slight wounds. Company B laid siege to the saloon, sporadically shooting through the windows while a soldier fetched a small cannon from headquarters. As the soldiers prepared to fire on the saloon with the cannon, the Denver city marshal arrived, entered the saloon, and arrested Harrison. After paying a $5,000 fine, Harrison left the territory for Kansas.[17]

In the summer of 1861, A. B. Miller, another secessionist, gathered men to join Confederate forces in Indian Territory. After Charley Harrison's trial, at which Colorado Territory Chief Justice Benjamin F. Hall said Miller's men "demonstrated," they left for the Cherokee Nation. Federal troops captured Miller's wagon train in Kansas, though Miller himself eluded capture.[18]

During the same summer, Joel McKee, a third Confederate sympathizer, competed with Governor Gilpin to control the arms supply in the territory. He and other southerners sought to buy as many munitions as possible, especially the vital item of percussion caps. McKee had gathered about forty men and was preparing to depart for Texas, when on September 29 Gilpin ordered the territorial marshal, Marshall Townsend, to arrest McKee. On vague charges, Townsend placed him in the Denver jail, whereupon McKee's friends initiated a *habeas corpus* suit to free him. Chief Justice Hass assumed a highly irregular power and denied the writ.[19]

On October 18, still another band of Confederates attempted to seize a government wagon train near Fort Wise on the Arkansas River, but cavalry from the fort came to the rescue and captured thirty-nine of the guerrillas without a struggle. Cook's mounted company came from Denver and returned with the prisoners to that city. They remained in jail with McKee until February 27, 1862, when they overpowered their jailers and escaped.[20]

Colorado Territory had become a dangerous environment for Confederates, and those remaining began to slip out of the territory in small groups. About the only open advocate of the South left in Denver was a young lady who still wore "secession rings" and professed "partiality for Palmetto 'chicken fixings'."[21]

Gilpin and his confidant, Chief Justice Hall, greatly exaggerated the Confederate menace in Colorado Territory. "The struggle with treason is a perpetual death-struggle," Gilpin claimed, which he waged "without a *single skilled assistant*."[22] But no one ever died in Gilpin's death-struggle. In correspondence with the United States War Department, Hall constructed elaborate scenarios involving secret Confederate fraternities. Both officials considered all political opponents secessionists. "There is not much difference," wrote Hall, for both "seem to have no idea of loyalty" and were drawn from "border ruffians of Kansas and the destroying angels of Brigham Young."[23] Actually there was no significant internal threat to the territory, for Union sympathies were preponderant. Gilpin also frequently spoke of the threat of Texan invasion. But when the expected incursion actually entered New Mexico in the summer of 1861, Gilpin was unexplainably slow to respond. Canby repeatedly pleaded with Gilpin to send troops to garrison Fort Wise, but Gilpin refused to do so until late December, even though the First Colorado Volunteer Infantry Regiment was available.[24]

Gilpin financed his military organization by issuing drafts on the United States Treasury, claiming that President Lincoln had given him a blanket commission to do whatever was necessary to combat secessionism. But when merchants in Colorado Territory sent the drafts to Washington, the Treasury refused them. Moreover, in response to a letter from a prominent attorney in Colorado Territory earlier in the year, Secretary of War Simon Cameron had stated that he desired no troops from the territory at that time.[25]

Meanwhile the First Colorado Volunteer Infantry Regiment, stationed two miles from Denver in Camp Weld, grew mutinous during the fall and winter of 1861-1862. The men of B Company unsuccessfully petitioned Gilpin to remove Logan, who had become their captain, for abusing his officers and men. The men of I Company, an all-German unit, defied their officers and claimed they were the victims of discrimination. Worst of all, in early November Slough tried unsuccessfully to muster in Companies K and G under Captain Charles P. Marion and Captain J. W. Hambleton. The men refused to take the oath because they had enlisted as mounted riflemen, and Slough was enlisting all his companies as infantry except for Cook's. Slough arrested Marion, stood off a march by the men of K Company to free him, then dismissed both Marion and Hambleton from service in the regiment. The two discontented companies were then mustered in.[26]

There also were naturally clashes with the Denver citizenry. Drunken soldiers frequently started saloon brawls and sometimes roamed the streets with revolvers, terrorizing citizens. Soldiers organized as "Company Q" made "jayhawking" expeditions to town and the countryside and rustled everything from melons to beeves. Whenever city authorities jailed such scavengers, Company Q rallied to the jail and forced their release. The worst offense of all came in January of 1862, when a score of soldiers barged into a clothing store and robbed the protesting owners of $1,200 in goods.[27]

Desertion became a problem especially because the volunteers were uncertain of their status after the rejection of the Gilpin drafts. Even President Lincoln in Washington understood the problems involved. Across the papers of a private of K Company sentenced to die for desertion, Lincoln scribbled: "Let him fight instead of being shot."[28] Indeed, the soldiers themselves longed for active duty. All but one of the regiment's officers signed a petition to Slough to secure their assignment to the New Mexico theater. "We consider that we have the right," they asserted, "to *demand* this of you."[29]

Gilpin left for Washington on December 24, 1861, to defend his policies before the government, but received a severe berating from Secretary of War Cameron for mismanagement in Colorado Territory. Gilpin returned to Denver in March, 1862, but even Francis Blair, who earlier had secured the governorship for Gilpin, admitted to Lincoln that the post in Colorado Territory required "some man of plain common sense."[30] In late March, Lincoln removed Gilpin and replaced him soon after with John Evans, a Chicago businessman.[31]

Nevertheless, the troops which Gilpin raised proved of great importance, for they played the key role in defeating the Confederacy's only real attempt to seize the West — Sibley's invasion of New Mexico. Confederate Brigadier General Henry Hopkins Sibley in late 1861 pushed up the Rio Grande River valley with nearly 3,500 Texas troops, and Colorado Territory troops answered Canby's pleas for aid. The first company to rush to Canby's side was an independent company under Captain Theodore H. Dodd, organized ninety-two strong in the fall of 1861 in Cañon City. After mustering in at Fort Garland, Dodd led the men south and arrived in Santa Fe, New Mexico Territory, on February 3, 1862, in time to join forces. Canby was marshaling at Fort Craig. Canby had 3,800 men, a mixture of volunteers and militia from New Mexico and regular troops, to face Sibley's Texans, dwindled in number to 2,600 by this time.[32]

The two armies clashed at ValVerde, on the Rio Grande River just north of Fort Craig. Union troops took up positions on the east bank of the river, with Dodd's company at the northern end of the lines. Three companies of Texas mounted lancers assaulted Dodd's position, but the Coloradoans held their fire until the lancers were only forty yards away, fired a first and a second volley, then rushed upon the decimated Texans with bayonets and nearly annihilated them. But later in the day Colonel Thomas Green, who had assumed command of Confederate forces, ordered a headlong charge for the Union batteries. In hand-to-hand fighting, the Texans put Union forces to rout, and Dodd's company was among those bearing the brunt of the fighting. The Coloradoans suffered losses of two killed, twenty-eight wounded, and nine missing in their retreat across the river as the Texans played double-barreled shotguns upon their backs.[33]

After ValVerde, Sibley followed Canby's retreating army into Albuquerque and Santa Fe. But more Col-

Courtesy of State Historical Society of Colorado

John Evans, the second governor of Colorado Territory and a Chicago businessman, vigorously raised militia forces during the Civil War for protection against hostile Indians.

orado Territory troops rallied to oppose the Confederates. First of these was another independent company from Cañon City under Captain James H. Ford. It reached Santa Fe on February 4, then proceeded to Fort Union to reinforce its garrison. The First Colorado Volunteer Infantry Regiment also prepared to enter the fray. In the winter, Companies B, H and F had gone to Fort Wise. On February 22, in accordance with orders from Major General David Hunter, commanding the Department of Kansas, which included Colorado Territory, the rest of the First Colorado Volunteer Infantry Regiment under Colonel Slough marched for New Mexico. The companies from Fort Wise united with them on the Purgatoire River to continue the trek, ten companies strong. On March 11 they reached Fort Union, their destination[34]

Slough asserted the seniority of his commission over that of Colonel Gabriel R. Paul, a regular army officer in command at Fort Union, and took control of troops there. He brushed aside protests by Paul and marched for Santa Fe with all the troops except a skeleton garrison left with Paul at Fort Union. On March 21 at Las Vegas, orders arrived from Canby directing Paul to remain with his forces at Fort Union, Canby being unaware that Slough had assumed command.

Nevertheless, Slough pushed on west. On March 25, Canby learned of the change of command and issued orders for Slough to return to Fort Union. But by the time Slough received the message, his forces already had advanced into Glorieta Pass, the gateway to Santa Fe, and fought the decisive battle of the New Mexico campaign.[35]

On March 25, Slough, encamped at Bernal Springs at the eastern entrance to Glorieta Pass, ordered Major John M. Chivington of the First Colorado Volunteer Infantry Regiment to proceed west with a striking force to try to surprise Confederate forces in Santa Fe. Chivington took 418 men, mostly soldiers of his own regiment along with a few regular troops. On the morning of March 26, twenty of Cook's mounted volunteers captured four Texas pickets, from whom Chivington learned that about 1,000 Confederates under Lieutenant Colonel William R. Scurry were advancing to meet him. Chivington advanced into Apache Canyon, near the western end of Glorieta Pass, where he met forward elements of Scurry's forces, perhaps 300 men.

The Battle of Glorieta Pass opened as the Confederates planted a battery in the road and Chivington deployed his troops, sending skirmishers to the left and right canyon walls. Flanking fire forced the Confederate battery to retreat twice. The second time the Union forces nearly encircled the retreating Texans, whereupon Cook's mounted company galloped down the canyon road, leaped into a deep crevice, and routed the Confederates. Flanking troops took seventy-one prisoners. By evening the Texans had suffered thirty-two dead and a similar number of wounded. Chivington's victory cost him five killed and fourteen wounded. Wary of the approach of Scurry's main force, he fell back to Coslosky's Ranch, near the east end of the pass.[36]

On March 28, both Scurry and Slough brought up their main commands. Slough sent Chivington and 430 men off on a rough road to the left of the pass to gain the Confederates' rear, while Slough and the remaining 800 or 900 men proceeded up the main road. At midmorning, Slough reached a place called Pigeon Ranch and sent his cavalry ahead to reconnoiter, when suddenly a concealed Confederate battery opened fire. Slough brought his battery and cavalry to the center and placed infantry on his flanks. For five hours the battle then surged through cedar-clogged terrain. An early attempt to take the Confederate guns by Companies D and I of the First Colorado Volunteer Infantry Regiment failed with heavy losses. Thereafter, the fighting took place mainly on the flanks, with the Texans advancing and the Unionists falling back. A vigorous Texan attack would have swept the Union force from the field, but Scurry was unsure of his adversary's strength. Slough's command finally retired toward its camp, having suffered twenty-nine killed, forty-two wounded, and fifteen lost as prisoners. Strangely, the Texans did not pursue, but came forward with a flag of truce and arranged a suspension of hostilities to bury

Courtesy of State Historical Society of Colorado
Colonel John M. Chivington of the First Colorado Volunteer Infantry Regiment saw extensive service in New Mexico Territory.

the dead.[37]

Slough was unaware that he actually had won the battle. Major Chivington's battalion, including five companies of Colorado Territory troops and a small number of regulars, had gained the Confederate rear by way of a rugged road. In the early afternoon, Chivington peered over a steep cliff at a place called Johnston's Ranch and saw below eighty wagons, containing all of Scurry's supplies and guarded by only 200 men and one field piece. Chivington's men clambered down the mountain face under ineffective fire from below. Next, Chivington sent part of his men up the opposite hillside to pick off the enemy artillerymen, while the rest seized the wagon train from the fleeing Texans. Chivington burned the wagon train and hastened back the way he had come, hoping to join Slough on the main battlefield.[38]

The significance of the Battle of Glorieta Pass was unclear at first, for both Union and Confederate forces retreated after the battle. Scurry reported to Sibley that he had won a victory, but had fallen back because of the loss of his supply train. Slough, unaware of Scurry's severe supply shortage, retreated to Fort Union. But the engagement was decisive; it ended the Confederate advance in New Mexico by blocking Scurry's move on Fort Union. Sibley then began a retreat down the Rio Grande valley.

Dual fears plagued Slough after his retreat to Fort Union: that Canby would press for a court-martial because of Slough's violation of orders; and that his own men might take his life. Enmities of vague origin between Slough and certain of his officers and men made him fear assassination attempts. At Pigeon Ranch a group of Slough's own men had fired a volley at him, whereupon he retired and directed the battle from the rear. Faced with such danger, Slough resigned his commission, but in August, 1862, President Lincoln rewarded him for saving New Mexico with a commission as a brigadier general and an Eastern command.[39]

The First Colorado Volunteer Infantry Regiment served further in New Mexico with Chivington as its new colonel. From Fort Union, it marched back to the Rio Grande River valley and helped Canby pursue the retreating Sibley, but fought no important battles. Chivington became commander of the District of Southern New Mexico, where his troops clashed more gravely with the populace than they had in Denver. One night four men of the First Colorado Volunteer Infantry Regiment and a regular officer, Captain Ira W. Claflin, attended a fandango at a place called Hutch's Ranch. A shooting fray broke out from which only Claflin and one of the other soldiers escaped alive. Later that night Colorado Territory troops returned and set fire to the entire village, then shot down eighteen New Mexicans as they fled the flames.[40]

On November 1, 1862, Major General Samuel R. Curtis of the Department of the Missouri sent the First Colorado Volunteer Infantry Regiment to Denver to be converted into cavalry. It absorbed two home guard companies and became a full twelve-company cavalry regiment. But its heaviest fighting was over, for thereafter it served as an Indian-fighting and guerrilla-hunting regiment. Chivington, its colonel, became commander of the District of Colorado on November 2.[41]

Other Colorado Territory troops took up the burden of battle. On February 17, 1862, Jesse H. Leavenworth, an experienced military man, had received authority from the War Department to raise six companies of infantry in Colorado Territory. He was to combine these companies with those of Ford and Dodd to form the Second Colorado Volunteer Infantry Regiment and become its colonel. Dodd became the lieutenant colonel and Ford the major of the new regiment. Leavenworth reached Denver and began recruiting in May, 1862, but found progress slow. Then, in August of 1862, Governor Evans authorized ubiquitous Colorado Territory politician William H. Larimer to raise a third regiment in the territory, even though the second was unfilled. Larimer later resigned, leaving his regiment only partially filled. Finally, in the summer of 1863, Leavenworth began recruiting an artillery company,

though he had no authority to do so.[42]

In March of 1863, the two partial regiments left Denver on orders from Major General Curtis. The Second Colorado Volunteer Infantry Regiment concentrated at Fort Lyon (formerly Fort Wise) while five incomplete companies of the Third Colorado Volunteer Infantry Regiment left for Leavenworth, Kansas. Further orders for the Second Colorado Volunteer Infantry Regiment arrived, and on April 6 Lieutenant Colonel Dodd also left for Leavenworth with six companies. En route he received orders from Major General James G. Blunt, commanding the District of the Frontier, to report to Fort Scott, Kansas. On June 20, the Colorado Territory troops left Fort Scott, escorting a supply train of 300 wagons bound for Fort Blunt in the Cherokee Nation.[43]

As a result of this trip, the Second Colorado Volunteer Infantry Regiment participated in the first engagement of Cabin Creek in Indian Territory on July 1-2, 1863. Dodd commanded the wagon train's escort, consisting of his Colorado Territory troops and elements of several other regiments, as it left Fort Scott. Later Colonel James. M. Williams, with the First Kansas Colored Volunteer Infantry Regiment and a company of Indian Home Guards, increased the column's strength to about 1,800 men. They came into contact with Confederate forces under Colonel Stand Watie at Cabin Creek on July 1 and engaged them on the next day. Dodd left a small guard with the wagon train while taking most of his troops to fight under the overall command of Williams. Three companies of the Second Colorado Volunteer Infantry Regiment were among troops who splashed across Cabin Creek and drove the Confederates from its banks. No Colorado Territory troops died in the engagement.[44]

After completing the escort, the Second Colorado Volunteer Infantry Regiment joined about 3,000 men under Blunt and fought in the Battle of Honey Springs, Indian Territory, on July 17. With the Colorado Territory troops on the left side of his assault line, Blunt boldly attacked a superior Confederate force under Brigadier General Douglas H. Cooper. After the successful assault, Dodd went to the rear with prisoners, and Major J. Nelson Smith commanded the Coloradoans, their role thereafter confined to the support of an artillery battery. Following this engagement, the Colorado Territory troops stayed with Blunt until he had driven Confederate forces in Indian Territory south across the Red River. They then went into quarters at Fort Smith, Arkansas.[45]

Meanwhile, Leavenworth and another company of the Second Colorado Volunteer Infantry Regiment had gone to Fort Larned, where he commanded briefly. Leavenworth, however, quarreled with Chivington over control of troops on the Santa Fe Trail, and Chivington's friends caused Leavenworth's discharge on September 26, 1863, on the pretext that he had raised an unauthorized artillery company.[46]

Because both the Second and Third Colorado Volunteer Infantry Regiments were incomplete, Major General John M. Schofield, commanding the Department of the Missouri, combined them and converted them to cavalry for service against guerrillas in Missouri. Ford became colonel of the new Second Colorado Volunteer Cavalry Regiment, consisting of twelve companies and 1,100 men. In November, 1863, its constituent parts marched from scattered posts to St. Louis to effect consolidation.

The new regiment next tackled an unpleasant task, the policing of Jackson, Cass and Bates counties in Missouri, with headquarters in Kansas City. Ford assumed command of the area on February 18, 1864, and quieted bushwhacker activity in the area initially. But soon Confederate guerrillas resumed harassment of the Union troops. In late April soldiers under Major Jesse L. Pritchard skirmished with guerrillas, dressed in Union uniforms, who had captured a Colorado Territory sergeant. A series of such clashes led up to an attack on Captain Seymour W. Wagoner and twenty-five Colorado Territory soldiers by 100 guerrillas under George W. Todd on July 6 near Independence. Eight men died on each side, including Wagoner, who fell at the head of his men with a revolver in each hand.[47]

The struggle between the troops and guerrilla bands under Todd and Colonel John C. Thornton became desperate. On July 13, Ford and 150 men inflicted heavy casualties on a large guerrilla force at Camden Point, Missouri, while losing only two men. But four days later, Captain Thomas Moses, with only forty-seven men, again ran onto Thornton's band and lost six men killed, four wounded and two missing. Moses himself emptied three revolvers and received five bullet holes through his clothing during the fight.[48]

In September, 1864, Confederate Major General Sterling Price posed a more serious problem by invading the western Missouri border. Ford formed a brigade and joined Blunt's First Division of the Army of the Border to oppose Price. Ford had with him 400 men of the Sixteenth Kansas Cavalry Regiment, 384 men of his own regiment, and the Independent Colorado Battery, consisting of 116 men under Captain William E. McLain. This battery, which was raised without authorization by Leavenworth, had seen service on the plains and in Lawrence, Kansas. Blunt formed his division near the Little Blue River on October 21, but Price forced the outnumbered Union forces back after spirited resistance. With his troops from Colorado Territory and Kansas, Ford covered the retreat of the Union Army toward Independence. Major J. Nelson Smith, a popular officer who was temporarily commanding the Second Colorado Volunteer Infantry Regiment, fell in this action. He and his regiment's nemesis, the guerrilla leader Todd, met face-to-face in battle and killed each other with simultaneous shots.[49]

Blunt's division again made a stand on the Blue River on October 22, with six companies of the troops from Colorado Territory fighting south of the river as skirmishers. But Price forced a crossing, and Blunt's forces fell back to Westport. There Union troops finally stood off Price later in the day, though Colorado Territory troops saw no action. The next day the Coloradoans again came to the front, crossed the Blue River, and aided in checking a spirited assault by Price. The Independent Colorado Battery did telling work, first destroying an enemy battery, and then inflicting such havoc in a column of enemy troops that the Confederates charged to try and silence the Coloradoans' guns. McLain fell back, and the Second Colorado Volunteer Cavalry Regiment and the Sixteenth Kansas Cavalry Regiment rushed forward and repelled the charge. The battery took a new positon on a commanding hill and repulsed another Confederate assault. In one of these fights, McLain suffered the loss of his right arm. Meanwhile, the rest of Ford's brigade advanced through wooded country and put the enemy to flight.[50]

Price began retreating south, and Colorado Territory troops took part in the pursuit of his forces and fought in several minor engagements. After the Price threat faded, the Second Colorado Volunteer Cavalry Regiment went west to garrison posts on the Santa Fe Trail. Governor Evans wanted the regiment sent directly home, however, for by late 1864 he needed additional troops. Starting in 1862 and intensifying thereafter, officials in Colorado Territory faced problems of guerrilla activity and Indian hostility.

Confederate guerrilla operations in Colorado Territory from 1862 to 1865 never posed a real threat, and resembled simple outlawry in many cases. But after the Denver jailbreak in February, 1862, and the parole of numerous Texan prisoners from the New Mexico campaign, an annoying secessionist element operated in Colorado Territory. Even while the New Mexico campaign was going on, a "Colonel" John Heffiner attempted to organize a Confederate regiment at Mace's Hole, south of Colorado City. He claimed 600 members in his invisible regiment, but only a small fraction of that number ever gathered at Mace's Hole. They escaped detection through the intelligence efforts of Zan Hicklin, owner of a local trail stop who jokingly called himself "Old Secesh" so that Union troops would think him a harmless old fool. Heffiner's men at one time plotted to seize Fort Garland, but broke up before the end of 1862 because of the pressure of Union patrols and internal dissension. Union troops rounded up many of the band, including Heffiner himself.[51]

There were other Confederate bands in Colorado Territory. Captain George T. Madison, or Mattison, formerly an officer with Sibley, led a party which captured the Fort Garland mail in August, 1862, but later left the territory. Most feared of the guerrillas was James Reynolds, who, after his escape from the Denver jail, led twenty-two men in capturing two government wagon trains on the Cimarron Cutoff. Reynolds then began a career of robbery in the mountains south and west of Denver, but vigilante groups pressed him into the foothills. In August, 1864, First Lieutenant George L. Shoup captured Reynolds and four of his men. Chivington tried them by military commission and, denied authority to execute them, sent them under guard south toward Fort Lyon with the understanding that they were not to reach their destination. The guards reported that the five shackled prisoners were shot in an "escape attempt."[52]

The major source of trouble for Colorado Territory, however, was the Indians, first the Utes and then the Plains Tribes. The Utes began depredations near Cheyenne Pass on the Overland Mail Route in June of 1863, causing Chivington to send several companies of the First Colorado Volunteer Cavalry Regiment, under Major Edward W. Wynkoop, in pursuit of them. Wynkoop fruitlessly pursued the Utes from North Park south almost into New Mexico before returning to Denver. Not long afterward, the offending Indians appeared at the Conejos Agency, near Fort Garland. There on October 7, Governor Evans met with them and concluded a treaty by which the Utes agreed to a reservation west of the Continental Divide. This brought peace with the Utes for the rest of the Civil War.[53]

Major Edward W. Wynkoop of the First Colorado Volunteer Cavalry Regiment was relieved of command because he practiced conciliatory policies toward the Indians of Colorado Territory.

Less easy to deal with were the Cheyenne and Arapaho tribes in eastern Colorado Territory. A treaty in 1861 had assigned to them a small reservation between the Arkansas River and Sand Creek. Prominent chiefs, including Little Raven of the Arapahos and Black Kettle of the Cheyennes, were signatories. This seemed to quiet Indian affairs, and in February of 1862, the United States government transported the principal chiefs to Washington for a visit. The Indians were uncowed, however. In late summer of 1863, Evans attempted to meet with non-treaty elements of the two tribes, with the object of securing clear title to the area between the north and south forks of the Platte River. But the Indians rebuffed Evans' emissaries.[54]

In April of 1864, the expected war began with an outburst of stock-stealing by the Indians. Because of long-held fears of attack by Confederates or Indians, and an Indian-hating attitude on the part of Colonel Chivington, the commander of the District of Colorado, the military forces of Colorado Territory overreacted. Soldiers of Chivington's First Colorado Volunteer Cavalry Regiment responded to minor incidents of cattle theft by Indians with swift attacks on Cheyenne camps. Most notable was a fight on May 3 in which Major Downing and twenty-five men attacked a camp of Cheyennes at Cedar Bluffs near American Ranch on the Overland Mail Route. The soldiers killed about twenty-five Indians. "The war," announced Downing, "has begun in earnest."[55] Later in May, troops from the Independent Colorado Battery killed twenty-five more Cheyennes at Big Bushes on the upper Smoky Hill River; four soldiers were also killed.[56]

On June 11, the Indians struck back with a wave of depredations uncomfortably close to Denver. Most sensational was the devastation of the Nathan W. Hungate Ranch on Box Elder Creek, with the scalped and mutilated bodies of Mr. and Mrs. Hungate and their two children being brought into Denver on June 13. Chivington and the First Colorado Volunteer Cavalry Regiment were in southern Colorado Territory at the time, and Evans found the militia so unorganized that he wired Secretary of War Edwin M. Stanton for authority to raise a regiment of 100-day men. Denver's citizens panicked, broke into a government warehouse containing 2,000 rifles, and armed themselves.[57]

The real danger was to outlying settlements. In July and August, Indians raided a number of ranches along the Overland Mail Route and destroyed several wagon trains, killing the ranchers and drivers. Governor Evans wired Secretary Stanton that he needed 10,000 troops to quell the uprising, while stage line officials began closing their stations on the Overland Mail Route. Indians also killed several soldiers near Fort Lyon, whereupon Major Wyncoop pursued and wounded four Indians in a running fight. Another detachment of troops killed ten Cheyennes near Valley Station.[58]

Evans on August 10 issued a proclamation calling on the men of the territory to form militia companies. "Any man who kills a hostile Indian is a patriot," he said, but he cautioned against attacking peaceable bands. Other observers were less discriminating, as the *Rocky Mountain News* commented: "A few months of active extermination against the red devils will bring quiet, and nothing else will."[59] On August 13, with Stanton's authorization, Evans called for recruits to fill a new Third Colorado Volunteer Cavalry Regiment of 100-day men. Evans narrowly averted disaster in late August when the allied Plains Indians planned a concerted attack by 1,000 braves on all settlements. Elbridge Gerry, an old plains trader, heard of the plans and warned Evans, who dispatched troops to key points. The Indians called off the assault. By the end of August, Chivington was dispersing the 100-day men to trouble points and the situation quieted.[60]

On September 4, messengers of Black Kettle and other chiefs came to Fort Lyon and offered to open peace negotiations. Wynkoop and 130 soldiers fearlessly visited the Indian camp at Big Timbers on the Republican River, where 600 to 800 warriors greeted them. Wynkoop agreed to escort the principal chiefs to Denver to meet with Governor Evans. But a council with Evans in late September accomplished nothing, for he and Chivington refused to treat with the Indians, who then returned to their bands. The major reason for the refusal was a wire from departmental commander Curtis dictating that "I want no peace until the Indians suffer more."[61]

Back at Fort Lyon, Wynkoop continued conciliatory policies. He allowed Left Hand's band of Arapahos to camp near the fort and issued rations to them. Curtis discovered this, and on November 2 Major Scott Anthony, with instructions to follow a stricter policy, relieved Wynkoop of command. When Cheyennes under Black Kettle came to the fort for a council, Anthony had them encamp on Sand Creek, not for peacemaking but for availability when forces could be raised to attack them. Meanwhile, Governor Evans had left for Washington to request more troops.[62]

During Evans' absence the most admired person left in Colorado Territory was Colonel Chivington, an able leader in the military, religious, and political arenas. The hero of the Battle of Glorietta Pass was a Methodist preacher, who took time off from military duties on Sundays to preach in Denver churches. More than a leader, he was a symbol. A religious soldier of the First Colorado Volunteer Cavalry Regiment once remarked to a bunk-mate that he should "Always put...trust in Jesus." "Jesus is played out," came the reply, "Colonel Chivington commands this regiment!"[63]

Chivington decided to deliver a telling blow to the Indians before the enlistment terms of the Third Colorado Volunteer Cavalry Regiment ran out. In late November he led most of that regiment and parts of the First Colorado Volunteer Cavalry Regiment toward Fort Lyon. There on November 28 he met Anthony and 125 more men. Chivington then marched his combined force of some 700 men toward Black Kettle's encampment of Cheyenne and Arapaho on Sand Creek. In the early morning of September 29, the soldiers, except for a company under Captain Silas S. Soule, who refused orders, swept upon the camp of sleeping Indians. The attackers ignored an American flag and a white flag displayed by Black Kettle. The Indians fled in confusion, reformed for resistance in the creek bed, and then wilted under the soldiers' fire. Soldiers pursued the fleeing Indians, but by midafternoon the fight was over and several hundred Indians lay dead, mostly women and children. Then Chivington's men commenced mutilation of the bodies. In his report, Chivington claimed 500 to 600 Indians killed.[64]

The truth of the engagement seeped out through military channels and set off an angry reaction against Chivington's brutality. Wynkoop replaced Anthony at Fort Lyon with orders to initiate an investigation, and his report condemned Chivington as an "inhuman monster." On January 4, 1865, Colonel Thomas Moonlight replaced Chivington in command of the Colorado District. Congressional committees and a military tribunal conducted several investigations of what became known as the "Chivington Massacre," but they could not wipe away disastrous results already accruing from the event. The Sand Creek affair incited the Indians to new uprisings. A series of raids destroyed most of the stage stations on the Overland Mail Route, with troops at Julesburg and Valley Station barely holding out against repeated assaults. The Indians cut off stage service and destroyed the telegraph line from Julesburg. Moonlight declared martial law in the territory and recruited new companies of ninety-day men; their dispersal along the Overland Mail Route quieted affairs temporarily. As the Civil War ended, Colorado Territory faced the prospect of renewed Indian hostilities in the summer.[65]

Just as the Civil War affected the Indian war, so also wartime national politics affected politics within territorial Colorado. The most important political action of this period in Colorado Territory was a statehood movement in which the territory became a pawn in an administration scheme. Early in 1864, an avid supporter of Lincoln, Senator James K. Lane of Kansas, introduced a bill to allow Colorado Territory to become a state. Opponents argued that the territory was ineligible for statehood because its population was too small to merit a congressman. However, administration congressmen passed the bill, and Lincoln signed it on March 21, 1864. The obvious intention was to obtain three electoral votes for Lincoln from a new state of Colorado in the 1864 election. Congress passed similar bills for Nebraska and Nevada Territories. But unlike Nevada, Colorado failed to cooperate. The Republican Party and press supported statehood, and a convention, meeting pursuant to a call by Governor Evans, completed a constitution on July 11. On the other hand, Democrats opposed the movement, and voters concluded it was a ploy by politicians like Evans to gain national office. The territory's small population was unready to support a state administration, and on September 13 the voters rejected the constitution by a 4,672 to 1,520 vote.[66]

The war affected the economy of Colorado Territory by intensifying a depression originally caused by a slump in gold mining. Placer gold deposits largely played out, and techniques for processing hard rock ore developed slowly. Quartz mill operators tinkered with extractive processes throughout the war years with only occasional profit, despite efforts by mining organizations and the press to disseminate technological information. There was plenty of gold-bearing quartz, but foreign elements in the ore interfered with the extraction of the gold, and each apparent advance in methods only spawned new difficulties. For instance, "Dr. Keith's desulphurizing process" removed sulphur from the ore by pulverizing it and burning it out. But the process proved impractical, because the crushers used to reduce the ore to powder wore out too quickly.[67]

Capital and labor were obvious needs in the mines of Colorado Territory. By 1864, Eastern investors had eased the need for capital and machinery. By then the shortage was labor, not capital. Thousands of workers left the mines to join the armed forces of Colorado Territory or of their home states, or rushed to new mines in Idaho and Montana Territories. Also, the war effort absorbed any excess labor in the East that otherwise might have come to Colorado Territory, while the Indian war also hampered immigration, which declined radically, except for a brief surge in 1863, and the territory suffered a significant net loss in population. In 1864, representatives of the territory opened an office in New York City to appeal to European immigrants to come to Colorado Territory and settle.[68]

Because of the mineral wealth of Colorado Territory, however, Congress in April, 1862, voted to establish a branch of the United States mint in Denver. Artisans from the Philadelphia mint began operations in September of 1863, turning out at first gold bars and later coins. Other manufactures remained in a primitive stage. Local enterpreneurs supplied such needs as bread and beer, but extensive industry was nonexistent.[69]

Agricultural development also was insufficient to meet the territory's needs, because of natural disadvantages and the shortage of labor. Vegetable raising in the Platte River and Arkansas River valleys provided plentiful produce at cheap prices, and by 1864 several thousand acres were sown with cereals. Yearly plagues of grasshoppers severely damaged these, however. Several flour mill operators began small-scale operations, but most flour still had to be imported.[70]

As Indian hostilities closed roads to the east, the high cost of living troubled Coloradoans. In 1861, provisions were plentiful, and flour cost $9 or $10 per 100 pounds. In January, 1865, the price of flour peaked at $25 to $30 per 100 pounds. Fortunately, there was an abundance of fish and game; elk, antelope, mule deer, prairie chickens, turkeys, waterfowl and fresh trout graced Denver markets.[71]

Transportation and communication were especially vital to Colorado Territory during the Civil War. Because of Southern secession, Congress transferred the daily mail route from its former southern route to a "Central Route" through Salt Lake City in 1861, and specified that Denver should be served by the main or a branch line. In the spring of 1861, a party of men from Colorado Territory, organized by E. S. Berthoud and guided by Jim Bridger, found a pass through the central Rockies which Coloradoans hoped would carry the mail route. But before Berthoud could return to mark and measure the route, mail service began by way of the Overland Trail up the North Platte River, with a branch line serving Denver three times weekly. In 1862, Overland Mail officials moved the mail to a route along the South Platte River through Denver. A weekly mail served southern Colorado Territory by way of the Santa Fe Trail. The territory also gained telegraph service during the Civil War period. The transcontinental line, completed in 1861, ran through Julesburg. In 1863, the citizens of Denver subsidized a branch line to their city. In addition, the people of Colorado Territory hoped to be on the route of the transcontinental railroad. Governor Evans even traveled to Chicago in late 1863 to address the Union Pacific Railroad directors and urge them to build via Berthoud Pass.[72]

A direct result of the war was the arrival in Colorado Territory of Negro refugees from Missouri, in numbers large enough that the *Rocky Mountain News* remarked on "pairs and parties of Missouri negroes of excessive blackness lying around."[73] The editor recommended that Congress put freedmen to work on the transcontinental railroad. Negroes in Denver formed their own church and a military company that was sent east for duty.[74]

Despite deprivations due to the Civil War and Indian uprising, society in Colorado Territory matured. Lawlessness lessened under the pressure of a formal legal system, and the earlier common practice of dueling died out. Organized churches were established and grew. The Methodists of the Rocky Mountain District in 1863 consisted of eight congregations and nineteen preachers, and by the next year Denver had seven different church denominations. The old days were over when in 1863 the courts of Denver began trials and convictions of "females for keeping improper and disorderly houses."[75]

Everyday life still could be hazardous. Mad dogs often were a problem, while pigs, allowed to run loose, often plopped unwitting children into the dirt. More serious were fire and flood. "The Great Fire" of April

19, 1863, destroyed a large portion of downtown Denver, and the Cherry Creek Flood of 1864 swept away City Hall and eleven citizens.[76]

Though affected by the war, residents of Colorado Territory enjoyed certain diversions. Amusements ranged from refined to brutal. Governor Gilpin's levee at the Broadwell House on October 1, 1861, was the territory's most exquisite event to that time. At a masquerade ball on January 17, 1862, Federal Marshal and Mrs. Townsend were the hit, he as a Continental soldier and she as the "Daughter of the Regiment" in a blue silk robe. Territorial Secretary Lewis Weld appeared as Shakespeare's Hamlet. The People's Theatres of Denver and Central City, and the Platte Valley Theatre of Denver, which opened with *Richard III* on October 26, 1861, always drew crowds. But on the day after a Shakespeare performance the same stage might host a dogfight, like the "Great Dog Fight" between "Malakoff" and "Old Brandy" at the Denver People's Theatre on March 22, 1863. Prizefighting was immensely popular, especially after Denver blacksmith Con Orem defeated a visiting professional named Enoch Davies in 109 bloody rounds on August 25, 1861. The "Colorado Champ" went on to a prizefighting career in the East. Others preferred more pacific sports, like the members of Denver's first baseball club or the fishermen who frequently pulled four-pound native cutthroat trout from the South Platte River.[77]

In February of 1864, Charles F. Brown, alias Artemus Ward, the famed humorist, visited Denver and Central City. The residents of Colorado Territory adored Brown; in fact, the Second Colorado Volunteer Cavalry Regiment in Missouri adopted Brown's usual lecture title, "Babes in the Wood," as their password for nighttime identification. Brown treated Denver and Central City to a spiel entitled "Babes in the Bedrock." Denverites so appreciated his humor that they gathered at his hotel window and called for him, whereupon he and they repaired to a local saloon for drinks. Fortunately, Brown could bring at least a few hours of hilarity to Colorado Territory, beset as it was by a welter of troubles during the war years.[78]

Settlement entered the Colorado region during years of economic hardship and sectional differences, and territorial organization came concurrent with the breakup of the Union. Fortunately, the Civil War found the people of Colorado Territory almost wholly on the side of the Union; any major difference of allegiance would have split the leaderless territory hopelessly. Unfortunately, Colorado Territory's first chief executive, Governor Gilpin, was visionary and imprudent. Though he efficiently organized a civil administration, his management of military affairs caused his undoing. The Gilpin drafts, the lack of coherent organization and discipline in the First Colorado Volunteer Infantry Regiment, and Gilpin's unfounded fears of Confederate activism all played a part in his downfall and in arousing resentments among the populace.

Still, Gilpin's military organization made possible the checking of Sibley's New Mexico invasion. Colorado's strategic position — an emphatically Unionist territory situated among less loyal territories — allowed it to play a key role in the conflict. Confederate victory in the Southwest would have had diplomatic and geopolitical implications that might have changed the course of the entire war. Victory for the Union at Glorietta Pass was Colorado Territory's outstanding contribution to the war effort. However, it also created a hero who, with the influence he thus acquired, did great damage to his home territory, as well as perpetrating offenses against humanity. The trail from Glorietta Pass led directly to Sand Creek, for Chivington was the principal actor in both dramas.

The contribution of the Second Colorado Volunteer Infantry (Cavalry) Regiment to the war effort was less conspicuous, for it blended into the efforts of larger Union armies. But like the First Colorado Volunteer Infantry (Cavalry) Regiment, the Second Colorado Volunteer Infantry (Cavalry) Regiment always acquitted itself well in battle. It aided Blunt in clearing Indian Territory of Confederate forces and served creditably against guerrillas in Missouri. The Second Colorado Volunteer Cavalry Regiment climaxed its career with important service against Price on the Missouri border.

Colorado Territory gave much to the war, but the war gave only hardship in return. It cut off immigration to a community that needed to grow to survive. It disrupted an economy that already was struggling against major difficulties. It aroused political rivalries for the sake of continuity in national war leadership. Finally, it brought an Indian war that continued after the sectional conflict was over. Colorado paid expensively for its organization as a territory of the United States.

NOTES

1. James H. Pierce, "With the Green Russell Party," *Trail,* Vol. XIV, No. 1 (June, 1921), p. 8.

2. *Ibid.,* pp. 6-10.

3. Thomas D. Isern, "The Making of a Gold Rush: Pike's Peak, 1858-1860" (Master of Arts Thesis, Stillwater: Oklahoma State University, 1975), throughout.

4. *Eighth Census of the United States, 1860* (4 vols., Washington: Government Printing Office, 1864-1865), Vol. I, p. 548; *Rocky Mountain News* (Denver, Colorado), July 11, 1861, p. 2.

5. J. L. Frazier, "Prologue to Colorado Territory," *Colorado Magazine,* Vol. XXXVIII, No. 3 (July, 1961), pp. 161-173, *Journal of the West XVI,* January 1977, pp. 63-65.

6. Blanche V. Adams, "Colorado in the Civil War" (Master of Arts Thesis, Boulder: University of Colorado, 1930), pp. 5-7; *Rocky Mountain News,* January 5, 1861, p. 2.

7. *Ibid.,* February 22, 1861, p. 2.

8. *Ibid.,* April 26, 1861, p. 2.

9. *Ibid.,* April 25, 1861, p. 2, April 27, 1861, p. 2, May 11, 1861, p. 2, May 23, 1861, p. 2, March 9, 1861, p. 2.

10. Thomas L. Karnes, *William Gilpin: Western Nationalist* (Austin: University of Texas Press, 1970), pp. 72-257.

11. *Daily Western Journal of Commerce* (Kansas City, Missouri), December 21,

1858, p. 2.

12. *Rocky Mountain News,* May 28, 1861, p. 2, May 30, 1861, p. 2.

13. Sheldon S. Zweig, "The Civil Administration of Governor William Gilpin," *Colorado Magazine,* Vol. XXI, No. 3 (July, 1954), pp. 183-190; *Rocky Mountain News,* August 28, 1861, p. 2; "Message of the Governor of Colorado Delivered at the First Session of the Legislature," Colorado Series, United States Department of State Territorial Papers, National Archives, Washington, D. C.; "Joint Resolution," October 28, 1861, *ibid.*; LeRoy R. Hafen, "Colorado's First Legislative Assembly," *Colorado Magazine,* Vol. XX, No. 2 (March, 1943), pp. 44-49.

14. United States Department of War, *The War of the Rebellion: A Compilation of the Official Records of the Union and Confederate Armies* (70 vols., 128 books, Washington: Government Printing Office, 1800-1901), Ser. III, Vol. I, p. 257.

15. *Ibid.,* Ser. I, Vol. IV, pp. 53-54, 68; *Rocky Mountain News,* July 25, 1861, p. 3, July 29, 1861, p. 3, August 22, 1861, p. 3; Ovando J. Hollister, *Boldly They Rode* (Lakewood, Colorado: Golden Press, 1949) pp. 2-3.

16. *Rocky Mountain News,* August 27, 1861, p. 2, August 29, 1861, p. 2.

17. Phyllis Flanders Dorset, *The New Eldorado: The Story of Colorado's Gold and Silver Rushes* (New York: Macmillan Company, 1970), pp. 143-145; *Rocky Mountain News,* August 26, 1861, p. 3.

18. *Official Records,* Ser. I., Vol. I, pp. 505-506, 636.

19. Dunham Wright, "A Colorado Incident of the Civil War," *Trail,* Vol. XIII, No. 5 (September, 1920), p. 13; William Gilpin to Marshall Townsend, September 29, 1861, Colorado Series, United States Department of State Territorial Papers, National Archives; "The Privilege of the Habeas Corpus under the Constitution," *ibid.*

20. Hollister, *op. cit.,* pp. 26-30; *Rocky Mountain News,* February 28, 1861, p. 2.

21. *Ibid.,* October 30, 1861, p. 3, October 11, 1861, p. 3.

22. *Ibid.,* December 14, 1861, p. 2.

23. *Official Records,* Ser. III, Vol. I, p. 637.

24. *Ibid.,* Ser. I, Vol. IV, pp. 63, 72.

25. Karnes, *op. cit.,* pp. 278-279; *Official Records,* Ser. III, Vol. I, p. 246.

26. *Rocky Mountain News,* September 7, 1861, p. 3, September 9, 1861, p. 2, October 31, 1861, p. 3, November 7, 1861, p. 3; Hollister, *op. cit.,* pp. 32-33.

27. *Ibid.,* pp. 33-36, 39-43; *Rocky Mountain News,* January 26, 1862, p. 2.

28. Abraham Lincoln to Joseph Holt, July 18, 1863, Roy P. Basler, ed., *The Collected Works of Abraham Lincoln* (9 vols., New Brunswick: Rutgers University Press, 1953-1955), Vol. VI, p. 335.

29. *Rocky Mountain News,* February 8, 1862, p. 2, February 12, 1862, p. 2.

30. Francis P. Blair, Jr., to Abraham Lincoln, March 10, 1862, Basler, ed., *op. cit.,* Vol. V, p. 174.

31. *Rocky Mountain News,* December 26, 1861, p. 2, February 26, 1862, p. 2, March 6, 1862, p. 2, March 28, 1862, p. 2.

32. Alonzo Ferdinand Ickis, *Bloody Trails Along the Rio Grande: A Day-by-Day Diary of Alonzo Ferdinand Ickis* (Denver: Old West Publishing Company, 1958), pp. 28-30.

33. *Official Records,* Ser.I, Vol. IX, pp. 493, 519-520; Ickis, *op. cit.,* pp. 31-33, 75-78.

34. William Clarke Whitford, *Colorado Volunteers in the Civil War: The New Mexico Campaign in 1862* (Boulder: Pruett Press, 1963), pp. 43-44, 75-79; Hollister, *op. cit.,* pp. 44-52.

35. Arthur A. Wright, "Colonel John P. Slough and the New Mexico Campaign, 1862," *Colorado Magazine,* Vol. XXXIX, No. 2 (April, 1962), pp. 91-97.

36. *Official Records,* Ser. I, Vol. IX, pp. 530-531; Hollister, *op. cit.,* pp. 61-67.

37. *Official Records,* Ser. I, Vol. IX, pp. 534-535; Hollister, *op. cit.,* pp. 68-71.

38. *Official Records,* Ser. I, Vol. IX, pp. 538-539; Whitford, *op. cit.,* pp. 115-120.

39. *Official Records,* Ser. I, Vol. IX, pp. 541-542; Wright, *op. cit.,* pp. 101-105.

40. Hollister, *op. cit.,* pp. 132-133.

41. *Ibid.,* pp. 148-149, 163; *Official Records,* Ser. I, Vol. XIII, p. 777.

42. *Rocky Mountain News,* April 24, 1862, p. 2, August 21, 1862, p. 2, July 23, 1863, p. 2; Blanche V. Adams, "The Second Colorado Cavalry in the Civil War," *Colorado Magazine,* Vol. VIII, No. 3 (May, 1931), p. 97.

43. *Ibid.,* p. 98; *Rocky Mountain News,* April 14, 1863, p. 3, August 5, 1863, p. 2.

44. *Official Records,* Ser. I, Vol. XXII, Pt. 1, pp. 379-381; *Rocky Mountain News,* August 5, 1863, p. 2.

45. *Official Records,* Ser. I, Vol. XXII, Pt. 1, pp. 447-448, 455.

46. William E. Unrau, "The Civil War Career of Jesse Henry Leavenworth," *Montana: The Magazine of Western History,* Vol. XII, No. 2 (Spring, 1962), pp. 81-82.

47. Adams, "The Second Colorado Cavalry in the Civil War," *Colorado Magazine,* Vol. VIII, pp. 101-102; *Official Records,* Ser. I, Vol. XXII, pp. 621-622, 627; *ibid.,* Ser. I, Vol. XXXIV, Pt. 1, pp. 903-904; *ibid.,* Vol. XLI, Pt. 1, pp. 49-50.

48. *Ibid.,* pp. 53-54; *Rocky Mountain News,* July 26, 1864, p. 2.

49. *Official Records,* Ser. I, Vol. XLI, Pt. 1, pp. 606-608; *Rocky Mountain News,* November 16, 1864, p. 2.

50. *Official Records,* Ser. I, Vol. XLI, Pt. 1, pp. 608-609.

51. Daniel Ellis Connor, *A Confederate in the Colorado Gold Fields* (Norman: University of Oklahoma Press, 1970), pp. 132-148.

52. Morris F. Taylor, "Confederate Guerrillas in Southern Colorado," *Colorado Magazine,* Vol. XLVI, No. 4 (Fall, 1969), pp. 310-322.

53. *Rocky Mountain News,* August 17, 1863, p. 2; *Official Records,* Ser. I, Vol. XXII, Pt. 2, p. 528; "Copy of Treaty with Tabaquache Band of Ute Indians," Colorado Series, United States Department of State Territorial Papers, National Archives.

54. *Rocky Mountain News,* June 13, 1863, p. 2, August 27, 1863, p. 2; Harry E. Kelsey, Jr., *Frontier Capitalist: The Life of John Evans* (Denver: State Historical Society of Colorado, 1969), pp. 129-131.

55. *Official Records,* Ser. I, Vol. XXXIV, Pt. 1, p. 907.

56. *Ibid.,* p. 935

57. Stan Hoig, *The Sand Creek Massacre* (Norman: University of Oklahoma Press, 1961), pp. 58-60; *Official Records,* Ser. I, Vol. XXXIV, Pt. 4, p. 449.

58. *Ibid.,* Ser. I, Vol. XLI, Pt. 2, pp. 644, 661; *ibid.;* pt. 1, pp. 238-239, 883.

59. *Rocky Mountain News,* August 10, 1864, p. 2.

60. *Ibid.,* August 13, 1864, p. 2, August 26, 1864, p. 2.

61. *Official Records,* Ser. I, Vol. XLI, Pt. 3, pp. 242-243; *Rocky Mountain News,* September 29, 1864, p. 1; *Official Records,* Ser. I, Vol. XLI, Pt. 3, p. 462.

62. *Ibid.,* Pt. 1, pp. 912-913; *ibid.,* Pt. 4, pp. 671-672.

63. *Rocky Mountain News,* May 27, 1863, p. 2.

64. Hoig, *op. cit.,* pp. 136-153; *Official Records,* Ser. I, Vol. XLI, Pt. 1, pp. 948-950.

65. *Ibid.,* Pt. 2, pp. 959-962; Hoig, *op. cit.,* pp. 163-173; *Official Records,* Ser. I, Vol. XLVIII, Pt. 1, pp. 726, 838-840.

66. *Congressional Globe,* 37th Congress, 3rd Session, p. 905; *ibid.,* 38th Congress, 1st Session, pp. 1166-1167; Kelsey, *op. cit.,* pp. 155-159.

67. *New York Times,* July 12, 1864, p. 8

68. Adams, "Colorado in the Civil War," pp. 114-126; *New York Times,* February 14, 1864, p. 5.

69. *Congressional Globe,* 37th Congress, 2nd Session, pp. 1551, 1789; *Rocky Mountain News,* September 29, 1863, p. 2.

70. *Ibid.,* August 31, 1864, p. 2; Adams, "Colorado in the Civil War," pp. 125-126.

71. *Ibid.,* pp. 130-134; *Rocky Mountain News,* October 31, 1861, p. 3, October 27, 1864, p. 2.

72. LeRoy R. Hafen, *The Overland Mail: Promoter of Settlement, Precursor of Railroads* (Cleveland: Arthur H. Clark Company, 1926), pp. 195-235; *Rocky Mountain News,* June 4, 1861, p. 2, January 25, 1864, p. 2.

73. *Ibid.,* March 13, 1863, p. 3, July 17, 1863, p. 2.

74. *Ibid.,* July 12, 1864, p. 3, January 29, 1864, p. 3.

75. *Ibid.,* March 4, 1863, p. 2; *New York Times,* July 12, 1864, p. 8; *Rocky Mountain News,* March 13, 1863, p.3.

76. *Ibid.,* April 20, 1863, p. 2; LeRoy R. Hafen, *Colorado and Its People: A Narrative and Topical History of the Centennial State* (4 vols., New York: Lewis Historical Publishing Company, 1948), pp. 290-291.

77. *Rocky Mountain News,* October 2, 1861, p. 2, January 18, 1862, p. 3, October 28, 1861, p. 2, March 21, 1863, p. 3, August 26, 1861, p. 2, March 13, 1862, p. 3, March 13, 1863, p. 3.

78. *Official Records,* Ser. I, Vol. XXXIV, Pt. 3, p. 92; *Rocky Mountain News, March 12, 1864, p. 2, February 27, 1864, p. 3.*

SELECTED READINGS

Blanche V. Adams, "The Second Colorado Cavalry in the Civil War," *Colorado Magazine,* Vol. VIII, No. 3 (May, 1931), pp. 95-106.

Stan Hoig, *The Sand Creek Massacre* (Norman: University of Oklahoma Press, 1961).

Daniel Ellis Connor, *A Confederate in the Colorado Gold Fields* (Norman: University of Oklahoma Press, 1970).

Ovando J. Hollister, *Boldly They Rode* (Lakewood, Colorado: Golden Press, 1949).

Alonzo Ferdinand Ickis, *Bloody Trails Along the Rio Grande: A Day-by-Day Diary of Alonzo Ferdinand Ickis* (Denver: Old West Publishing Company, 1958).

Thomas L. Karnes, *William Gilpin: Western Nationalist* (Austin: University of Texas Press, 1970), pp. 253-298.

Harry E. Kelsey, Jr., *Frontier Capitalist: The Life of John Evans* (Denver: State Historical Society of Colorado, 1969), pp. 115-168.

Morris F. Taylor, "Confederate Guerrillas in Southern Colorado," *Colorado Magazine,* Vol. XLVI, No. 4 (Fall, 1969), pp. 304-323.

William Clarke Whitford, *Colorado Volunteers in the Civil War: The New Mexico Campaign in 1862* (Denver: State Historical and Natural History Society of Colorado, 1906).

Arthur A. Wright, "Colonel John P. Slough and the New Mexico Campaign," *Colorado Magazine,* Vol. XXXIX, No. 2 (April, 1962), pp. 89-105.

Nebraska Territory

By Larry D. Duke

In March, 1860, the statehood question was put before the voting population of the Territory of Nebraska; 2,094 favored the issue, while 2,372 opposed it. The election did not reflect the overall statehood sentiment of the people, but was based solely on the political issue of anti-slavery laws. Although Nebraska was then a nearly solid Democratic territory, the question of secession was never seriously considered. Although organized as a territory in 1854, together with Kansas, her policies were not fully developed until after Kansas was admitted as a state in 1861.

Nebraska politicians came during the 1850's from Iowa, Missouri, Indiana, Illinois, the North, the South, and the East. Many settlers came with the single purpose of establishing themselves in the newly formed territorial government; others came by United States government appointment, and some came as pioneers eager to build a new land. In 1860, the territorial governor was Samuel W. Black, an appointee and loyal supporter of President James Buchanan. Although Black was a strong Democrat from Virginia and a vigorous Southern sympathizer, he did not support the new secession talk then beginning throughout the nation. The territory had been created by a Democratic Congress and administration, and all of her first judges, secretaries, and officials were Democrats; even the counties bore Democratic names. But in the territory itself, party lines were not so sharply drawn.

A change in the territory came with the election of Abraham Lincoln to the presidency in 1860. That year the People's Party, afraid to adopt the Republican name in 1859, quickly changed to come in line with Lincoln. The change of administration in the spring of 1861 was the beginning of a long Republican reign and was the sunset for the Democratic politicians of the territory. On May 18, 1861, Governor Black turned over his office to Alvin Saunders, a Republican Lincoln appointee from Mount Pleasant, Iowa.[1]

The outbreak of the Civil War seriously affected Nebraska even though it was still a frontier territory, and Governor Black was eager to relinquish his duties to his Republican successor. Before leaving office, Black issued an order for all volunteer military companies to report immediately. On April 30, he issued a proclamation recommending the organization of military companies throughout the territory because of the large withdrawals of United States troops from the forts of Nebraska and because of conditions over the nation

at large. Immediately on coming to office in May, 1861, Governor Saunders issued the first proclamation for the territory calling for volunteers for the Civil War.

Though the Federal government never doubted its hold on the territory, there was the ever present fact that until Lincoln's election, the territory had been strongly Democratic. Moved by the necessity of saving the Union to make common cause with the Republicans, the Democrats nevertheless refused to forget their differences, especially with the Radical Republican elements. At times, refusal to disband the party for the sake of unity against the enemy was looked upon as

Alvin Saunders, governor of Nebraska Territory throughout the Civil War, was a Republican from Iowa appointed by President Abraham Lincoln.

giving aid and comfort to the enemy. Surprisingly, the Democrats were able to maintain considerable strength in the territory throughout the Civil War. It was not until the territory began to fill up with Union veterans and newly Republicanized immigrants that the Democrats fell into a hopeless minority.

Though the territory and the Federal government were sometimes at odds as to priorities of funds and troops, the relationship was never really strained. The grim business of war in the East and Indian trouble at home had taken the place of partisan politics. There was much controversy as to the ability of the territory to defend itself against border ruffianism on the southern and Indian depredations along the whole western border. The strongest opposition to the Federal government arose over sending the First Infantry Regiment out of the territory.

Aside from the overriding necessity of preserving the Union, the Republicans in Nebraska Territory were greatly aided by the passage in 1862 of the Federal Homestead Act, a measure the previous Democratic administration had consistently opposed, and the funding for the building of the Union Pacific Railroad, which would start in Nebraska. But the Republicans still did not reign supreme; so in 1864, Phineas W. Hitchcock, a

Union Party member, was sent to Congress as the territorial delegate. But the overwhelming victory of the Republicans in the presidential election of 1864 demonstrated that the people had had enough of political sniping at the conduct of the Civil War. In the nation, the Republicans went on to a successful conclusion of the war, and in Nebraska, they turned full attention to bringing the territory into statehood.[2]

In 1864, Lincoln was having trouble holding the support of some of the elements of the Republican Party. In that same year, Nebraska's territorial legislature asked Congress to give Nebraska a special invitation to join the Union. Men in Congress friendly to the president believed that Nebraska as a state would provide welcome support. Lincoln was liked in the territory because of the Homestead Act, and also because the Union cause was favored. An act was passed by Congress at its last session in 1864 to enable the territory to form a state government. In 1864, the territorial legislature accepted a hurriedly-written constitution prepared by a secret committee. For Lincoln, it was too late, since the voters did not get to act on the new constitution until June 2, 1866.[3]

The complete contrast between the attitude of the first and seventh territorial legislatures in Nebraska

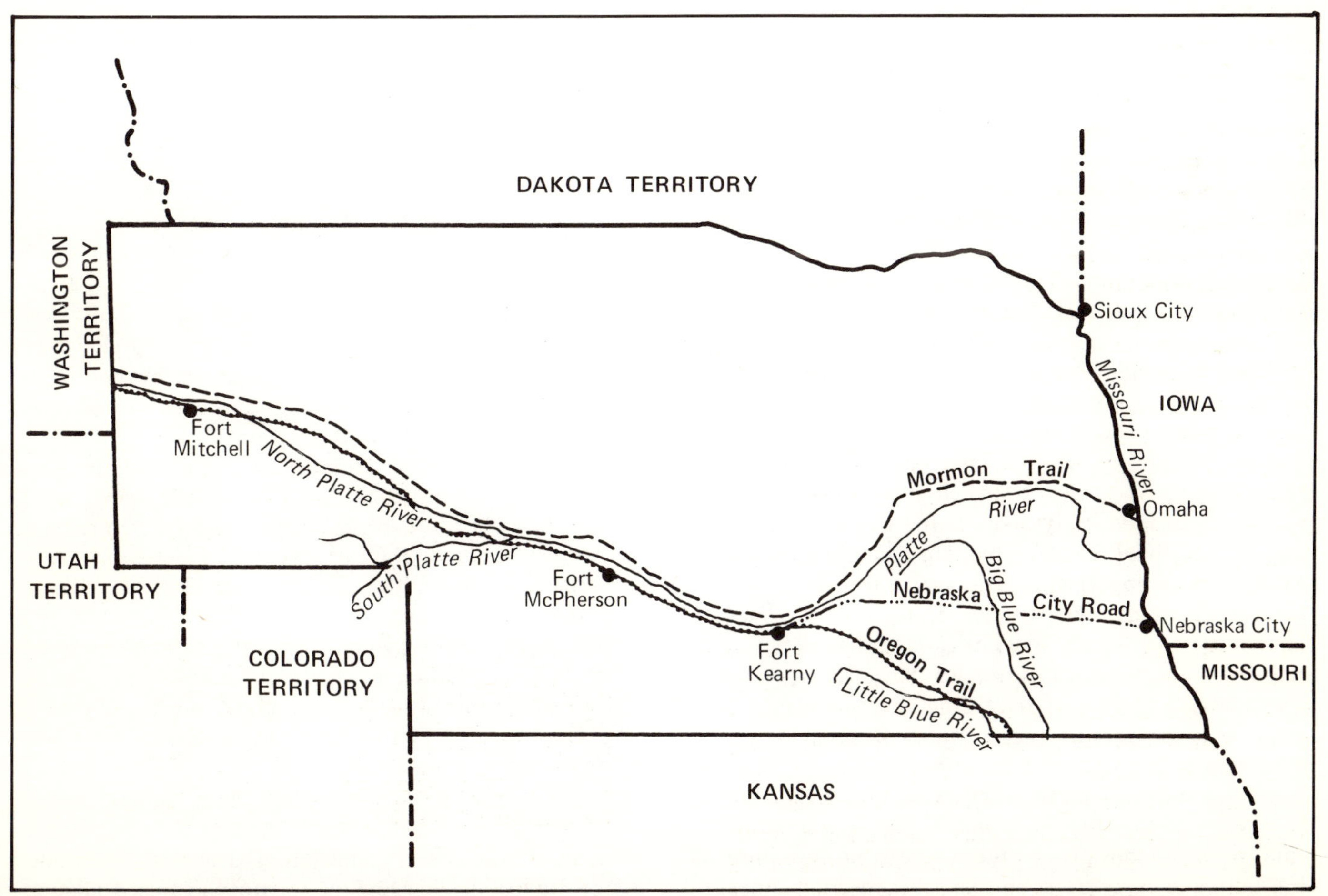

Map Drafted by Georganne T. Bartow

Nebraska Territory During the Civil War

toward the Negro question indicates the rapid growth of anti-slavery sentiment after the passage of the Kansas-Nebraska Act in 1854. A bill prohibiting the settlement of free Negroes and mulattoes in the territory passed the lower house of the first legislature. In the sixth legislature, a bill of the same type was introduced but was loaded with an amendment prohibiting slavery, and the enacting clause was stricken from the bill. The closer the legislators lived to the slave state of Missouri, the farther away they wanted to keep slavery. At the seventh session of the legislature, the prohibitory measure was enacted into law, being passed with only two dissenting votes. Governor Black vetoed it, citing that it would hurt economically because it would keep companies with slaves from coming into the territory. The bill was finally passed over his veto. While the Democrats had cooperated with the Republicans in prohibiting slavery in the territory, they persisted in their opposition to anti-slavery principles or tendencies.

The slavery question in Nebraska was handled oddly. Both parties generally opposed the institution, but it was hard to pass prohibitive and abolitionist legislation. The Democrats would say that slavery did not exist and that the issue was unnecessary. Republicans would generally agree or say it was very slight, but that it would not hurt to have anti-slavery laws on the books. The census of 1860 had listed only fifteen slaves in the territory.[4]

John Brown's underground railway led through a corner of Nebraska and through Nebraska City. Many newspapers of that region characterized Brown as a typical Republican, being both a horse and a ''nigger thief.'' Few Nebraskans wanted slavery, but first and foremost, hardly any wanted Negroes, slave or free, in the territory. Because of the few Negroes who were in the state, hard conflict never arose. When statehood finally came in 1867, the United States Congress forced Nebraska to accept Negro suffrage and equality.[5]

Another problem that arose concerned the Copperheads. Their objections to the Lincoln administration were mostly economic. They felt the North and the East had begun the war for financial profit, and, as it happened, the West was left to help pay the cost, which hurt them economically and left the frontier open to attack. Sectional loyalty characterized most of the Midwestern Copperheads. The loss of transportation, banking relations, and Southern capital hit the West hard, along with high freight rates and the loss of Southern river trade. Copperheadism was basically a clash of the industrial Northeast and the agricultural West. As elsewhere, the Copperheads in Nebraska pointed to all the faults of Republicans, including the failure of the war effort and the collapse of the economy. Finally, war prosperity came to the West, and William T. Sherman's capture of Atlanta proved the war was not a failure. Farmers and laborers soon experienced good times, thus undermining the Copperhead protest. The Nebraska Copperhead movement was never strong, and the only organization it had was in the secret protest societies then popular across the nation.[6]

For military preparedness at the outset of the Civil War, Nebraska was ahead of many territories and states. To begin with, nearly every adult male in the territory owned a gun of some type. There were already many United States troops in the territory guarding the numerous trails and defending settlements and forts. For the war effort, the territory furnished a remarkably large quota of 3,157 men out of a total population of a little less than 30,000. Nebraska ranked second in the number of men furnished by the territories to aid the Union. Perhaps as many as 2,000 more Nebraskans fought in the war under different surrounding states as well as a few for the Confederacy. Scarcely a regiment from either Kansas, Missouri, Iowa, or Illinois did not have at least a few Nebraskans in it. Ohio, Indiana, and other places frequently had soldiers who listed Nebraska Territory as their home. The Fifth Regimental Missouri State Militia had nearly a company from Nebraska.[7]

On May 3, 1861, Lincoln had issued a call for 500,000 troops. Nebraska furnished only 91 men, and they enlisted for only one year. Under the call of August, 1862, for 300,000 men for nine months of service, Nebraska furnished 1,228 men. There was never a quota for Nebraska Territory as there was for the states, and of the 3,157 Nebraska men who enlisted during the war, only 2,175 selected the three-year standard enrollment.[8]

The initial unit to organize was the First Nebraska Infantry Regiment, enlisted at Omaha from June 11 to July 21, 1861. It was attached to the Department of Missouri until November, 1864, meanwhile becoming the First Nebraska Cavalry Regiment. The organization at last came to the District of Nebraska, where in July, 1865, it became the First Nebraska Veteran Cavalry Regiment. The second group to organize was the Second Nebraska Cavalry Regiment. Organized at Omaha in October of 1862, this unit remained in the territory, except for brief service in Dakota Territory, until mustered out on December 23, 1863.

In 1864, the First Nebraska Cavalry Battalion was organized and attached to the District of Nebraska. It saw duty in Colorado and at Fort Laramie before being consolidated with the First Nebraska Veteran Cavalry Regiment in July, 1865. Two independent companies of Indian scouts were organized in 1865, but their duty was solely against Indian insurgents. They were the Independent Company A of Pawnee Scouts organized on January 13 and the Independent Company of Omaha Scouts organized on May 3. Both companies were mustered out by July, 1866.[9]

Other preparations for operations against enemy forces included the constant struggle for the procurement of supplies, transportation, arms, and munitions for the troops guarding the territory against Indian attack. Lack of money was also a problem at the beginning of the Civil War. A part of the preparation for action was the actual replacement of the United States troops which had been recalled for service in the South, along with Nebraska's own men, and those units campaigning in neighboring states. Nebraska was faced with preparing new recruits to take over the duties of veteran troopers and Indian fighters.

The civilian attitude in Nebraska during the Civil War was displeasure and fear. The foremost reason the war was not more popular was because so many men were off fighting the Confederates that settlements and overland trails were left largely unguarded. Civilians constantly believed that they were being ignored by Washington in favor of the safety of the North. They were of the impression that the Federal government should, and could, do more to help and protect them and their property. When Indian trouble was least, sympathy for the war was highest. The attitudes of the territorial government were those of its people. The government was in perpetual request for more of everything: transportation, arms, munitions, troops, and money. Officials repeated continually that they could not do what they were expected to do without further Federal aid and cooperation.

Military activity within the territory was confined primarily to fighting Indians, guarding forts, escorting travelers west, and scouting expeditions. The scouting expeditions were for the purpose of discovering what trails the Indians were using and in what locations they might be gathering or hiding. Fort McPherson was built in 1863 across a major Indian trail to discourage Indian uprisings. The escorting of stages and wagon trains tied up companies of troops. Sometimes it was the duty of the troops to gather or direct emigrants to the various forts, to be organized into larger groups, thereby insuring safety, while releasing men for other duties. The manning of the forts themselves was a job which required more and more men as the Indian troubles increased, especially from 1862 to 1864.

The records list 31 troop engagements, skirmishes, and operations in Nebraska Territory from April, 1863, until midsummer, 1865. Of these, Nebraska troops were involved in 13 of the actions, sustaining 2 killed and 6 wounded. The groups participating were the First Cavalry Regiment, the Second Cavalry Regiment, the First Cavalry Battalion, and the Omaha Scouts. Of the 3,157 men listed from Nebraska in the army for Civil War service, a total of 239 died. Of this number, 35 were killed or mortally wounded in battle, 1 died as a prisoner of war, death by accident claimed 23, death from causes except battle killed 21, and 159 died of various diseases, the most common cause of death during the Civil War. [10]

Fort Kearny was the main headquarters for troops in Nebraska Territory. At the outbreak of the war in April, 1861, the fort commander was Captain Charles H. Tyler, a Virginian and a secessionist. He promptly resigned and soon became a colonel in the Confederate Army. Tyler had made an effort to subvert the fort and

had ordered the guns spiked, but the men remained loyal and would not allow the orders to be executed. In June, regular troops were withdrawn to aid in the Southern campaigns, and for the duration they were replaced by volunteer regiments. All the heavy ordnance was transferred to Kansas and was not replaced until after the war. [11]

Despite heavy emigration and military and freighting traffic passing through Nebraska westward, the period from 1861 to 1863 remained relatively peaceful, except for a two-month long Sioux Indian uprising. The Sioux uprising in nearby Minnesota in 1862 alarmed the settlers of Nebraska. The South had an unwitting ally in the West, the awesome Sioux. Citizens immediately began appealing to the government of Nebraska and its governor for military protection. In September, 1862, because the people were so alarmed, the governor asked for, but was denied, authority to raise a regiment for the defense of the Nebraska border. Since April, 1862, Nebraska had had no active home guard and no volunteer troops in service except for two regiments fighting in the East. In September of that year, Major General John Pope, in command of the Department of Missouri, returned to the West from retreats in the East. Pope did not get results, for lack of support, since the Confederate yell in Washington was closer and drowned out the Sioux war whoop. Pope "recommended to the Government to gather the Indians around military posts, disarm them, and compel them either to become good farmers and Christians, or to starve." [12]

By early fall, 1862, the Sioux had closed the overland trails for a month, cut the telegraph, halted the mail and stage, and driven the white population in terror to the East and to the forts; rumors spread that Confederates were leading the Indians. It was determined that a general campaign was needed to stop these depredations. For this purpose, a new Nebraska regiment would need to be organized, and after a brief quarrel between Governor Saunders and the military, the governor authorized its formation.

At this point, one of the two most distinguished Nebraskans in the army came into action. This was Robert W. Furnas, publisher of both the *Nebraska Advertizer* and the *Nebraska Farmer*. At the outbreak of the Civil War, Furnas promoted home defense forces for the frontier, and though he had a large family, he longed for active participation in the war effort. He became the colonel of the First Indian Regiment of Indian Territory, but after becoming disgusted at the behavior of the troops, returned to Nebraska, where he was authorized to raise a company of men for the new Second Cavalry Regiment intended for home defense. The unit was organized on October 23, 1862, and assigned to duty at Fort Kearny where it guarded and operated against the Indians until April, 1863, when it was ordered to participate in a campaign against the Sioux in Dakota Territory.

Brigadier General Alfred Sully, in command of the First Military District at Sioux City, Iowa, was the ranking officer in charge of the campaign of 1863. Colonel Furnas was in charge of nine of the twelve companies of the Second Nebraska Cavalry Regiment on the expedition. After joining up at Sioux City, Iowa, and spending some three weeks in preparing to meet the Indians, the expedition marched north into Dakota. July and August brought no hostilities, but, on September 3, scouts reported a camp of 600 lodges. Parts of the expedition began surrounding the Indians as combat opened; the battle raged for several hours until dark. Losses of the Second Nebraska Cavalry Regiment were limited to 7 killed, 14 wounded, and 10 missing in action. Estimated Indians killed ranged from 80 to 150, and as many as 300 wounded. During the night, the Indians stole away from camp, leaving everything, including 15 to 20 women and children; the regiment did not give pursuit because of the lack of supplies. After serving a few weeks of garrison duty at Fort Randall, Dakota Territory, the regiment made a leisurely journey back to Omaha. On December 23, 1863, the Second Nebraska Cavalry Regiment was mustered out of the service three weeks short of the nine months enlistment period. At last a blow had been struck by the military,

Brigadier General Alfred Sully of Nebraska Territory commanded the campaign against the Sioux Indians in Dakota Territory in 1863.

and both Colonel Furnas and Brigadier General Sully termed the campaign a decided success. By keeping the Sioux on the move, the army had forced them to use up or to lose their supplies, and they suffered a harder winter because of the campaign.[13]

In the summer of 1864, another Sioux outbreak occurred with wholesale destruction of ranches, farms, and stage stations, including the butchery of their inhabitants. Soldiers were kept in constant movement during the hostilities, but never managed to catch up with the raiders to inflict sufficient harm to stop the attacks. Finally, in October, 1864, troops halted raids for a few weeks by burning the prairie from Fort Kearny to Julesburg and south to the Republican River. In November, 1864, the newly organized First Nebraska Cavalry Regiment, formerly the First Nebraska Infantry Regiment, was returned to the territory on furlough, but was recalled and ordered to Fort Kearny. Major General Samuel R. Curtis, commandant of the Department of Kansas and the Curtis Horse Cavalry Regiment, came out from Fort Leavenworth, Kansas, with a small force, and with Brigadier General Robert Mitchell, in command of the District of Nebraska, organized an expedition against the Sioux. Though Curtis did not have enough men to move against the Sioux in force, he provided escorts for stages and freighter

Colonel Robert W. Furnas, a Nebraska Territory newspaper publisher, initially commanded the First Indian Regiment of Indian Territory and then campaigned against the Sioux Indians in Dakota Territory in 1863.

wagons, and reopened traffic along the overland trails. The Sioux, somewhat awed, made no further concerted attacks, confining themselves to hit and run raids against isolated spots.[14]

On November 29, 1864, Colonel John M. Chivington, commanding the Third Colorado Cavalry Regiment and a former elder in the Nebraska Methodist Conference, attacked a group of Sioux and Cheyenne on Sand Creek. These were peaceable Indians who had voluntarily surrendered. The Sand Creek Massacre enraged the Indians and by January, 1865, the Great Platte River Road was again paralyzed. Major General Grenville M. Dodge, commanding the Department of Missouri of which Nebraska Territory was a district, ordered out additional military units to give full protection to the overland trails. Soldiers were quartered at several rebuilt Overland Stage Company stations along the Platte River, and slowly commerce began to revive. At times in 1864 it appeared that the hostilities might bring a general retreat of the white population. These sagging defenses were filled by six regiments of "Galvanized Yankees," officially United States volunteers but actually captured Confederates who were willing to swear allegiance to the Union upon assurance that they would not be asked to fight their brothers in the South. In Nebraska, they were stationed at Fort Kearny, Fort McPherson, Camp Mitchell, and Plum Creek. They had skirmishes with the Sioux from the Little Blue River to the border, but their main service in the territory was protection of stage and railroad stations in the Platte River Valley.[15]

Who would help defeat the Sioux? That thorny question would remain until after the South had laid down its arms, for 1865 did not see the end of Indian trouble in Nebraska or anywhere in the West. In 1865, the Civil War ended in the North and South, but not in Nebraska, for there wars would continue off and on until the 1880s. In the final year of the Civil War, volunteer troops which had performed so gallantly were gradually replaced by United States Army regulars, battle-hardened veterans of the Civil War.

There were many reasons that prevented the army from containing the Sioux. The very way of life of the Indians and the vastness of the territory served to keep the army and the Indians from coming to blows more often. Ammunition was not always plentiful in Nebraska for army use, but was usually adequate. The lack of arms or munitions or both from time to time was not unique in Nebraska or the West in the war years, but was on the whole analogous to the general situation of the nation. The Sioux, on the other hand, were not merely supplied with only bows, arrows, or lances. Shotguns and even rifles were in common use among them. Another problem was the difficulty in retaining troops, as well as finding them, because of the increasing need to release more soldiers for service in the South.

Military activity outside of the territory during the Civil War was confined mainly to a Nebraska battalion in the Curtis Horse Cavalry Regiment and to the First Nebraska Infantry Regiment. The Nebraska men who served in the Curtis Horse Cavalry Regiment were not an actual Nebraska unit but were instead a part of the Fifth Iowa Cavalry Regiment. This group was noted for action in Tennessee, Alabama, and Kentucky. Lieutenant Colonel Matthewson T. Patrick commanded the Nebraska battalion. Organized in December, 1861, the unit kept in active service in Tennessee and Kentucky until June 25, 1863, when it was assigned to duty in the state of Iowa. This regiment saw constant activity until the conclusion of hostilities.[16]

The First Nebraska Infantry Regiment served with distinction. Organized as ten companies on July 21, 1861, at Omaha, it was attached to the Department of Missouri, Third Division, Army of the Tennessee. Colonel John M. Thayer was appointed by Governor Saunders to command the Regiment; Thayer had formerly served in the territorial legislature. In July, 1861, the regiment was ordered to St. Joseph, Missouri, and from there was sent on to reinforce Brigadier General Ulysses S. Grant, who was holding Pilot Knob, Missouri. From the time Colonel Thayer reported to Grant in his quarters, the two became lifelong friends; Thayer went on to serve under Grant for two years. The

Courtesy of Nebraska State Historical Society

Brigadier General John M. Thayer, Nebraska Territory's ranking officer, commanded the First Nebraska Infantry Regiment and other army units at the capture of Fort Donelson and in the Battle of Shiloh.

regiment's first action came against Springfield, Missouri, in October, November, and December, 1861, in a campaign against bushwhackers. The regiment's first major fighting came on December 18, 1861, when it participated in an engagement at Shawnee Mound, Missouri; the battle resulted in a Union victory with the capture of 1,300 prisoners.[17]

Grant had begun a campaign to break the Confederate defense line in Tennessee and had already taken Fort Henry, when Thayer and his division were sent by steamboat up the Cumberland River toward Fort Donelson, which was Grant's next target. As the fort was surrounded, the First Nebraska Infantry Regiment landed and spent its first night at Fort Donelson in the bitter cold without benefit of fires. Colonel Thayer was put in command of a brigade and Lieutenant Colonel William D. McCord assumed direct command over the Nebraska men. After spending another night without fires and in the snow, the regiment awoke to gunfire. The fighting was ahead of the First Nebraska Infantry Regiment and along the road on which it was situated. Soon the wounded began coming down the road and the forces began fallng back. The First Nebraska Infantry Regiment was to hold one side of the road and another regiment the other. As the artillery fell back to reposition, the Nebraska regiment was left on the front line as the Confederates came charging down the road. As the Confederates neared this position, cannons blazed away; the Nebraska regiment fired along with the other regiments, and the Confederates were soon headed back toward Fort Donelson. The next day, as the Federals began advancing on the fort, the Confederates surrendered all 14,000 men. The Union had lost 2,600, the Confederates 2,000, and the Nebraska forces 9. Thus, the First Nebraska Infantry Regiment and Colonel Thayer had played important roles in holding the line of battle the day before the Confederate surrender.[18]

In April, 1862, at the Battle of Pittsburg Landing (Shiloh), the First Nebraska Infantry Regiment again saw major action. Other actions occurred at Arkansas Post, Fort Smith, and the Battle of Jenkins Ferry, all in Arkansas; nearly all the regiment's action in 1863 was confined to Arkansas. In late August of that year, however, the regiment was transferred to St. Louis, and in November it became the First Nebraska Cavalry Regiment and was returned to Nebraska Territory.[19]

Colonel Thayer, after the battles of Fort Donelson and Shiloh, had been recommended for promotion and was commissioned a brigadier general on October 4, 1862. Later, in 1863, he would be named to command the Army of the Frontier, with headquarters at Fort Smith. In July of 1865, after seeing the Union safe, he resigned to be with his family and to return to his home in Nebraska. He had begun his career as the ranking officer from Nebraska Territory and retained that distinction for the duration of the Civil War; since many Union veterans settled in the territory in later years,

this honor proved to be of great political significance to him.[20]

Just as the military in Nebraska had been kept busy since the outbreak of the Civil War, the Nebraska economy long stagnated began to come alive. The increased demand for goods of all types provided Nebraska's two main enterprises the encouragement they had needed. The economic activity in the territory during the Civil War years was confined mainly to agriculture and freight transportation. Agriculture was not the chief economic activity of the territory in the beginning; land speculation had been the primary interest in Nebraska from its opening in 1854 until the Panic of 1857. Until the panic hit, farming was not lucrative enough and proved too expensive. Pressed by the aftermath of the panic, many people turned to farming, some because they could find nothing else to do, and others because it would pay better than any other business. The United States Census of 1860 showed Nebraska to have 118,889 acres of improved farm land; the cash value of those farms was listed as $3,851,326. Of grain produced, the census showed bushels of wheat at 147,867, Indian corn or sod corn at 1,482,080 bushels, oats at 74,502 bushels, and potatoes at 162,188 bushels. By 1862, much change had taken place in the territory's agriculture. For the first time, the territory was exporting enough produce to more than counterbalance the goods imported, and thus exchange was running in favor of the territory. Though its agriculture was widely diversified with large quantities of fruit grown, Indian corn was the staple crop. Cotton may have been king in the South, but in Nebraska corn was king.

For several years after the initial settlement of Nebraska, it was common belief that wheat could not be grown, but finally it began to be pushed by the newspapers and came more and more into production. Soon wheat became the second most important crop, and territorial farmers were constantly urged to plant more. Many other agricultural products were also grown in Nebraska; some grew well, others did not. There was an abundance of wild fruits in the eastern part of the territory; wild grapes were one of the favorites.

In 1861, one might expect to pay $1.25 to $2.50 per bushel of corn; for flour, $5 to $7 per 100 pounds; potatoes brought $2 per bushel; butter was 25 cents a pound; and eggs about 25 cents a dozen. Profit could be made in agriculture, especially if a farmer was in the right location. Farming during the Civil War years was not without its hazards though. Droughts were bad anywhere, but in dry territory like Nebraska, they could spell doom quickly. The years 1859, 1860, 1863, and 1864 all had average annual rainfalls of less than sixteen inches. Grasshopper plagues also occurred periodically; 1860, 1865, and 1866 were bad years. Grasshoppers were quicker than droughts and could ruin a farmer in a day; often in the spring, grass on the prairie would be burned to kill young grasshoppers. Despite all the hardships, agriculture continued to be

Nebraska's primary economic asset, and the Civil War years were its beginning, due chiefly to persistent food demand caused by the war.

All forms of manufacturing and industry were slow to catch on in Nebraska Territory. The United States Census of 1860 gives the best picture of this. To begin with, there were only 107 manufacturing establishments in the whole territory. Their total capital investment was only $266,575, with a valued product of $607,328 annually. Only 336 persons were employed. The primary business was lumber, followed by gristmills; shoe and bootmakers came in third; and printing and publishing ranked fourth. Only one blacksmithing business was listed, but there was probably at least one in every town. [21]

Mining for coal and salt during the early 1860's proved to be uneventful. In 1863, gold was found in southern Dakota Territory, and it was hoped that Nebraska might have a little of the vein, but it proved not to be. In fact, the territory did not have raw materials to sustain heavy industry, and it became apparent by 1865 that Nebraska industry would consist largely of the processing of agricultural products.

The biggest business by far, except for agriculture, was freight transportation, both overland and steamboat. The importance of overland freighting cannot be excessively emphasized, and the towns along the Missouri River developed proportionally to the amount of steamboat freight transfer business they were able to secure. Heavy emigration west, the Colorado gold rush of 1859, and the rushes to Montana and Dakota in 1862 and 1863 created an immense demand for goods and supplies throughout the territory. The military forts and increased number of soldiers added to the demand in the years 1862 through 1865 and beyond. There was only one satisfactory way to get goods from the Missouri River or the Mississippi River to the territory or farther west, and that was to freight it overland. Nebraska's river towns were established to outfit emigrants going west, and they were developed into important freighting terminals as steamboats unloaded goods and people to be transferred and shipped by wagon across the Great Plains.

By its very nature, the freighting business tended to concentrate itself in a relatively few large firms. The cost was high as well as the risk, but profits were usually high also. Largest of all the freighting companies was Russell, Majors, and Waddell. In 1857, they secured a contract to supply troops in Utah, and in early 1858 they moved their headquarters from Leavenworth, Kansas, to Nebraska City. Heavy freight wagons carrying three to five tons of freight were pulled usually by six to twelve yoke of oxen or as many mules. The big companies concentrated on hauling grain, food, and military supplies. Everything under the sun was hauled west; cats, apples, frozen eggs, and even oysters made the trip.

Nebraska City and Omaha were the main Nebraska freighting terminals. Nebraska City had sixty-four such businesses at one time and Omaha had twenty-four. It was at these two points that river freight was transferred to westward bound freight trains. Most of these trains followed the Platte River into Colorado and went from there to Montana, Utah, and California.

Wagon freighting on the plains and in Nebraska increased every year from 1858, probably reaching its height from 1863 to 1866. It was during this time that Russell, Majors, and Waddell had an estimated 6,250 wagons and 75,000 oxen on the trails. A census of 1865 showed that the freighting of supplies out of Nebraska City employed 7,365 wagons, 7,231 mules, 50,712 oxen, and 8,385 men. The amount of freight leaving the city totaled 31,445,428 pounds. [22]

During the Civil War, the freighting business began to change. Much of the river trade to the South had been cut off, and companies began to pick up freight at the western-most terminals of the existing railroads. Fewer steamboats were available for what trade there was. The Civil War had caused a boom in the freighting business in Nebraska. With the war raging, the Southern trails were closed or hazardous at best, and many shippers moved their operations into the territory.

Finally, in the late 1860s, the freight wagon, like the steamboat, fell prey to the railroad. Both had been very beneficial to Nebraska, bringing the roots of civilization and society to the territory, and helping also to fill its vast void. These big operators had provided an outlet for the produce of the territory and the employment of thousands of men.

The development of transportation in Nebraska Territory from 1860 to 1865 is almost unequaled in American history. The reason for this is that more and more people began to move west, and they wanted to get there quicker, safer and more comfortably with the passing of each year. Once in the West, they began demanding a faster flow of goods and supplies, and most especially, the faster flow of mail and news from the East.

River navigation was the main source of freight and passenger service between the Great Plains and the East. In 1859, the steamboat advertisements in St. Louis stated that more boats left St. Louis for the Missouri River than for both the upper and lower Mississippi River. This would not long be true. The years from 1855 to 1860 proved to be the zenith of river freighting on the upper Missouri. From 1861 to 1865 the navigation of this river was interrupted from time to time because of the Civil War and the often fierce struggle in Missouri and farther south. After 1865, steamboats found it hard to compete with the ever-lengthening railroads from the East, and fell into sharp decline. To the river towns of the territory, however, the steamboat provided the necessary links with the East. They brought settlers, carried goods to stock frontier stores, and supplies to be shipped across the territory in the freight wagons; they also brought mail and newspapers. Though the steamboats carried a great and varied quantity of freight, many of them from 1853 to 1865 were designed and used almost solely for passenger service and many of them were referred to as floating palaces.[23]

If a person in the period from 1860 to 1865 was traveling west to settle, after arriving at Omaha by steamboat with his goods, he had the option of either buying a wagon, loading his belongings into it, and joining a wagon train, or he could take a stagecoach west and have his possessions shipped by freight wagon. If he chose to buy a wagon and haul it himself, he was in for a long, hard, uncertain journey. Wagon trains of that period were usually forming in the early spring in St. Louis, St. Joesph, Omaha, and even Nebraska City.

For the emigrant, the wagon he was traveling in was literally his home. It contained all his worldly goods and served as his kitchen, bedroom, and family place. It also served as a boat across streams; it was the only shelter he would know for months. Despite their shortcomings, these wagons were often referred to as rather tight, roomy, and comfortable. These "prairie schooners" were generally pulled by six animals, either horses, mules, or oxen. The heaviest items, such as plows and machines, were loaded in the bottom, followed by a few pieces of furniture or household goods, and on top of the load would be bedding, coats, and clothes, so as to make a soft place to sit or ride. Actually, there was very little riding in the wagons, for everyone that could, walked alongside to lighten the load and speed the trip.[24]

While passing through Nebraska these wagon trains usually enjoyed the best conditions and roads of the long trip to California, Denver, Salt Lake City, or Oregon. Fort Kearny was the main point after leaving the Missouri River. Conditions eastward from the fort were generally excellent while those toward the West were good to acceptable. It was here that the grade became steeper as one approached the Rocky Mountains. The road that these trains, as well as the Pony Express and stage lines followed, was that of the Great Platte River Road, as it was called in Nebraska. Most of the trains and stages used the road on the south side of the river, but the annual Mormon emigrants stayed on the north side so as to avoid contact with the "Gentiles." Fort Kearny lay along both these routes, and because of the great amount of traffic it saw, it was considered a hub of Western frontier transportation. Wagon trains were the main source of transportation for the masses of people who crossed the territory until the late 1860s, when the transcontinental railroad was finally connected. Wagon trains were the best way to cross Nebraska in the 1860s, and 1864, when the Civil War still raged and the Sioux uprising flared, proved to be one of the heaviest years for civilian emigration during the war or any other period. The wagon train was suitable for moving the family west, but if one wished to go quickly, he could find no better transportation than the stagecoaches of the middle 1860s.[25]

In Nebraska, the most noted point that the stages would pass was Fort Kearny. It was here that the Oregon Trail, Mormon Trail, and other westward trails, as well as the telegraph line, converged. The coaches used were the heavy Concord type usually drawn by four to six horse teams. Mules were used some, but horses were faster. On making the crossing from Omaha to Nebraska City, the stages traveled ten to twelve miles before stopping at swing stations to change teams, and they stopped every fifty miles at home stations to allow passengers to depart, to relax or eat. Drivers were also changed at this point. Fort Kearny, in central Nebraska, was a major home station. Meals at these home stations consisted primarily of bacon, bread, coffee, canned vegetables, and sometimes fresh pies and fruit. During the war, the price of such food far out on the Great Plains ranged from $1 to $2.50, quite high for the time.

Nebraska had always been an important territory in stage travel, but after the Civil War began, the Southern travel route closed, and the central route through Nebraska became the major highway. Some of the lines doing business over it were the Butterfield, Holladay, Western, Central Overland, Californian, and Pike's Peak Express, the latter being that of Russell, Majors, and Waddell. The terminals for these lines varied at times, but the two most important were St. Joseph and Atchison. Omaha and Nebraska City were also important and did great amounts of business. Destination terminals were Denver, Salt Lake City, or Placerville, California. Average fares for the ride in 1863 ran about as follows: Atchison to Denver, $75; Atchison to Salt Lake City, $150; and Atchison to Placerville, $225. By the end of the Civil War, prices had doubled.

Although the Civil War had changed the stage routes to Nebraska and added even more impetus to the Platt River Road, the Sioux wars of 1862 and 1864 served to hinder or shut down the lines altogether. Until 1864, the stage lines had had little trouble with the Sioux, but the depredations suffered during the autumn of that year were the worst ever experienced by the companies. All stations in Nebraska, except home stations towns, were burned, had their stores looted, and stock run off. Commerce came to a halt, and the overland mail, which for three years had been on a daily schedule, ceased to operate. After about two months, traffic began on an irregular basis and continued until 1865, when, because of the previous year's Indian trouble, the lines found it hard to secure stage drivers. One of the new drivers hired that summer was William F. Cody, a former rider of the Pony Express. His run was usually from Fort Kearny, which he had scouted out of many times, to Plum Creek, a distance of about thirty-five miles. After 1865, when hostilities ended across the nation and work began on the Union Pacific Railroad, the stagecoach across Nebraska saw its days numbered. The stagecoach had rendered adequate and never-to-be forgotten service to not only Nebraska Territory but also to the nation and the thousands of emigrants eager to travel west quickly.[26]

The Pony Express died out somewhat earlier than the stagecoach. The idea of the Pony Express had been around for some years prior to its beginning operations in April of 1860. As early as 1854, Senator William M. Gwin of California had proposed the establishment of such an enterprise. By 1859, Gwin had persuaded William H. Russell, of Russell, Majors, and Waddell fame, to undertake the operation of the Pony Express from St. Joseph, Missouri, to San Francisco, California. The first run began on April 3, 1860, at the two terminals. Nebraska was to be traversed from east to west by the Pony Express. The first 300 miles was relatively easy, for the land was flat and the road good, but from Fort Kearny on Indians might strike at any moment. The first riders carried a carbine and two revolvers, but the rifle and one revolver were soon discarded and the Navy Colt (1860) became the standard arm. Extra cylinders already loaded were sometimes carried.

Soon after the Pony Express was put into service, it was put to its test, and carried urgent news of the impending national crisis and later the firing on Fort Sumter. The price of dispatches or letters carried by the Pony Express in the beginning was about $5 per half ounce plus regular United States postage. The main problem was that the government mail contract Senator Gwin had promised the Pony Express never materialized. Without the contract, the operating cost of the service was overwhelming. The project ended costing the promoters some $2,000,000. The distance the route covered became shorter and shorter by early 1861 as the telegraph lines began to cross the Nebraska plains. When Civil War hostilities finally broke out, the lines had already reached Fort Kearny. The Pony Express ceased to operate on October 24, 1861, when the lines coming east and west met some distance west of Fort Kearny.

The first telegraph line to cross Nebraska was that of the Missouri and Western Telegraph Company. Fort Kearny was unusually important in both the history of the Pony Express and telegraph because it was at this post that the freighters, wagon trains, and stages came to the first telegraph and main mail station west out of Omaha, Atchison or Nebraska City as they traversed the Oregon Trail.

The actual building of a telegraph line across Nebraska was no easy job. The transportation of supplies and building material alone required the use of over 1,000 oxen, 200 mules, and 400 wagons. Red cedar was the type of tree desired to make poles, and because of the barrenness of timber along the laid out route, poles had to be shipped from as far away as the Missouri River. The work in eastern Nebraska proceeded very smoothly to Fort Kearny, and though the laborers proceeded more cautiously west of the fort, the line went up without any major difficulties. The telegraph's abil-

ity to send messages much faster than the pony inspired awe in the Indians, so they seldom bothered the lines. Outlaws were a greater menace. The telegraph was an immediate success. It connected the territory to the nation as no other means could, not even the railroad. Although the people of the territory looked to the railroad as the way of giving them new markets and goods, the telegraph served as no other device in the quick dissemination of news.

One of the most important results of the Civil War in Nebraska Territory was the transfer of major travel routes of the South to the central route; this was what clinched the building of the Union Pacific Railroad across the central route and through Nebraska. In fact, the struggle over the location of a transcontinental railroad was Nebraska's initial reason for being. It was on July 1, 1862, that Congress chartered the Union Pacific Railroad Company to build the Eastern end and provided help to the Central Pacific Railroad Company to build the Western end. For Nebraska, the matter of greatest importance was where the Eastern terminal would be located. Though construction of the railroad would not begin for over a year, President Lincoln decided that the terminus would be on the Missouri River opposite Omaha. Though this was actually in Iowa, it was Omaha that would benefit. At the end of the Civil War, when men had been released for civilian jobs and scarce material once again could be secured, the Union Pacific Railroad was ready to move. By the end of 1865, however, only forty miles of track had been laid in Nebraska. But the railroad had its problems, for along the route in western Nebraska, Indians looted supply and attacked survey and building crews. In 1866, as the track began to move faster, ''end-of-track'' settlements sprang up, while other towns moved to be near the track and thereby secure its blessings. By 1867, the Union Pacific Railroad had completely crossed Nebraska Territory, and the Platte River Valley became an ever strengthening link in the highway to hold the West to the East.

The transportation facilities also aided in the settlement of the territory. As the means of communication and transportation became better developed, people began settling in the territory rather than passing through it. Immediately preceding and following the Civil War, Nebraska gained its initial population, but it was land speculation which had first attracted people to Nebraska. For those who wished to keep the land they had settled on, they had to pay $1.25 for each acre, which often meant going into debt. Interest on these loans ran as high as 120 percent, thus causing many to lose their land. By 1857, the territory had been thrown into frenzied speculation in farm land, but the boom finally ended by 1859, and people began turning to farming and gave up the get-rich-quick schemes which had monopolized the economy of Nebraska since 1854. But wild interest rates and speculations would not improve dramatically until wartime prosperity hit in

1862.[27]

That same year also brought another boom to Nebraska, for in May President Lincoln signed the Homestead Act. In general, the law provided that any United States citizen at least twenty-one years of age and the head of a household could, upon paying a $10 fee, file a claim on public lands for up to a quarter section, and after living on it five years, receive a final deed to it. Applications for filing homesteads were not to be accepted in local land offices until January 1, 1863, to give the officials time to prepare for the expected rush. The homestead of Daniel Freeman, near Beatrice, Nebraska, was later selected as the site of the Homestead National Monument. The location of the monument was not inappropriate, for Nebraska, ranked with Montana, North Dakota, and Colorado in the number of homestead filings carried to deed stage. The original homestead entries in Nebraska for the Civil War years were 349 entries for 50,775 acres in 1863; 769 entries for 114,649 acres in 1864; and 812 entries for 114,875 acres in 1865. The land near the timbered regions of the Platte River Valley was most highly prized and was confined mostly to eastern Nebraska. In western Nebraska, especially after the war, people would settle wishing to graze sheep and cattle. Though agriculture and land usage in the territory was good, it was the lack of sufficient moisture that kept agriculture from developing more extensively.[28]

The exact number of emigrants traveling through Nebraska is unknown for the Civil War period, but a few rough estimates of travel westward along the Oregon Trail by way of the Platte River give this picture: 1859 — 30,000; 1860 — 15,000; 1861 — 5,000; 1862 — 5,000; 1863 — 10,000; 1864 — 20,000; 1865 — 25,000; 1866 — 25,000. These estimates show the results which the beginning of the Civil War had not only on the flow of foreign immigrants but also on domestic emigration as well. These figures also show that as the war slowly began to turn toward Union victory, more people moved west. By 1865, Nebraska Territory had a population of just under 50,000, compared with just under 30,000 in 1861. Thus Nebraska grew considerably during the war years, and nearly all this growth was due to emigration.[29]

As these emigrants moved out onto the Nebraska plains, they found very little in the line of civilization or social life except what they themselves brought. Settlements were far and few between, and towns numbered less than ten by 1865. Though to some it seemed that Nebraska was thoroughly uncultured, as the pioneers moved in, they brought their ideas of religion and education. They were eager to secure a foothold on the land to implement these ideas. In March, 1855, a free public school act was passed by the First Territorial Legislature. By this act, counties were to be divided into school districts and money raised for the organization of schools. Funds were to be distributed on the basis of the number of white children between the ages

of five and twenty-one years. It became a matter of custom for people to add children to the school census in order to get a larger share of school funds.[30]

The average pay for a male teacher was about $30 a month; a woman would get about $26. On the prairie, many male teachers boarded with the parents of pupils during the six months school was held. Students were often as old as the teacher. A typical frontier school would be made of sod and doubled as the local meeting house or a church. Maps, dictionaries, and similar teaching aids were nearly nonexistent. There was no such thing as a standard textbook. Bibles, song books, and almanacs often stood in for readers.[31]

From the earliest settlements came the desire to have colleges or academies of higher learning. All of the early colleges were backed by religious orders. The Baptists at first were not too successful with their schools, but met in 1860 at their territorial convention to discuss the subject of higher education. In 1863, a school for the education of women was organized near Omaha and was under the control of the Episcopal Church. The University of Nebraska was not founded until early 1869. Congregationalists, Presbyterians, Catholics, Methodists, and Christian churches all attempted to bring higher education to Nebraska during the late 1850s and early 1860s. Their most important contribution in the field of college training was not their success or failure but rather the fact that they kept the idea of education alive and constantly before the populace.[32]

Aside from all that was being done to give Nebraska education, few found the time or means to go to school, even when it was available. In 1859, out of a total of 4,767 children of elementary school age, only 1,310 attended any school at all. Seven of the organized counties reported no elementary schools at all. In the school year ending in June of 1860, a total of 3,296 children had attended school. There were eighty-five public schools with ninety-three teachers reported in the census. Though Nebraska's educational system during the Civil War was greatly lacking, the people pushed steadily for more education, and once the Morrill Land-Grant College Act was passed in 1862, and Nebraska had become a state, progress began to bound.[33]

Churches, like schools, found it hard to get started and keep going. The Methodists first organized a church in 1854 in Nebraska City under the pastorship of the Reverend W. D. Gage. Other churches were quickly organized; according to the United States Census of 1860, Nebraska had sixty-three organized churches. The Methodist Episcopal Church led with thirty-four congregations followed by the Presbyterians, with fourteen. The Congregational Church had four. The Baptist, Episcopal, and Catholic churches had three each, while the Christians and Lutherans had only two. There were undoubtedly several other meeting houses or groups which were not listed.[34]

The best view of religion and churches in early Nebraska comes from the Reverend George W. Barnes, a pioneer Baptist preacher of Omaha, who said: "There were but few Christians among that varied population, and religion met only a left-handed favor. The great mass seemed in a terrible hurry to build their houses, and push their enterprises to success. . . .The Sabbath was painfully disregarded. You could hear the whiz of the saw and the click of the hammer, at all hours . . .The Lord's day found only a few who honored its claims."[35]

The churches of Nebraska provided even more than religion and education; they also formed the center of territorial social life. For many, the only social contacts they would know would come from the church meetings. Because of the great distances separating neighbors and settlements, normal visiting with friends would often take two days even in the 1860s. Community projects were welcomed events, and an occasional county fair was eagerly awaited.

In the towns, social life was much like it was on any frontier. The lack of single women led to the playing of rough games as a substitute for fun. Saloons were usually one of the first buildings to go up in any town. As corn was the number one crop, corn whiskey was inexpensive and flowed freely. Omaha, because it was the capital, was the social city, followed by Nebraska City, which housed many large freighting operations. The forts of the frontier had an even greater imbalance of men to women and rough-housing and drinking were even more prevalent there; desertions sometimes occurred because of loneliness and the desire for female companionship. What women, usually married, there were at the forts and towns were treated with the utmost courtesy. Often soldiers would have whirlwind romances with the daughters of the thousands of emigrants who passed the forts in the 1860s. During the opening years of the Civil War, many soldiers assigned to duties in Nebraska wanted to go south to see combat action for a change of pace.

By the end of the Civil War, it appeared that even though Nebraska Territory had made significant contributions to the war effort and had suffered many hardships during the time, the benefits which it gained outweighed the hardships brought on by the war. Nebraska had offered several thousand of her men for military service, and it could be proud to claim such leaders as John M. Thayer, Robert W. Furnas, and William F. Cody. Nebraska's First Infantry Regiment had proven itself outside of the territory at the capture of Fort Donelson and at the Battle of Shiloh. On the home front, however, Nebraska provided its greatest service. Thousands of emigrants passed west on its roads, and it had done all possible to insure them safe passage. Without the cooperation of Nebraska, the movement of people and goods to the West would have come to a standstill. When the Southern trails were forced to close, it was Nebraska that took up the slack in providing a line to the West over which people and goods could travel.

While providing avenues of commerce and men for the Civil War, Nebraska Territory and its inhabitants were forced to contend with many hardships. Indian depredations, partly caused by the war and loss of frontier troops, caused the death of hundreds and the loss of many thousands of dollars in real and personal property. Forced as they were to defend millions of acres with reduced troop strength, the soldiers and civilians of Nebraska spent many hours on alert. Economically, too, the territory was at first hurt. Before 1860, it had close ties with Southern financial interests and markets. Its former thriving Missouri River trade was all but destroyed by the war.

Nebraska, politically, was a great joy to Washington. Lincoln had been quickly accepted and the territory's allegiance was never seriously questioned. Its vast open areas had become home to hundreds of Union sympathizers dispossessed by the fighting in the border and Southern states. As the Northern states lost their Southern food supply, Nebraska and the other Western states increased agricultural production to feed the North.

During the years of the Civil War, Nebraska Territory had contributed greatly in proportion to its population; its people had been forced to contend with problems they might not otherwise have confronted, but above all, the territory gained. Its population increased impressively, its political status improved to the point of statehood invitations, and, for the first time, its economy thrived. Before the war, agriculture was only subsistence farming, but new profitable markets opened during the war. More people began to settle in Nebraska with the passage of the Homestead Act in 1862. One of the most direct results was the Union Pacific Railroad across the territory. Because of the great importance of its trails, Nebraska gained political advantages it might not have enjoyed. No one in Nebraska was happy the Civil War had come, but few would deny that had it not been for the war, many improvements and gains would not have been made or at least delayed for years.

NOTES

1. J. Sterling Morton, *Illustrated History of Nebraska* (3 vols., Lincoln: Western Publishing and Engraving Company, 1911), Vol. I, pp. 432, 460-461, 463, 473-474.

2. *American Annual Cyclopaedia and Register of Important Events of the Year 1864* (New York: D. Appleton and Company, 1865), p. 773.

3. *Congressional Globe,* 38th Congress, 1st Session, pp. 1310, 1558, 1607, 1639, 1802; *American Annual Cyclopaedia and Register of Important Events of the Year 1864,* p. 773.

4. Morton, *op. cit.,* Vol. II, pp.*Population of the United States in 1860, Eighth Census* (Washington: Government Printing Office, 1864), pp. 554-557.

5. Morton, *op. cit.,* Vol. II, pp. 63-64.

6. Frank L. Klement, "Economic Aspects of Middle Western Copperheadism," *Historian,* Vol. XIV, No. 1 (Autumn,

1951), p. 27; Frank L. Klement, "Middle Western Copperheadism and the Genesis of the Granger Movement," *Mississippi Valley Historical Review*, Vol. XXXVIII, No. 4 (March, 1952), pp. 679-694.

7. Morton, *op. cit.*, Vol. II, pp. 169, 171.

8. United States Department of War, *War of the Rebellion: A Compilation of the Official Records of the Union and Confederate Armies* (70 vols., 128 books, Washington: Government Printing Office, 1880-1901), Ser. III, Vol. IV, pp. 73-74, 1264-1270.

9. Frederick H. Dyer, *A Compendium of the War of the Rebellion* (3 vols., New York: Thomas Yoseloff, 1959) , Vol.III, p. 1345.

10. *Ibid.*, Vol. II, pp. 982, 987; *ibid.*, Vol. I, pp. 14-15.

11. Francis B. Heitman, *Historical Register and Dictionary of the United States Army* (2 vols., Washington: Government Printing Office, 1903), Vol. 1, p. 976.

12. *American Annual Cyclopaedia and Register of Important Events of the Year 1864*, p. 773.

13. Robert C. Farb, "The Military Career of Robert W. Furnas," *Nebraska History*, Vol. XXII, No. 1 (March, 1951), pp. 32-41, 18; Dyer, Vol. I, *op. cit.*, p. 1345.

14. *Ibid.*, p. 1344; *ibid.*, Vol. II, pp. 987-982.

15. D. Alexander Brown, *The Galvanized Yankees* (Urbana: University of Illinois Press, 1963), pp. 1-11.

16. Morton, *op. cit.*, Vol. II, p. 171.

17. *Official Records,* Ser. I, Vol. VII, p. 650; Earl G. Curtis, "John Milton Thayer," *Nebraska History,* Vol. XXVIII, No. 4 (October, 1947), pp. 225-238; Dyer, *op. cit.,* Vol. III, p. 1345; Benjamin Franklin Cooling, "The First Nebraska Infantry Regiment and the Battle of Fort Donelson," *Nebraska History*, Vol. XLV, No. 2 (April, 1964), p. 133.

18. *Official Records,* Ser. I, Vol. VII, pp. 252-253, 236-248, 169.

19. Dyer, *op. cit.*, Vol. III, p. 1345.

20. Curtis, *op. cit.*, pp. 236-238.

21. *Agriculture of the United States in 1860, Eighth Census* (Washington: Government Printing Office, 1864), pp. 172-175; Morton, *op. cit.*, Vol. II, p. 266; *Manufactures of the United States in 1860, Eighth Census* (Washington: Government Printing Office, 1865), pp. 663-665.

22. Lyle E. Mantor, "Stage Coach and Freighter Days at Fort Kearny, " *Nebraska History,* Vol. XXIX, No. 4 (December, 1948), pp. 336-338.

23. Morton, *op. cit.*, Vol. I, pp. 99-103.

24. *Ibid.*, p. 92.

25. Merrill J. Mattes, *The Great Platte River Road* (Lincoln: Nebraska State Historical Society, 1969), pp. 218, 20.

26. Mantor, *op. cit.*, pp. 324-338.

27. Morton, *op. cit.*, Vol.pp. 95-96, 98-99; Paul Gates, *Agriculture and the Civil War* (New York: Alfred A. Knopf, 1965), pp. 282-283.

28. *Ibid.*, p. 292; Thomas C. Donaldson, *The Public Domain* (Washington: Government Printing Office, 1884), p. 351.

29. Mattes, *op. cit.*, pp. 23-24; *American Annual Cyclopaedia and Register of Important Events of the Year 1865* (New York: D. Appleton and Company, 1866), pp. 784-785.

30. Helen Siampos, "Early Education in Nebraska," *Nebraska History,* Vol. XXIX, No. 2 (June, 1948), pp. 115-116.

31. *Ibid.*, p. 116; Everett Dick, *The Sod-House Frontier, 1854-1890* (New York: D. Appleton-Century Company, 1943), pp. 320-323.

32. Siampos, *op. cit.*, pp. 117-133.

33. *Mortality and Miscellaneous Statistics of the United States in 1860, Eighth Census* (Washington: Government Printing Office, 1866), pp. 494, 497-501.

34. *Ibid.*

35. George W. Barnes, "Pioneer Preacher — An Autobiography," *Nebraska History,* Vol. XXVII, No. 2 (April, 1946), pp. 79-80.

SELECTED READINGS

Benjamin Franklin Cooling III, "The First Nebraska Infantry Regiment and the Battle of Fort Donelson," *Nebraska History,* Vol. XLV, No. 2 (April, 1964), pp. 131-145.

Earl G. Curtis, "John Milton Thayer," *Nebraska History,* Vol. XXVIII, No. 4 (October, 1947), pp. 225-238.

Everett Dick, *The Sod-House Frontier, 1854-1890* (New York: D. Appleton-Century Company, 1943), Chapters XX,XXIII,XXIV.

Robert C. Farb, "The Military Career of Robert W. Furnas," *Nebraska History,* Vol. XXXII, No. 1 (March, 1951), pp. 18-41.

Lyle E. Mantor, "Stage Coach and Freighter Days at Fort Kearny," *Nebraska History,* Vol. XXIX, No. 4 (December, 1948), pp. 324-328.

Merrill J. Mattes, *The Great Platte River Road* (Lincoln: Nebraska State Historical Society, 1969), pp. 19-21, 192-237.

J. Sterling Morton, *Illustrated History of Nebraska* (3 vols., Lincoln: Western Publishing and Engraving Company, 1911), Vol. I, pp. 432, 460-474, 91-111; Vol. II.

New Mexico And Arizona Territories

By James A. Howard II

A Texas brigade, which had only a short time earlier volunteered for service with the Confederate States of America, was in full parade as it passed Brigadier General Henry H. Sibley. He was about to lead the unprepared brigade on a daring but disastrous invasion of New Mexico Territory. The troops anticipated an easy victory and seemed excited about the coming battles. As Sibley viewed his troops, one of the companies marched over a hill and out of sight because it failed to hear an order to turn. While Sibley watched the company disappear over the hill, he remarked, ''Gone to Hell,'' and unknowingly he predicted the results of the Confederate invasion of New Mexico.[1]

The brigade began the invasion of New Mexico on that same day, October 26, 1861. Leaving Camp Sibley and friendly San Antonio, Texas, behind, marching in small groups, weeks later the brigade entered the territory controlled by the Apache Indians. Though they suffered a shortage of supplies and a series of Apache Indian raids, the brigade, by February 20, 1862, was massed only three miles east of Fort Craig, New Mexico.[2]

Colonel Edward R.S. Canby, the Union commander of Fort Craig, approved a plan to surprise and panic the Confederate forces confronting him. The plan, as submitted by Captain James ''Paddy'' Graydon, was to load howitzer shells onto pack mules and release the mules near the Confederate horses. Under the cover of darkness, Graydon and a small company led two mules packed with twelve, twenty-four pound howitzer shells

Courtesy of Arizona Historical Society
Colonel Edward R. S. Canby, Federal commander in New Mexico Territory, led his forces to defeat at the Battle of Val Verde.

Courtesy of National Archives
Brigadier General Henry H. Sibley of Texas, the commander of the Confederate invastion of New Mexico Territory in 1861-1862.

to within sight of the Confederate horses. The fuses were lit and the mules released, but instead of walking in among the Confederate horses, the mules turned and followed the fleeing Graydon company. The surprised Confederates prepared to repulse the invaders, but found they were already in a hasty retreat.[3]

These incidents indicate the character of the Civil War in New Mexico Territory. Though it would enjoy early success in its invasion of New Mexico Territory, due primarily to mistakes made by its Union counterparts, the Confederate brigade because of its own mistakes would be, as unknowingly predicted by Sibley, "Gone to Hell."[4]

New Mexico Territory, located in the semi-arid southwestern region of the United States, had as its first white settlers Spaniards, who arrived perhaps as early as 1605. During the 200 years of Spanish control, settlements were located along the three major rivers in the region. Villages were founded in the fertile valleys of the Gila, the lower Colorado, and the Rio Grande Rivers. The village of Santa Fe, located along the Rio Grande River, became the center of Spanish settlement in the region. The area north of Santa Fe was termed the Rio Arriba settlement, while that area settled to the south was called Rio Abajo. Spanish settlement ended at the treacherous and uninhabitable area known as the Jornado del Muerto (Journey of Death). Though control of the area passed through the hands of two governments, the patterns of settlement established by the Spaniards were still the same at the outbreak of the Civil War.[5]

In 1821, the region had come under the control of the Republic of Mexico, but within twenty-five years the area was invaded and claimed by the United States. In August of 1846, an American force under the leadership of Brigadier General Stephen W. Kearny, in conjunction with the overall military operations of the United States in the Mexican War, invaded the region and occupied Santa Fe. It was from Santa Fe on August 22, that Kearny issued a proclamation in which he announced the organic law of New Mexico Territory. The proclamation served as the law until formal territorial status was granted on September 9, 1850, even though the section granting United States citizenship to residents of the new territory was repudiated by President James K. Polk.[6]

The issue of the extension of slavery was the dominant factor which delayed the United States Congress in formally admitting New Mexico as a territory. From the ratification of the Treaty of Guadalupe Hidalgo on May 26, 1848, several attempts to formally admit the region as either a territory or a state were initiated.

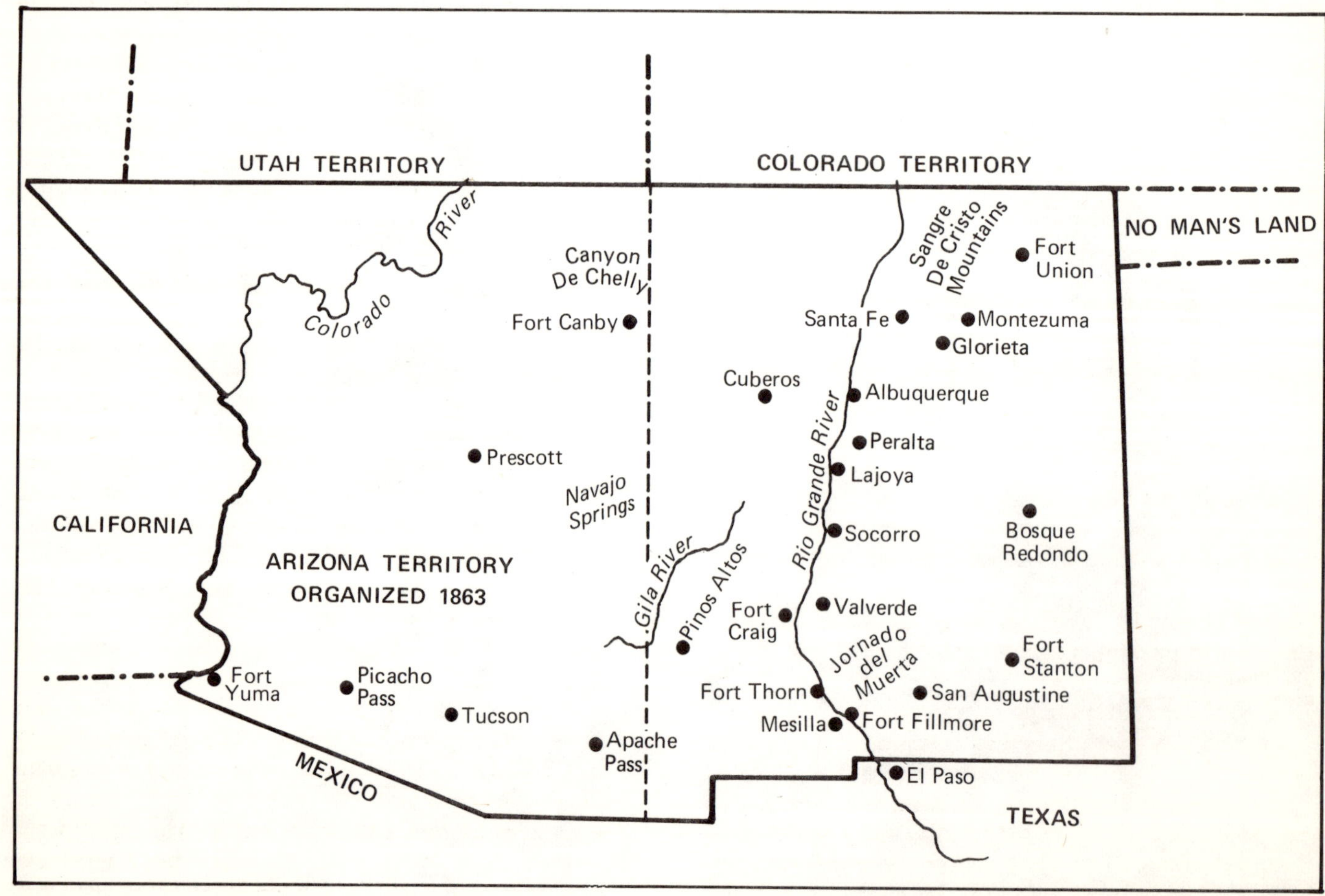

Map Drafted by Georganne T. Bartow

Arizona and New Mexico Territories During the Civil War

During the congressional truce between the Northern and Southern legislators, known as the Compromise of 1850, New Mexico failed to achieve statehood but was admitted, with rather vague boundaries, as a formal territory of the United States.[7]

The southern boundary of the territory was firmly established by the purchase of 45,000 square miles of land from the Republic of Mexico. The land, located between the Colorado and Rio Grande Rivers and purchased by the United States for a total price of ten million dollars, was added to New Mexico Territory. The Gadsden Purchase, as this acquisition is known, was completed on December 30, 1853. The other boundaries of the territory, with the exception of the eastern or Texas boundary, were ambiguous and provided political debate and controversy before, during, and after the Civil War; the Texas boundary had been firmly established by the same act which granted formal territorial status to New Mexico.[8]

The pre-Civil War period in New Mexico was characterized by cultural and political tension. Natives of the territory had cultivated a resentment toward Americans. Their resentment was based in part on the cultural differences of the two groups and in part on the period of United States military occupation. The domination of governmental positions of authority by the Americans also contributed to the tensions. Though they dominated the political scene during the period, Americans resented, mistrusted, and feared the consequences of native political control. "We are fully convinced that there is no hope for the improvement of our Territory unless Americans rule it," said Jacob Houghton and other American territorial residents in a memorial to the President of the United States. The memorial further stated "that the spirit of Mexican rule must be corrupt, ignorant, and disgraceful in a Territory of the United States."[9]

The pre-Civil War political scene in New Mexico Territory was also characterized by a series of separatist movements. Residents of various sections of the territory would periodically join together and petition the United States Congress for separate territorial status. In 1855, James A. Lucas, a citizen of Mesilla, presented a petition to create the new territory of Pimeria in southern New Mexico. Two petitions for the creation of Arizona territory were introduced in 1856. One of these originated in Mesilla, and the other in Tucson. During 1857, George Kippen, a citizen of Tucson and the residents of the western part of the territory, petitioned for separate status, and the same year citizens of the Mesilla region, primarily the Mexican-Americans, again petitioned for separate territorial status.[10]

The failure of the attempts to separate the territory and the failure of the territory to achieve statehood were due primarily to the issue of the expansion of slavery. Even after the United States Congress passed the act admitting New Mexico as a formal territory, the issue of the expansion of slavery continued to dominate the attitudes and actions of that body in relation to New Mexico Territory. Leaders of the territory did not by their actions enhance their opportunities with the anti-slavery states for admittance to the Union. The slave code enacted by the territorial legislature in 1859 led many people to believe that New Mexico had accepted slavery. During the United States Senate debates on the Colorado Territory bill, Senator Stephen A. Douglas of Illinois questioned whether the effect of that bill would be "to abolish slavery in that part of the territory thus cut off, and make it a free territory."[11] The Colorado Territory bill, which established Colorado Territory from parts of Kansas and New Mexico, was signed into law by President James Buchanan on February 28, 1861. Miguel A. Otero, the New Mexico Territory delegate to the United States Congress, issued a statement to his constituents which brought him into conflict with journalist Horace Greeley. The statement, issued by "Her Delegate in Congress," according to Greeley, was "intended to disaffect them [the New Mexican people] toward the Union, and incite them to favor the Rebellion."[12]

The advent of the Civil War found New Mexico Territory in a peculiar situation. In relation to the conflict beginning between the Northern and Southern states, the native population was apathetic. Because of the Indian hostilities preceding the Civil War, a large number of United States troops were stationed throughout the territory, but a considerable number of these men and many of their officers were Southern sympathizers. Territorial Governor Abraham Rencher and Territorial Secretary A.M. Jackson, both Southern Democrats, resigned their respective positions and returned to their home states following the outbreak of war. Of the 83,000 non-Indian population, only 85 were Negroes, and therefore the appeals of both the abolitionist groups and the pro-slavery groups did not gain many supporters among the citizens of the territory.[13]

An important factor, however, in determining the early sympathies of the citizens of New Mexico Territory was the feeling of isolation created by the geographic features of the territory and the southwestern United States. The territory, largely isolated from the United States, was separated into a northern area and a southern area by the Jornado del Muerto region. The southern section of the territory, sharing a common border with Texas, and having a larger number of former Texans among its population, was decidedly more aligned with the Southern states than it was with the northern part of the territory. The alignment with the Confederate States was also promoted as much by fear and the need for security as it was by the loyalty of its citizens to the Confederate cause. The isolation of southern New Mexico Territory from northern New Mexico Territory and the United States, created by the uninhabitable Jornado del Muerto region, caused the

Rio Abajo citizens to believe that they would be left on their own to repel an invasion from Texas, and if they failed, the Texans would then be free to take out their vengeance on any who had resisted.[14]

At the beginning of the war, the Confederacy was more interested in acquiring the territory than the Union was interested in holding the territory. The Confederacy needed additional territory, and it believed that it could acquire much needed mineral wealth if it could control New Mexico Territory. Confederate leaders were also hoping to open an economic trade route to California and the Pacific ports by controlling New Mexico Territory. They also believed, though in error, that the population was decidedly sympathetic to the Confederate cause, and therefore there was little hesitancy among Confederate leaders in deciding to invade or liberate the territory.[15]

The Union attitude toward the territory was completely opposite that of the Southern states. Union leaders did not attach much importance to the territory. They had, for the most part, ignored the territory in the years preceding the war, and they viewed the territory as a burden rather than as an attribute. In fact, during the opening months of the war orders were received in New Mexico to transfer Union officers and troops to the Eastern theater of the war. Union leadership within the territory protested and then reacted slowly to this order because of the rumored Confederate invasion that was expected to begin at any moment. As early as May 11, 1861, Caleb B. Smith, the Secretary of the Interior, warned Simon Cameron, the Secretary of War, of "the condition of New Mexico and the imminent danger now existing that the southern counties will be invaded from Texas." Smith continued, claiming that "Colonel Loring, now in command there, [Fort Fillmore, New Mexico Territory] is disloyal to the Government," and Smith then recommended that "he [Loring] should be superseded in his command."[16] Secretary of War Cameron, displaying the normal attitude of Union officials, replied to Smith that "measures have been or will be taken communsurate with its [New Mexico's] importance."[17]

Shortly after the outbreak of war, June, 1861, there was an aggregate of 2,466 troops assigned to the Union New Mexico Military Department. During May and June of that year, several prominent officers assigned to the New Mexico Military Department resigned from the United States Army, left the territory, and accepted commissions in the Army of the Confederate States. Among those who resigned were some of the better known and respected officers in the New Mexico Military Department. These included Lieutenant Joseph Wheeler, Lieutenant Colonel George B. Crittenden, Colonel William W. Loring, Majors James Longstreet and Henry H. Sibley, Captains Richard S. Ewell, Carter L. Stevenson, and Cadmus M. Wilcox. Each resignation had a negative impact on the morale of the Union forces in the New Mexico Military Department, while they had an equally positive effect on the morale of Southern sympathizers within and adjacent to the territory. Some enlisted men also left the Union Army in New Mexico in order to join the Confederate Army. However, the actions of these soldiers, unlike the similar actions of some of their officers, were considered desertion.[18]

Following the resignation of the civilian territorial officials, Rencher and Jackson, President Abraham Lincoln appointed Henry Connelly as territorial governor and Miguel A. Otero as territorial secretary. Connelly, a Democrat who was born in Virginia and had moved to New Mexico in 1828 and married into a prominent family, quickly quelled the Radical Republicans in the United States Senate, who were voicing some opposition to his appointment, by recommending to the legislature of New Mexico Territory that Eastern investments in the economic institutions of the territory should be sought. After receiving confirmation of his appointment by the United States Senate, Connelly served throughout the Civil War as the governor of New Mexico Territory. Otero's appointment, however, was vigorously opposed by the Radical Republicans of the United States Senate. Otero, like Connelly, was a Democrat from a prominent New Mexican family, but to his detriment, he had acquired a reputation as an advocate of slavery. The Radical Republicans, who were hoping to exploit the territory's political and economic resources, believed that Otero's drive for New Mexico's statehood during the 1850's would continue with ultimate success in the 1860s. Therefore, the United States Senate in July of 1861 refused to confirm his nomination.[19]

Following the rejection of Otero's nomination, Lincoln appointed James H. Holmes, a New York Republican, to the post of secretary of New Mexico Territory. Holmes, like Charles Sumner and James H. Lane who had recommended him to Lincoln for the position, was a Radical Republican, and he had little trouble being confirmed by the United States Senate. Holmes, however, found a great deal of opposition from the local New Mexican politicians during his one year tenure as the territorial secretary. The opposition to Holmes culminated in a petition for his removal. John S. Watts circulated the petition accusing Holmes, among other things, of neglect of duty, irresponsibility, and misuse of funds, and following a receipt of the petition, Lincoln removed Holmes.[20]

Lincoln then appointed Willian F.M. Arny, a Kansas Republican, to replace Holmes as the territorial secretary. Arny was one of a group of Kansans who earlier had hoped to exploit the territory economically by controlling United States political appointments to the territory. Arny, who served from July 31, 1862, through 1867, promoted and advanced the interest of the Republican Party within the territory. Due to the illness of Connelly during most of the war, Arny performed many of the duties of governor in addition to his own duties as secretary. Working in this dual position, he was able to extend economic benefits to both Northern and Eastern corporate groups.[21]

Lincoln again clashed with the United States Senate Radical Republicans when he decided to retain Kirby Benedict as chief justice in New Mexico Territory. Benedict, a Unionist Democrat, was considered by Lincoln as necessary in holding the territory against the secessionists. The Radicals, who had opposed the reappointment of Benedict, rose quickly to the support of Brigadier General James H. Carleton, the Union commander of the New Mexico Military Department, who clashed with Benedict in the summer of 1862. When Carleton instituted martial law throughout the territory, Arny with his associates attempted to gain political and economic advantages while the territory was under military rule. Benedict challenged Arny and his associates, however, who in turn contacted Washington influentials. The Washingtonians then reported to Lincoln that Benedict conducted court while drunk. To this accusation Lincoln replied, "Well, gentlemen, I know Benedict. We have been friends for thirty years. He may imbibe to excess, but Benedict drunk knows more law than all others on the bench in New Mexico sober. I shall not disturb him."[22]

Anticipating the political defeat of secession, the Union loyalists anxiously awaited the convening of the legislature of New Mexico Territory. Membership of both the house and the council was heavily pro-Union. Southerners had failed to elect a majority of their delegates, although there were a number of pro-Southern delegates present at the opening session, which met on January 1, 1862, at Santa Fe. The territorial legislature quickly passed a declaration of loyalty to the Union and then repealed the slave code which had been passed by the 1859 territorial legislature. The legislature then turned its attention to military developments within New Mexico Territory. The governor was directed "to repulse and drive from the soil, the now invading army," and to accomplish this, he was made commander in chief of the militia.[23] Under this law, the governor was authorized to act accordingly to necessity, taking whatever measures he needed to combat the invading army.[24]

The territorial legislature was temporarily interrupted by the invading Confederate brigade. Upon reconvening after the Confederates had withdrawn from the territory, the territorial legislature became embroiled in internal political struggles taking place among the various factions. The conflicts were closely aligned with the two major political parties. Arny, leading the Republican Party, was attempting to wrest control of the territory from the Democrats led by Connelly. Membership and support for the two factions changed frequently, but the struggles remained bitter.[25]

Factionalism within the territory surfaced on various issues during the remainder of the war. The 1863 territorial delegate to Congress contest which Colonel

Francisco Perea, a Democrat, won against Republican Jose Gallegos resulted in charges of corruption against Governor Connelly and the territorial legislature. The Indian policy of Brigadier General Carleton and his rule of the territory became major issues debated by the two factions. Arny and his associates, hoping to profit from the Indian reservation policy, could not control Carleton and therefore launched an all out attack to belittle Carleton and his policies. Wanting to control the lucrative postmaster's position, Arny attempted to replace Augustine M. Hunt, the Santa Fe postmaster. This action led to another bitter struggle between the two factions. Yet another struggle erupted while Arny was out of the territory on official business. He had appointed the territorial librarian, Theodore Greiner, to serve as acting secretary. Connelly appointed Demetrio Perez to the position of territorial librarian, having declared the position vacant on the grounds that one official could not fill two positions. This struggle was finally settled in favor of Connelly by the New Mexico courts. Factionalism such as this continually impeded the development of New Mexico Territory during the Civil War.[26]

The most significant political development in New Mexico Territory during the Civil War period was the creation of Arizona Territory by the Confederate States. The failure of several pre-war attempts to gain separate territorial status induced some prominent citizens to request admittance to the Confederate States in 1861. Consequently, following the withdrawal of Union troops from the southern half of New Mexico Territory, Confederate Colonel John R. Baylor issued a proclamation on August 1, 1861, annexing the territory south of the 34° parallel. Baylor's proclamation was approved by the Confederate Congress on January 24, 1862, and a formal proclamation was issued by Confederate President Jefferson Davis on February 14, 1862.[27]

Citizens of the new Confederate territory had previously convened at Tucson on March 16, 1861, prepared a constitution, and petitioned the Confederate States for territorial status. In his proclamation, Baylor recognized the proceedings of the Tucson convention, and he promised to establish a civil government as soon as expedient. The provisional military government established by Baylor served the territory until March 13, 1862, when civilian appointments were named by President Davis. With the exception of Baylor, who was appointed governor of Arizona Territory, the majority of the appointees did not reach the territorial capital at Mesilla before it was reoccupied by Union forces in August, 1862.[28]

The United States Congress, having ignored the numerous petitions for territorial status by the citizens of southern and western New Mexico, was not affected by the establishment of the Confederate Territory of Arizona. Finally, on February 24, 1863, President Lincoln signed a bill creating Arizona Territory. Congress had passed the bill, not because the territorial legislature of New Mexico or its citizens favored it, nor because Brigadier General Carleton supported it, but because many congressmen, having lost in the recent election, hoped to receive appointments as territorial officials. The law creating the territory established the eastern boundary at the 109° meridian and specified that the capital should not be located at Tucson.[29]

Lincoln appointed John N. Goodwin of Maine as governor, Richard C. McCormick of New York as secretary of state, and with other appointed officials they entered the territory on December 27, 1863. Two days later, at Navajo Springs, they staged a ceremony which set Arizona Territory in operation. Then the governing officials established Prescot as the provisional capital of the new territory on May 30, 1864, and began the development of Arizona Territory.[30]

Military action within New Mexico Territory can be divided into three phases: (1) the initial Confederate defeat and subsequent capture of the Union garrison at Fort Fillmore, (2) the Confederate invasion of New Mexico Territory, and (3) the Confederate occupation of Arizona Territory. Although each of these actions was marked by early Confederate success, poor planning and the attitude of Confederate soldiers toward New Mexican citizens determined final Union victory in the territory.[31]

In July, 1861, Lieutenant Colonel John R. Baylor led a small Confederate force, the Texas Mounted Rifles, into El Paso, Texas, where the unit occupied Fort Bliss. Even though little resistance was met in occupying Fort Bliss, Baylor was concerned about holding El Paso. He therefore decided to launch an offensive against Fort Fillmore, located at Mesilla. By July 24, Baylor's force was camped only 600 yards from Fort Fillmore. Major Isaac Lynde, the Union commander of the fort, learned of the attack planned for daybreak on July 25 from a Confederate deserter. To counter the Confederate move against Fort Fillmore at nearby Mesilla, Lynde led 380 troops in a halfhearted attack against Mesilla. After marching the six miles from Fort Fillmore to Mesilla, Lynde demanded that the Confederate force surrender. Failing to achieve the surrender, Lynde fired two harmless howitzer shells, which fell short of their mark, and then ordered his troops to attack the Confederates at Mesilla. The Confederates opened fire, killing two and wounding five, thus forcing the Union troops to withdraw from the field of battle and return to the fort.[32]

Because of the construction and the terrain surrounding Fort Fillmore, Lynde did not believe that he could repel a Confederate attack. Therefore, on July 26, when he received a report that the Confederate forces would soon be reinforced with artillery, he decided to abandon Fort Fillmore in favor of the more defensible Fort Stanton, located about 100 miles distant. Supplies that could not be transported were destroyed, and early on July 27, the Union garrison began the march toward Fort Stanton. All went well on the march until the intense heat combined with the lack of water began to fatigue the Union troops. Upon reaching San Augustine Springs, Lynde and a small advance guard gathered all the water they could transport and began the journey back along the road to relieve the fatigued troops.[33]

As Lynde approached the troops scattered along the road, he learned that a large Confederate force was approaching from Mesilla. With only 100 infantrymen capable of fighting, Lynde was forced to surrender his command to Baylor. Following the surrender, Baylor pardoned the prisoners and supplied them with enough food and equipment to travel through the Apache Indian country to Fort Craig. The pardoned troops were assigned to non-belligerent duties for the remainder of the war, and Lynde was court martialed and stripped of his rank. On July 28, 1866, however, he was reinstated to his former rank by President Andrew Johnson.[34]

The Confederate occupation of Arizona Territory was conducted by Captain Sherod Hunter. Hunter and the Arizona Volunteers, an independent company, were ordered by Sibley to occupy Tucson. Hunter was welcomed to Tucson on February 28, 1862, where he remained until the following May 4. A Union patrol from the California Column came into contact with a Confederate patrol at Picacho Pass on April 15, 1862. The engagement at Picacho Pass, forty miles west of Tucson, ended with a Confederate withdrawal to Tucson, and was the westernmost combat action during the Civil War. On May 4, 1862, realizing that he could not contend with the larger California Column then approaching Tucson, Hunter decided to evacuate the territory.[35]

The major military action in New Mexico resulted from Sibley's Confederate invasion of the territory. Although Sibley's forces were successful in the military aspects of the engagements in which they fought, through poor preparation and a negative attitude toward the native population, they were forced to withdraw from New Mexico Territory. The Confederate retreat quickly became a rout as disasters continually struck Sibley's units.

Sibley's forces, which had left San Antonio on October 26, 1861, and stopped at Fort Thorn, New Mexico Territory, to rest for over three weeks, approached Fort Craig on February 16, 1862. By February 20, the Confederate units were camped only two miles distant, but on the opposite bank of the Rio Grande River from Fort Craig. The final action which took place on that day was the mule attack led by Graydon. On the following morning, Sibley ordered the majority of his command of 2,000 troops to cross the Rio Grande River at Val Verde about six miles above Fort Craig. Sibley and the remaining troops faked a frontal assault against Fort Craig, hoping to distract the Union troops, while his main force crossed the river.[36]

Colonel Canby, in command of Fort Craig, had anticipated such a maneuver and had various companies of his 3,810 troops stationed at strategic locations along

Courtesy of National Archives

Fort Craig, New Mexico Territory, a major United States Army post, at the time of the Civil War.

the Rio Grande River. However, Colonel Benjamin G. Roberts, ordered by Canby to prevent the Confederates from reaching the river, arrived at ValVerde at about the same time the Confederates reached the river. Roberts ordered the Third United States Cavalry Regiment to cross the river and engage the Confederates. Fighting on foot, this unit was able to push the Confederates away from the river, and this allowed Roberts to send his artillery across the river. By 10:00 a.m., the artillery of both forces had been deployed and for the following four hours the battle raged back and forth with both sides receiving reinforcements, and the Union troops consistently gaining ground.[37]

At 2:45 p.m., Colonel Canby arrived at the battle and assumed personal command of the Union forces. He had determined that Fort Craig was not in danger and that if the Battle at ValVerde could be won, the Confederates would be forced to withdraw from New Mexico Territory. Canby surveyed the positions of the two forces and decided to launch an attack against the Confederate left. He began a reorganization of his lines to facilitate his coming assault, but before he had all of his troops in place, he was surprised by a Confederate attack.[38]

Confederate Colonel Tom Green had ordered the assault against the two Union batteries because he believed it was the only possible way for the Confederates to win the battle. The Confederate attack on the Union's left battery failed, and they sustained heavy casualties, but the main assault on the Union right carried the battery after bloody hand-to-hand combat. The Confederates then turned the cannon on the retreating Union troops.[39]

The Union loss at ValVerde has been attributed to Canby, because all had gone well until he assumed command; it has also been attributed to the New Mexico volunteers because they refused to support the artillery battery against the Texans' assault; and it has likewise been attributed to Colonel Tom Green, who planned the assault which carried the field. Union forces sustained casualties of 68 killed, 157 wounded, and 35 men missing, while Confederate casualties were 40 killed and 200 wounded.[40]

After allowing his troops two days of rest, Sibley proceeded to Albuquerque, leaving Canby and his Union force in control of Fort Craig. Canby sent special couriers and the New Mexico Volunteers around the Confederate camp with orders to the quartermasters and private citizens in the Confederate line of march to destroy all supplies that might be of use to the Confederates.[41]

One of the detachments was ordered to Socorro to engage and delay the Confederate foraging parties until the supplies could be destroyed. After a warning shot was fired, however, most of the volunteers either deserted or went into hiding. After comparing the Confederate force confronting him with the remnants of his own command, Captain Nicolas Pino agreed to surrender at 2:00 a.m. on February 25, 1862. The surrender allowed the Confederates to capture 250 small arms which they desperately needed. Until this capture of arms, two of the Texas companies had been armed only with lances. By the time Sibley reached Albuquerque, however, Union supplies in the town had been destroyed and the troops had withdrawn to Santa Fe.[42]

Though the citizens of Albuquerque could not offer Sibley the supplies that he needed, they welcomed him to their town. An official ceremony, complete with the firing of a salute, was held at the plaza of the city on March 7, 1862. On March 13, Sibley issued a proclamation to the people of New Mexico: "Those of you who volunteered in the Federal service were doubtless deceived by designing officials," Sibley reasoned, and therefore, "I deem it proper and but just to declare complete and absolute amnesty to all citizens who...within ten days lay aside their arms and return to their homes and avocations."[43] The proclamation did not produce the results that Sibley had expected, how-

ever, and there was no great number of desertions from the Union Army.[44]

The citizens of Cubero proved to be more useful to the Confederate Army than the residents of Albuquerque. On March 3, 1862, residents of Cubero, a Mexican village sixty miles west of Albuquerque, led by Dr. F. E. Kavenaugh, demanded the surrender of the Union depot located in the village. Captain Francisco Aragon, the commander of the depot, realized that he was outnumbered and surrendered the depot and the supplies it contained. A detachment from Sibley's brigade arrived at Cubero on March 5, 1862, and escorted twenty-five wagons loaded with the captured supplies to Albuquerque. With these supplies, Sibley renewed his invasion of New Mexico by sending Major Charles L. Pyron into Santa Fe on March 13, 1862.[45]

As the Confederates burned and looted their way north, Union leaders were requesting reinforcements

Courtesy of the National Park Service

A modern aerial view of Fort Union showing the classic design of the Civil War Fort with the remains of the post used till 1890 in the background.

and volunteers. The pleas for help were heeded by Governor Gilpin of Colorado. Gilpin ordered Colonel John P. Slough and the First Colorado Infantry Regiment to New Mexico Territory. Three companies under the command of Slough were stationed in southern Colorado at Fort Wise on the Arkansas River. On February 22, 1862, Slough started the troops stationed at Fort Wise on a difficult winter march into New Mexico Territory and at the same time, he ordered Major John M. Chivington and the remainder of the regiment, which was stationed at Camp Weld near Denver, to also start the march to New Mexico Territory.[46]

By mid-March, the First Colorado Infantary Regiment had reached Fort Union, and a short time later the determining battle of the Civil War in New Mexico Territory was fought. At Glorieta Pass, on the southern end of the Sangre de Cristo Mountains between Santa Fe and Las Vegas, Confederate and Union forces staged the battle sometimes referred to as the Gettysburg of the Southwest.[47]

On March 26, 1862, Chivington and a detachment of the First Colorado Infantry Regiment marched into Apache Cañon at the western end of Glorieta Pass on their way to Pigeon's Ranch at the opposite end of the pass. At the same time, a detachment of about 300 Confederates under Major Pyron was entering Glorieta Pass from the east. Thirty Confederate scouts and their officer were captured while they were resting in a thicket of trees on the afternoon of March 26. News of the capture was sent to the main body of Union troops, and Chivington ordered the Coloradoans forward. They threw their equipment aside and raced into Apache Cañon, and as they rounded a bend in the cañon, they saw the Confederates. Pyron saw the charging troops, deployed his men in an orderly manner, and opened the battle with howitzer fire. The Coloradoans panicked, and for a short time confusion reigned among Chivington's command. Chivington gained control of his troops, however, and deployed them for an attack against the Confederates, who had formed a skirmish line across the floor of the cañon. Chivington sent his infantry up the sides of the cañon and ordered his cavalry to make frontal assaults against the Confederate line. After the first charge failed because it started prematurely, Chivington ordered a second charge. This time the Union cavalry carried the Confederate line, and the Confederates began a confused withdrawal from the cañon. As night fell, the Union force withdrew to Pigeon's Ranch, while the Confederates regrouped at Johnson's Ranch.[48]

Both Pyron and Chivington sent for reinforcements. The following day, on March 27, 1862, a force of about 700 Confederates under the command of Colonel William R. Scurry waited at Johnson's Ranch for the expected Union assault. Chivington's force had run out of water at Pigeon's Ranch and had withdrawn to Kozlowski's Ranch, where they joined the Union force

under Slough. The following morning both commanders ordered their troops toward the opposing force, and contact was finally made at Pigeon's Ranch where the Union forces had stopped to rest.[49]

The engagement at Pigeon's Ranch raged back and forth most of the day. The action was fought with artillery, small arms, and bowie knives, and was marked with extreme bravery on both sides. The Confederate assaults were intended to capture the Union artillery, and although the Confederates reached the Union guns in the final assault of the day, an inspired counterattack by the Coloradoans prevented the capture of the guns. This final assault, however, drove the Union troops from the field of battle.

The Confederate victory was a costly one, for while they were engaged in battle at Pigeon's Ranch, their supply wagons left at Johnson's Ranch were destroyed. Major Chivington had led a Union detachment through the mountains and destroyed the sixty-four inadequately protected supply wagons left at the ranch. Chivington then retraced his path through the mountains and rejoined the Union force which had regrouped at Kozlowski's Ranch. In addition to the supply train, the Confederate losses at the Battle of Glorieta Pass were approximately 60 killed, 100 wounded, and 91 captured, while the Union losses were 51 killed, 78 wounded, and 24 captured or missing.[50]

With their supplies destroyed and little hope for acquiring adequate supplies in New Mexico Territory, the Sibley forces decided to withdraw from the territory. The units began the march to Texas from Santa Fe. They were hampered in the retreat by a lack of food, blankets, and medical supplies. They were low on ammunition, were harrassed by Union forces, and fought skirmishes at Albuquerque, and then at Peralta, located on the Rio Grande River. Confronted by a Union force, Sibley's units abandoned the remaining baggage near Lajoya, and after nightfall dissolved into the San Mateo Mountains. Sibley's men then straggled back into Texas, leaving over half of the original force dead in New Mexico Territory.[51]

New Mexican troops did not, as a unit, fight outside the territory of New Mexico. Because of the military policies, the increased Indian hostilities, and the rumors of a second Confederate invasion, New Mexico forces were totally occupied within the territory. There were individuals, who had at one time resided in the territory, and were considered New Mexico Territory citizens, who fought with other units in the Eastern theater of the Civil War.[52]

The Civil War brought an increase in Indian hostilities in New Mexico Territory. As the tribes witnessed the conflict between the whites, and the movement of both military and civilian personnel, as well as what they believed to be the withdrawal of these groups from the territory, they came to believe that the whites were fleeing because they feared the Indians. This belief, particularly among the Navajo and the Apache tribes, created a feeling of victory, which resulted in enlarged bravery and boldness, and led to increased hostilities, attacks and raids against the white settlements. This action brought a reaction from the whites that resulted in the eventual defeat and relocation of these tribes on reservations. For a brief period of time, however, the Indians were quite successful in their war against the whites, and this created a state of panic among the whites.[53]

The territorial newspapers reported every minor incident in emotionally charged language, and were quick to assign the responsibility for any loss of person or property to the Indians. Most lost or strayed livestock was reported as stolen by Indians. Other property damages were also reported as resulting from Indian depredations. Indians were blamed for almost everything, including racial discrimination; according to reports, Indians were not making war on Mexican-Americans, but only on whites in the territory. A freight train owned and operated by whites was attacked by Indians, while another train in the same vicinity was allowed to pass unmolested because it was owned and operated by Mexican-Americans. Newspapers also editorialized in favor of a strong Indian policy. ''The Indians must be destroyed or in some manner subdued,'' claimed the *Santa Fe New Mexican,* because, ''If not, progression and safety can be but slightly realized.''[54]

The policy of the military reflected the attitude of the citizens of the territory. Under Carleton's leadership, the Union Army was directed to conduct a war of total destruction against the Navajo and Apache tribes. Other tribes, in particular the Ute, Zuni, and Moquis, were considered friendly and in some cases were even employed as spies and scouts for the army. In directing his forces against the Navajos, Carleton ordered that ''All prisoners [should be brought] to Santa Fe,'' and from there either he or the Superintendent of Indian Affairs would determine their final destination. ''All horses, mules or other stock . . . will be turned over to your chief quartermaster . . . and used in the public service,'' and continuing his orders, Carleton explained that ''Troops and employees [would receive] a bonus of $20 apiece . . . as prize money on the delivery to the chief quartermaster of every sound, serviceable horse or mule.''[55] Carleton also authorized the payment of one dollar per head of sheep captured and delivered to the chief commissary. Troops were also ordered to destroy or capture all Indian property, and it was this policy of destruction which brought the final surrender of the Navajo tribe.[56]

To subdue the Navajo Indians, the First New Mexico Volunteer Infantry Regiment was ordered into action. Under the command of Colonel Christopher ''Kit'' Carson, the unit was to undertake an expedition to bring the tribe to a reservation. In the campaign against the Navajos, Carson and the New Mexico unit conducted search-and-destroy type operations. They would go into Navajo country, live off the land, destroy crops, capture livestock and fight only minor skirmishes with small groups of Navajos. The First New Mexico Volunteer Infantry Regiment was headquartered at Fort Canby during the Navajo campaign, and it was from there that Captain John Thompson led a small detachment into the Cañon de Chelly for the purpose of destroying the Navajo peach orchards located there. Thompson and his thirty-five men left Fort Canby on July 29, 1864, destroyed approximately 4,150 peach trees, captured 1,500 sheep, accepted the surrender of Barboncito, the leader of the Cañon de Chelly Navajos, and returned to Fort Canby on August 10, 1864. Although by the time of the expedition, a majority of the Navajos were already relocated on the Bosque Redondo Reservation, the thirteen days of massive destruction caused by Thompson and his small detachment brought to a close the resistance of the Navajos that remained in the Cañon de Chelly area.[57]

The Apache Indians were not as easily subdued as the Navajos. They numbered approximately 6,500 at the advent of the Civil War, and because of their nomadic tribal life, the military found it much more difficult to conquer them. The various bands of the Apache tribe were for the most part located in the southern part of the New Mexico Territory, and when the Civil War erupted they too erupted. During the first year of war, the Apache tribe controlled the southern part of the territory. Communication, travel, and economic pursuits outside of the larger settlements were hazardous, if not impossible.[58]

In order to combat the Apaches, Thomas J. Mastin of Pinos Altos organized the Arizona Guards on July 18, 1861. The Arizona Guards, assigned to Baylor's Confederate Army, remained in Arizona to protect the territory from the Indians. The Arizona Guards conducted an aggressive war against the Apaches and at one point pursued them into Mexico. Mastin and fifteen of the Arizona Guards defended the town of Pinos Altos against an attack of 250 to 300 Apaches on September 27, 1861. Mastin was wounded in the engagement and died on October 7, 1861. He was replaced by Lieutenant Thomas J. Helm, and the Arizona Guards were then transferred to San Antonio to provide a rear guard for Sibley's invasion of New Mexico Territory.[59]

The arrival of the California Column in southern New Mexico Territory did not immediately end Apache hostilities, but by the end of 1862 the territory was once again in control of the whites. The first meetings of the California Column and the Apache Indians, however, came under a flag of truce presented by the Apaches at Apache Pass near Tucson. After the conference ended, the Californians discovered the mutilated bodies of two of their comrades. At the same place a short time later, a superior force of Apaches attacked another detachment of the California Column. The Californians employed howitzers against them and were able to drive them off. After seeing the graves of his men at Apache Pass, Carleton, who had originally issued orders not to fire upon the Indians, revoked those orders and the Apache Indian war was begun, not to end until after the Civil War.[60]

The economic growth of New Mexico Territory, already burdened by inadequate communication, transportation, and population, and also suffering continual Indian hostilities, for the most part was adversely affected by the Civil War. The Confederate invasion of the territory resulted in widespread destruction and disruption of production facilities, wealth, and investment capital. The invasion also stimulated the Indian tribes to increased hostilities against the white population. The only positive effects that the Civil War had on the economic growth of the territory was in the form of increased spending in the Santa Fe region, and the improvement and protection of some wagon roads along the major trade routes.[61]

Political leaders who were aware of the economic problems of New Mexico Territory continued throughout the Civil War period to attempt to alleviate them and to improve them. New industry was encouraged to locate in the territory, and newspapers advertised and editorialized in favor of the opportunities that existed for various industries or industrious individuals to locate profitably within the territory. Appeals to the California Column volunteers, in the form of bounties and editorial encouragement, to remain in the territory and work in the profitable mining industry were commonplace after Confederate withdrawal from the territory. Several suggestions were offered to the United States government, which if approved, would have allowed New Mexico Territory to collect reparations for damages from the Confederate government, from Texas, or from Confederate sympathizers within New Mexico Territory.[62]

The only measure that was implemented in an attempt to collect reparations for war damages was the confiscation and sale of property belonging to Confederate sympathizers who resided within the territory. The confiscated property was offered for sale to the highest bidder, and the sales were advertised in the territorial newspapers. The most noted of these cases was that of Sylvester Mowry of Tucson. Mowry, a retired United States Army officer and owner of the Patagonia Silver Mine, was believed by General Carleton to be a secessionist and an instigator of rebellion in the territory. Mowry was arrested by order of Carleton on June 12, 1862. Within a month, Mowry's property had been confiscated and he had been assigned to Yuma Prison, only to be released without comment on November 4 of the same year. Following his banishment from the territory, however, Mowry's silver mine and other property were sold for $2,000 on April 1, 1864, by the United States District Court of the Second Judicial District.[63]

At the outbreak of the Civil War, mining for gold, silver, and copper was one of the major industries of New Mexico Territory. Located within the territory were fifteen mines employing a total of 822 men. Several gold strikes along the Gila and Colorado Rivers just prior to the outbreak of war had produced a rush of prospectors in the territory. This rush, as well as the mining industry, was slowed considerably by the war. The abandonment of several forts and increased Indian hostilities during the early stages of the war created a hazardous environment for the miners. However, as the military reoccupied the forts and extended protection to the mining areas, the industry was resumed with increased vigor and was stimulated also by investments of Eastern capital. The miners soon found that the soldiers sent to protect mining regions were instead joining in the search for gold.[64]

Agriculture was the leading industry of New Mexico Territory at the outbreak of the Civil War. Although the average farm was 277 acres 4,490 of the 5,088 farms in the territory had less then 50 acres per farm. The main agricultural products of the New Mexican farmers were livesock, orchards, corn, grain, and market-garden products. The primary livestock production was sheep, followed by cattle and dairy products. In addition to the orchards, corn, grain, and market-garden products, New Mexican farmers also produced barley, tobacco, hay, molasses, and wine. Unlike the mining industry, agriculture received a stimulus from the Civil War in the form of military purchases of farm products. Government agents advertised frequently in the territorial newspapers their desire to purchase farm products not only for military consumption, but also for distribution on the Indian reservations. The government purchases resulted in speculation and inflated prices, particularly on staple products, but many producers realized an even higher profit by shipping their products to the Colorado Territory gold camps. In general, the Civil War produced a period of prosperity for New Mexican farmers.[65]

Although limited in number, there were located within New Mexico Territory the necessary manufacturing concerns. Blacksmiths, carpenters, and millers were found in all of the major counties. The manufacture of sawed lumber was pursued in some counties. Arizona, Taos, and Mora Counties had liquor distilleries, and in addition Arizona County was served by a cobbler, a men's clothier, and a willow furniture producer. By the end of the war, Santa Fe was served by two jewelers and the local newspapers advertised profit for a hatter who would locate in the city.[66]

Marketing, particularly in Santa Fe, did not suffer as a result of the Civil War. During the war period two concerns built and opened new stores in Santa Fe. General merchandise stores advertised the arrival of products from the states, which included lager beer, notions, clothing, hardware, groceries, and personal items. One Santa Fe merchant, Louis Zeckendorf, advertised the arrival of "two regiments [of] Cavalry and Infantry, and other curious toys for the youngsters."[67]

W. R. Shoemaker, chief ordnance officer of the New Mexico Military Department, offered the territorial residents 2,390 French muskets at an auction held at Fort Union on September 12, 1864. The Byers and Andrews jewelry business additionally offered the citizens of Santa Fe "dental operations under the supervision of Dr. E. Andrews, who is confident of giving satisfaction to all who may desire his services."[68] Other specialty stores offered the citizens of the territory the finest Mexican goods and other foreign products.[69]

The economic system of New Mexico Territory during the Civil War was in part dependent upon the maintenance of the class structure of the society. The peonage system provided the major source of inexpensive labor, and within this system, the peon class was composed primarily of Mexican-Americans. Another source of cheap labor was the system of Indian slavery that existed in the territory. The class structure of the society provided the upper class with a comfortable life style and much political power. Therefore, the maintenance of the system was an important factor in many of the social decisions made by the political leaders of the territory in the Civil War years.[70]

During the Civil War period, with two exceptions, social institutions and social activities continued in a normal manner. The invasion by Sibley's Confederate forces, for the most part, brought all activities except military to a standstill, but normalcy returned to New Mexico Territory with the withdrawal of the Confederate forces. The other exception was Arizona Territory. Under the constant threat of Indian attacks, the isolated residents of the territory did not return to normal social pursuits throughout most of the Civil War.

In May of 1863, measures were undertaken for the relief of the suffering inhabitants of Socorro County. The Confederate invasion, Indian depredations, and drought had so thoroughly destroyed agricultural production that starvation was widespread throughout the county. The military and civilian population located in the other more prosperous counties joined together to raise money for the relief of the citizens of Socorro. Soldiers and citizens alike contributed liberally to this charitable cause, and the territorial newspapers aided in the effort by printing articles and editorials supporting the relief campaign.[71]

A totally inadequate common school system served the territory during the Civil War period. Inadequately financed, and under the supervision of the courts, a school was established in each settlement by the 1859-1860 New Mexico Territorial Legislature. Improvement of the school system was strongly opposed by the upper socio-economic class of New Mexican society. This group, primarily Spanish or Mexican-American, hoped to maintain the peonage system that existed for their benefit throughout the territory. The recent American immigrants to the territory, and particularly the appointed territorial officials, recognized the need for an adequate school system, and supported measures to improve the educational system within the territory. Governor Connelly, addressing the New Mexico Territorial Legislature in December, 1863, explained: "There is no want that is so widespred among our people as that which is occasioned by the absence of a school system." Connelly further explained: "Education refines, strengthens, and elevates the intellect of man," and continuing he claimed that "It purifies society and relieves it from crimes and offenses of every grade and character."[72] Even though the need was recognized and affirmative action for the establishment of adequate common schools was recommended, it was primarily the private schools that served the territory during the Civil War.[73]

Though they were quite limited, private schools in New Mexico Territory served ably throughout the war years. Private schools were for the most part sponsored by Protestant missionaries; even though the Catholic clergy lacked the finances to establish schools throughout the territory, they were opposed to educating Catholic children in the Protestant schools. Santa Fe was the location of two Catholic schools, one for males, and the other for females. It was claimed that "the two schools" exemplified "the progress...being made in education in New Mexico," and further that "Yearly...these institutions increase in their usefulness and spread their good influences throughout the territory."[74] The Santa Fe New Mexico Institute, another private school, established by the Reverend W. I. Kermott, a Baptist missionary, was welcomed to Santa Fe in September, 1864. The school, with a staff of three instructors, was designated as "a first class English school."[75]

The lack of institutions for formal education does not seem indicative of the literacy level of the population. Augustine M. Hunt, for example, opened a subscription and circulating library at Santa Fe in September, 1864. This successful venture offered to its subscribers, for a fee of five dollars per quarter, such varied works as *China and the Chinese, West Point Love Story,* and *Don Quixote de la Mancha.* The territorial citizens were also reading enough to keep at least eight newspapers in circulation. In order to profitably publish a newspaper, it apparently required a minimum of 600 subscribers.[76]

Following the withdrawal of the Confederate forces, holidays, celebrations, parties, dances, and other festive occasions were frequent throughout the territory. The only negative effect the war seemed to have on these observances was exemplified by a warning to "the gay and festive people...at the fandangos," published in the *Santa Fe Gazette.* "There are Provosts about," explained the *Gazette,* "and they march to the guard house, those who flourish knives and pistols. These are war times."[77] At least on one occasion, and probably several more, the people did not heed the warning of the *Gazette.* A "shameful' incident was reported by the *Gazette* which involved a fight, "at a fandango" between "two of the females [who] became insulted and outraged at each other . . . .American men present endeavored to inflame the ill will of the two women," the report continued, and "a ring was formed and knives placed in the hands of each, for a desperate fight."[78] Other events were not marred by such violence, and most seemed to be joyous and festive occasions.[79]

New Mexico Territory citizens benefitted from the two cultures present in the territory, in that the Catholic religious holidays and the traditional American holidays were observed and celebrated by the total society. The annual Feast of Corpus Christi, a Catholic holiday, was celebrated in Albuquerque in 1863 with the "accustomed ceremonies" and a procession which included the Fifth United States Infantry Regiment Field Band. One year later Santa Fe's observance of the holiday was highlighted by a procession which included 200 scholars from the Convent La Sonora de la Luz, the bishop and priests, school children, and the Fifth United States Infantry Regiment Field Band. Christmas, a town's patron saint's day, and other religious holidays were all observed in a festive atmosphere. Traditional American holidays were also observed in a joyous and festive spirit. The 1863 observance of George Washington's birthday included the firing of a thirty-five gun salute and a ball at which "the Guests were merry . . .and enjoyed the dancing with a zest."[80]

The citizens of the territory also enjoyed other social activities such as concerts, the theater, and the performances of various traveling troupes. The citizens of Santa Fe boasted of a theater which "the managers" exerted "themselves to make it a place of pleasant resort for every class of our citizens."[81] Concerts by local citizens were frequent and usually attended by large crowds. Traveling troupes, such as the Hawes, Barry, and Company's Ethiopian Minstrel Troupe, the Red Man of Agar, the California Acrobatic Troupe, and the Contraband Serenaders all performed before large crowds throughout the territory.[82]

Both spectator and participant sports were popular activities among the territorial population during the Civil War. Fishing and hunting for sport were two such pastimes enjoyed and often boasted of by the citizens. Mountain climbing was another participant sport as exemplified by General Carleton who took time from his military duties to climb the mountains in the Santa Fe area. However, horse racing seemed to be the most popular sport enjoyed by both participants as well as spectators. In 1864, at the urging of the local newspaper, Albuquerque organized a Jockey Club and developed a race course at Val Verde. In addition to these organized race meets, citizens were frequently matching their horses against each other in less organized but heavily attended races. One of the most notable races reported in the territory during the Civil War period "was run by an officer of the United States Army from Montezuma on foot, against Alderman Strachan's

celebrated pony 'No Name'. Distance, 40 yards and repeat," and according to the report, "the Montezuman won."[83]

The institution of marriage was not adversely affected by the war, as bachelors were encouraged to seek out brides. One young man who followed this advice found a prospective bride, secured a marriage license, and repeated the marriage vows with his bride before a local clergyman. While awaiting breakfast the following morning, the young man was shocked to read in the newspaper that he had married a different woman. After reading his marriage certificate, on which the name of his bride had indeed been incorrectly recorded, he announced to his bride: "I am married to the wrong woman. You are not my lawful wife." After reading the document herself, his bride casually replied, "It's no use fretting, Jeremiah — it's too late now!"[84] A brother of Abraham Staab, a prosperous Santa Fe businessman, was married in New York during January, 1864. On the day that the marriage took place, Staab celebrated in Sante Fe by inviting his friends to a dinner and dance honoring the marriage of his brother.[85]

There were social and fraternal organizations within New Mexico Territory during the Civil War. The Ancient Free and Accepted Masons were active in the territory, maintaining the Montezuma Lodge Number 109 at Santa Fe, the Chapman Lodge at Fort Union, and a number of Masons were reported living at Taos, although there was no lodge there. The New Mexico Masonic Order was said to exemplify the ancient organization particularly well; the most prominent men of the territory were listed as members. A Lodge of Good Templars was organized by some of the members of Company A, First California Infantry Regiment. Other Good Templars among the troops also became active in the promotion of temperance.[86]

Temperance groups were probably quite busy because there appeared to be an abundance of spirits of every type for those territorial citizens who were not abstaining. The Union Hotel of Albuquerque advertised that "their bar will always be furnished with the best . . .Foreign and Domestic Liquors."[87] Merchants advertised their present liquor stocks as well as the anticipated arrival of any supply of liquor. In addition to the imported liquors, drinking citizens could partake of wines produced within the territory or beer from the Pacific Brewery of Santa Fe.[88]

There was one solemn occasion on which temperance was observed by all citizens of the territory. Due to the isolation of the territory from the United States, it was the first week of May, 1865, before the citizens of New Mexico Territory learned of the assassination of President Lincoln. On May 7, 1865, the Reverend Kermott presented a sermon on the assassination to the citizens of Santa Fe. "He saw the fall of Sumter and of Charleston. The fall of Richmond and the surrender of Lee," explained Kermott, and now, "The man the people loved, trusted, and honored is dead."[89]

The most important factor affecting New Mexico Territory during the Civil War was its geographic isolation. The citizens believed they were being ignored and neglected by the United States government. Inadequate transportation and communication facilities, and the failure of the United States government to improve these facilities contributed to the territorial citizens' feelings of neglect. Feelings of isolation were further intensified by the geographic features within the territory. The uninhabitable regions of the territory isolated the various population centers from each other. For example, the Jornado del Muerto region between Santa Fe and Mesilla created a weak allegiance to Texas by the citizens of Mesilla and the southern part of the territory. The allegiance was founded in the fear that neither the New Mexican government at Santa Fe nor the United States would protect them from a Confederate invasion.

At the advent of war, New Mexican citizens were not strongly allied with either the Northern or Southern cause. Although they felt isolated from and neglected by the United States government, New Mexican citizens owned no slaves and had developed a dislike for Texans. The attitude and conduct of the invading Sibley forces toward the territorial citizens caused many of them to support the United States.

The military scene within the territory was characterized by individual bravery, such as Colonel Tom Green's assault at ValVerde, but the outcome was determined by the mistakes and blunders of commanders. Lynde's surrender of his superior force to Baylor after the former had abandoned Fort Fillmore is one example. The destruction of the unguarded Confederate supply train during the Battle at Glorieta Pass, Sibley's failure to adequately supply his invasion force, and his policy of taking supplies from New Mexican citizens, all eventually forced the withdrawal of his brigade and the loss of the territory by the Confederacy.

The Colorado and California troops sent to New Mexico Territory contributed to the final Union victory. The destruction of the Confederate supply train at the Battle of Glorieta Pass was conducted by Chivington and the First Colorado Infantry Regiment. Al-though they did not participate in a major engagement, the approach of the California Column forced Hunter to withdraw from Arizona and contributed to Sibley's decision to evacuate New Mexico Territory.

These troops, particularly the California Column, remained in the territory following the Confederate withdrawal, and contributed to the reconstruction of the territory. The California troops also participated in quelling the Indian hostilities. Carleton, as commander of the New Mexico Military Department, initiated the severe policy which eventually subdued the Indians. The Californians also contributed to the economy, participated in the political struggles, and joined in many of the social activities of the territory.

Following the withdrawal of Sibley's Confederate forces, political factionalism resurfaced within the territory. However, these political struggles were between the Republican appointed office holders and the Democratic leaders who had controlled the territory prior to the war. Arny and his followers were attempting to gain economic advantages for Eastern financiers, and they were strongly resisted by Connelly and his supporters.

Economically, the citizens of the territory, with the exception of the Santa Fe merchants, suffered mildly as a result of the war. The Confederate invasion, Indian hostilities, and bad weather all combined to forestall economic growth.

For the most part, the social institutions, following the withdrawal of the Confederates, returned to their pre-war status. The military troops stationed within the territory participated individually in most of the social activities and at times as units. The social pursuits, although many and varied, reflected the isolation of the territory. Activities in some cases were dependent upon the arrival of supply trains from the United States, and they were almost always regional within the territory.

With one exception, the creation of Arizona Territory, New Mexico Territory was allowed to return to its pre-war isolation and neglect. Office seeking politicians in Washington created Arizona Territory, a move which was welcomed by citizens of both territories, and then the two territories, Arizona and New Mexico, shared the continued feelings of isolation and neglect until statehood came in 1912.

NOTES

1. Odie B. Faulk, "Confederate Hero at Val Verde," *New Mexico Historical Review,* Vol. XXXVIII, No. 4 (October, 1963), p. 302.
2. William A. Keleher, *Turmoil in New Mexico, 1846-1868* (Santa Fe: Rydal Press, 1952), pp. 143-145.
3. Faulk, *op. cit.,* p. 303; George H. Pettis, "The Confederate Invasion of New Mexico and Arizona," Clarence C. Buel and Robert U. Johnson, eds., *Battles and Leaders of the Civil War* (4 vols., New York: Thomas Yoseloff, 1956), Vol. II, pp. 105-106; Ray C. Colton, *The Civil War in the Western Territories: Arizona, Colorado, New Mexico, and Utah* (Norman: University of Oklahoma Press, 1959), pp. 26-28.
4. Faulk, *op. cit.,* p. 302.
5. Ralph H. Brown, *Historical Geography of the United States* (New York: Harcourt, Brace and World, 1948), pp. 78-82, 492-501.
6. Keleher, *op. cit.,* pp. 13-18, 38-42, 126.
7. William I. Waldrip, "New Mexico During the Civil War," *New Mexico Historical Review,* Vol. XXVIII, No. 3 (July, 1953), pp. 126, 196; Keleher, *op. cit.,* pp. 126-127.
8. *Ibid.*
9. Robert W. Larson, *New Mexico's Quest for Statehood: 1846-1912* (Albuquerque: University of New Mexico Press, 1968), pp. 72-73.
10. Loomis Morton Ganaway, "New Mexico and the Sectional Controversy, 1846-1861," *New Mexico Historical Review,* Vol. XIX, No. 1 (January, 1944), pp. 55-64; Larson, *op. cit.,* p. 88.
11. *Ibid.,* p. 83.
12. *Ibid.;* Keleher, *op. cit.,* pp. 126-127; Ralph Emerson Twitchell, *The Leading Facts of*

New Mexican History (5 vols., Cedar Rapids: Torch Press, 1912), Vol. II, p. 358.

13. William I. Waldrip, "New Mexico During the Civil War," *New Mexico Historical Review*, Vol. XXVIII, No. 4 (October, 1953), pp. 274-276; Twitchell, *op. cit.*, p. 361; United States Department of the Interior, *Eighth Census of the United States, 1860: Population* (Washington: Government Printing Office, 1864), pp. 566-568.

14. Waldrip, *op. cit.*, No. 4, pp. 276-280; Ganaway, *op. cit.*, pp. 55-65.

15. Waldrip, *op. cit.*, No. 3, pp. 163-168; Colton, *op. cit.*, pp. 3-7.

16. United States Department of War, *War of the Rebellion: A Compilation of the Official Records of the Union and Confederate Armies* (40 vols., 128 books, Washington: Government Printing Office, 1880-1901), Ser. I, Vol. LIII, p. 490.

17. *Official Records*, Ser. I, Vol. I, p. 605; Waldrip, *op. cit.*, No. 3, p. 168.

18. Waldrip, *op. cit.*, No. 3, p. 170; *Official Records*, Ser. III, Vol. I, p. 301; Colton, *op. cit.*, p. 8.

19. Waldrip, *op. cit.*, No. 4, p. 275; Vincent G. Tegeder, "Lincoln and the Territorial Patronage: The Ascendency of the Radicals in the West," *Mississippi Valley Historical Review*, Vol. XXXV, No. 1 (June, 1948), pp. 82-84.

20. *Ibid.*, p. 84.

21. *Ibid.*, pp. 82-84; Lawrence R. Murphy, "William F. M. Arny: Secretary of New Mexico Territory, 1862-1864," *Arizona and the West*, Vol. VIII, No. 4 (Winter, 1966), pp. 323, 325, 326.

22. Tegeder, *op. cit.*, pp. 84-85; Murphy, *op. cit.*, pp. 330-331; Ralph E. Twitchell, "Chief Justice Kirby Benedict," *Old Santa Fe: The Story of New Mexico's Ancient Capital* (Santa Fe: Santa Fe New Mexican Publishing Corporation, 1925), p. 351.

23. Keleher, *op. cit.*, p. 166.

24. *Ibid.*

25. Waldrip, *op. cit.*, No. 4, p. 280; Murphy, *op. cit.*, p. 330.

26. *Ibid.*, pp. 332-335, 331.

27. Adlai Feather, "The Territories of Arizona," *New Mexico Historical Review*, Vol. XXXIX, No. 1 (January, 1964), pp. 16-19; Waldrip, *op. cit.*, No. 3, p. 174; Colton, *op. cit.*, pp. 198-202; *Official Records*, Ser. I, Vol. IV, p. 20.

28. *Ibid.*; Ganaway, *op. cit.*, pp. 63-67, 70-74; Feather, *op. cit.*, pp. 16-19.

29. *Ibid.*, pp. 16-17; Colton, *op. cit.*, pp. 202-203; Rufus Kay Wyllys, *Arizona: The History of a Frontier State* (Phoenix: Hobson and Herr, 1950), pp. 165-167.

30. *Ibid.*, pp. 166-171; Colton, *op. cit.*, pp. 203-204.

31. Martin H. Hall, *Sibley's New Mexico Campaign* (Austin: University of Texas Press, 1960), pp. 21-28, 225-226.

32. A. F. H. Armstrong, "The Case Of Major Issaac Lynde," *New Mexico Historical Review*, Vol. XXXVI, No. 1 (January, 1961), pp. 9-11; Pettis, *op. cit.*, p.103.

33. Armstrong, *op. cit.*, pp. 15-18.

34. *Ibid.*, pp. 18, 25, 33.

35. Wyllys, *op. cit.*, pp. 146, 148-149; Hall, *Sibley's New Mexico Campaign*, pp. 53, 205; Martin H. Hall, "The Skirmish of Picacho," *Civil War History*, Vol. IV, No. 1 (March, 1955), pp. 24-35.

36. Faulk, *op. cit.*, pp. 302-305; Waldrip, *op.*

cit., No. 3, pp. 177, 178; Pettis, *op. cit.*, pp. 106-107. *Official Records*, Ser. I, Vol. IX, pp. 507, 487-490.

37. United States Senate, 37th Congress, 3rd Session, *Senate Report 108* (Washington: Government Printing Office, 1863), pp. 367-378; *Official Records*, Ser. I, Vol. IX, pp. 489-490, 493-494; Colton, *op. cit.*, p. 29; Hall, *Sibley's New Mexico Campaign*, pp. 83-88.

38. *Ibid.*, pp. 89-100; Faulk, *op. cit.*, p. 304.

39. *Ibid.*; Hall, *Sibley's New Mexico Campaign*, pp. 89-100; United States Senate, 37th Congress, 3rd Session, *Senate Report 108*, p. 367; *Official Records*, Ser. I, Vol. IX, pp. 490-492, 506-510.

40. Hall, *Sibley's New Mexico Campaign*, pp. 100-103; *Official Records*, Ser. I, Vol. IX, p. 493.

41. Hall, *Sibley's New Mexico Campaign*, pp. 104-106, 108-109.

42. *Ibid.*, pp. 110-113.

43. *Ibid.*, p. 117; *Santa Fe Gazette*, April 26, 1862, p. 1.

44. Hall, *Sibley's New Mexico Campaign*, pp. 113-117.

45. *Official Records*, Ser. I, Vol. IX, pp. 528-530.

46. David Westphall, "The Battle of Glorieta Pass: Its Importance in the Civil War," *New Mexico Historical Review*, Vol. XLIV, No. 2 (April, 1969), p. 141; Hall, *Sibley's New Mexico Campaign*, pp. 116, 118-123; Agnes Wright Spring, "Why Did John P. Slough Resign?" *The Colorado Magazine*, Vol. XXXIX, No. 2 (April, 1962), pp. 81-88; Waldrip, *op. cit.*, No. 4, pp. 251-254.

47. *Ibid.*, p. 255; Colton, *op. cit.*, p. 49; Spring, *op. cit.*, p. 81.

48. Waldrip, *op. cit.*, No. 4, p. 255; Westphall, *op. cit.*, pp. 144-146; Spring, *op. cit.*, p. 97; Colonel J. M. Chivington, "The First Colorado Regiment," *New Mexico Historical Review*, Vol. XXXIII, No. 2 (April, 1958), pp. 148-149; *Official Records*, Ser. I, Vol. IX, pp. 530-531; Pettis, *op. cit.*, p. 109; Hall, *Sibley's New Mexico Campaign*, pp. 133-140.

49. *Ibid.*, pp. 140, 142-143; Westphall, *op. cit.*, pp. 146-147.

50. *Official Records*, Ser. I, Vol. IX, pp. 533-535, 538-539, 540-541, 542-543; Hall, *Sibley's New Mexico Campaign*, pp. 143-153, 156-158; Westphall, *op. cit.*, pp. 146-149; Chivington, *op. cit.*, pp. 150-152.

51. Hall, *Sibley's New Mexico Campaign*, pp. 166-169; Waldrip, *op. cit.*, No. 4, pp. 256-259; Ovando J. Hollister, *Boldly They Rode: A History of the First Colorado Regiment of Volunteers* (Lakewood, Colorado: Golden Press, 1949), pp. 92-96, 108-110; *Official Records*, Ser. I, Vol. IX, pp. 550-551.

52. Waldrip, *op. cit.*, No. 4, pp. 259, 263-265, 268-269; *Santa Fe Gazette*, August 27, 1864, p. 2.

53. Waldrip, *op. cit.*, No. 4, pp. 263-267; Lee Myers, "Military Establishments in Southwestern New Mexico: Stepping Stones to Settlement," *New Mexico Historical Review*, Vol. LXIII, No. 1 (January, 1968), pp. 5, 8-9, 15, 18, 21-25, 27; Clarence C. Clendenen, "General James Henry Carleton," *New Mexico Historical Review*, Vol. XXX, No. 1 (January, 1955), pp. 39-43; Colton, *op. cit.*, pp. 126-127.

54. *Santa Fe New Mexican*, 1863-1865, throughout; *Santa Fe Gazette*, 1863-1865, throughout; *Rio Abajo Weekly Press*, Albuquerque, 1863, throughout; *Santa Fe New Mexican*, August 19, 1864, p. 2, January 31, 1864, p. 1.

55. *Official Records*, Ser. I. Vol. XXVI, Pt. 1, pp. 235-236.

56. *Ibid.*, Colton, *op. cit.*, p. 125.

57. Stephen C. Jett, "The Destruction of the Navajo Peach Orchards," *Arizona and the West*, Vol. XVI, No. 4 (Winter 1974), pp. 365-371; *Official Records*, Ser. I, Vol. XXVI, Pt. 1, pp. 232-238, 250-261; Colton, *op cit.*, pp. 141, 144-146.

58. Wyllys, *op cit.*, pp. 187-192; Keleher *op. cit.*, p. 71.

59. Martin H. Hall, "Captain Thomas J. Mastin's Arizona Guards, C.S.A.," *New Mexico Historical Review*, Guards, C.S.A.," *New Mexico Historical Review*, Vol. XLIX, No. 2 (April, 1974), pp. 144-145.

60. Clendenen, *op. cit.*, pp. 39-40.

61. Myers, *op. cit.*, pp. 14-15; Robert M. Utley, "Fort Union and the Santa Fe Trail," *New Mexico Historical Review*, Vol. XXXVI, No. 1 (January, 1961), pp. 44-45; Waldrip, *op. cit.*, No. 4, pp. 283.

62. *Ibid.*, pp. 283-284.

63. Keleher, *op cit.*, pp. 245-250, 269-270; Constance W. Altshuler, "The Case of Sylvester Mowry: The Charge of Treason," *Arizona and the West*, Vol. XV, No. 1 (Spring, 1973), pp. 63-82; Constance W. Altshuler, "The Case of Sylvester Mowry: The Mowry Mine," *Arizona and the West*, Vol. XV, No. 2 (Summer, 1973), pp. 149-174.

64. United States Department of the Interior, *Eighth Census of the United States, 1860: Manufactures*, pp. 666-667; George Ernest Webb, ed., "The Mines in Northwestern Arizona in 1864: A Report by Benjamin Silliman, Jr.," *Arizona and the West*, Vol. XVI, No. 3 (Autumn, 1974), pp. 247-252.

65. United States Department of the Interior, *Eighth Census of the United States, 1860: Agriculture*, pp. 178-179, 220-222; *Santa Fe New Mexican*, 1864-1865, throughout; *Santa Fe Gazette*, 1864-1865, throughout.

66. United States Department of the Interior, *Ninth Census of the United States, 1870: The Wealth and Industry* (Washington: Government Printing Office, 1872), pp. 638-696; *Santa Fe New Mexican*, February 17, 1863, p. 2.

67. *Rio Abajo Weekly Press*, July 14, 1863, p. 3.

68. *Santa Fe New Mexican*, September 23, 1864, p. 2, April 28, 1865, p. 2.

69. *Ibid.*, 1863-1865, throughout; *Santa Fe Gazette*, 1863-1865, throughout; *Rio Abajo Weekly Press*, 1863-1865, throughout.

70. Twitchell, *The Leading Facts of New Mexican History*, Vol. II, pp. 324-325.

71. *Rio Abajo Weekly Press*, May 12, 1863, p. 3.

72. *Santa Fe New Mexican*, December 12, 1863, p. 1.

73. Twitchell, *The Leading Facts of New Mexican History*, Vol. II, pp. 321-322.

74. *Santa Fe Gazette*, June 4, 1865, p. 2.

75. *Ibid.*, September 24, 1864, p. 2.

76. *Santa Fe New Mexican*, November 14, 1863, p. 3, September 9, 1864, p. 2, February 6, 1864, p. 2; *Rio Abajo Weekly Press*, June 30, 1863, p. 3; Larson, *op. cit.*, p. 377-379.

77. *Ibid.*, November 7, 1863, p. 1.
78. *Ibid.*, January 23, 1864, p. 2.
79. *Santa Fe Gazette*, 1863-1865, throughout; *Sante Fe New Mexican*, 1863-1865, throughout; *Rio Abajo Weekly Press*, 1863-1865, throughout.
80. *Santa Fe New Mexican*, February 27, 1864, p. 2; *Rio Abajo Weekly Press*, June 9, 1863, p. 2; *Santa Fe Gazette*, June 4, 1864, p. 2; *Rio Abajo Weekly Press*, August 4, 1863, p. 3; *Santa Fe New Mexican*, January 6, 1865, p. 2; *Rio Abajo Weekly Press*, June 2, 1863, p. 2, February 24, 1863, p.3.
81. *Santa Fe Gazette*, November 5, 1864, p. 2.
82. *Santa Fe New Mexican*, February 6, 1864, p. 2; *Santa Fe Gazette*, November 19, 1864, p. 2, September 23, 1864, p. 2, September 17, 1864, p. 2, November 12, 1864, p. 2, December 31, 1864, p. 2.
83. *Santa Few New Mexican*, December 19, 1863, p. 2; *Santa Fe Gazette*, August 7, 1864, p. 2; *Rio Abajo Weekly Press*, June 2, 1863, p. 2, January 27, 1863, p. 2, June 23, 1863, p. 2, May 19, 1863, p. 2, July 14, 1863, p. 3.
84. *Santa Fe New Mexican*, February 6, 1864, p. 1.
85. *Santa Fe Gazette*, May 28, 1864, p. 2; *Santa Fe New Mexican*, January 23, 1864, p. 3.
86. *Ibid.*, January 6, 1865, p. 2, January 2, 1864, p. 2; *Santa Fe Gazette*, December 31, 1864, p. 2, September 17, 1864, p. 2.
87. *Rio Abajo Weekly Press*, July 17, 1863, p. 3.
88. *Santa Fe New Mexican*, September 23, 1864, p. 2, May 12, 1865, p. 1.
89. *Ibid.*, May 12, 1865, p. 1.

SELECTED READINGS

A. F. Armstrong, "The Case of Major Isaac Lynde," *New Mexico Historical Review*, Vol. XXXVI, No. 1 (January, 1961), pp. 1-35.

Ray C. Colton, *The Civil War in the Western Territories: Arizona, Colorado, New Mexico, and Utah* (Norman: University of Oklahoma Press, 1959).

Adlai Feather, "The Territories of Arizona," *New Mexico Historical Review*, Vol. XXXIX, No. 1 (January, 1964), pp. 16-31.

Loomis Morton Ganaway, "New Mexico and the Sectional Controversy, 1846-1861," *New Mexico Historical Review*, Vol. XIX, No. 1 (January, 1944), pp. 55-79.

Martin H. Hall, *Sibley's New Mexico Campaign* (Austin: University of Texas Press, 1960).

Stephen C. Jett, "The Destruction of Navajo Orchards in 1864," *Arizona and the West*, Vol. XVI, No. 4 (Winter, 1974), pp. 365-378.

William A. Keleher, *Turmoil in New Mexico, 1846-1868* (Santa Fe: Rydall Press, 1952), pp. 143-458.

Robert W. Larson, *New Mexico's Quest for Statehood: 1846-1912* (Albuquerque: University of New Mexico Press, 1968), pp. 41-94.

Lawrence R. Murphy, "William F. M. Arny, Secretary of New Mexico Territory, 1862-1867," *Arizona and the West*, Vol. VIII, No. 4 (Winter, 1966), pp. 321-338.

Ralph Emerson Twitchell, *The Leading Facts of New Mexican History* (5 vols., Cedar Rapids: Torch Press, 1912), Vol. II, pp. 329-451.

William I. Waldrip, "New Mexico During the Civil War," *New Mexico Historical Review*, Vol. XXVIII, No. 3 (July, 1953), pp. 163-182, No. 4 (October, 1953), pp. 251-290.

Rufus Kay Wyllys, *Arizona: The History of a Frontier State* (Phoenix: Hobson and Herr, 1950), pp. 139-162.

A drawing by combat artist James R. O'Neill of the Battle of Honey Springs, July 17, 1863, the Gettysburg of the Indian Territory.

Indian Territory
By James W. Ware

On April 17, 1861, a train moved out of Washington, D.C., headed for Missouri, many of its passengers already concerned with the new war which would soon affect them all. One of these people was a United States Army Second Lieutenant, William W. Averall, only recently returned from an extended sick leave. This experienced soldier was bound for the unorganized Indian Territory, carrying special orders for the Union troops stationed there. Averall left the railroad at Rolla, Missouri, and traveled by stage through a countryside torn by the talk of secession and war. Finding Fort Smith, Arkansas, in the hands of the Confederates, he traded some money and his gold watch for an unbroken horse. After taming his mount, Averall headed west for Fort Arbuckle on the Washita River in southern Indian Territory. Pursued by secessionists, endangered by roving packs of wolves, lost in a blinding wind and rain storm, Averall struggled west, finally reaching the already retreating United States column on May 2. With the delivery of his orders to Major William H. Emory, commander of the Indian Territory detachment, Second Lieutenant Averall completed one of the most courageous individual missions of the Civil War. His message to evacuate all United States troops north to Kansas marked the beginning of a war which would shatter the lives of those living in Indian Territory, just as it split the nation into two warring camps.[1]

Withdrawal of Union troops from Indian Territory deeply divided the Five Civilized Tribes. But these divisions were not new ones; they only reopened old wounds which had been created by tribal histories and institutions. The Cherokee, Creek, Seminole, Choctaw, and Chickasaw tribes had occupied the unorganized territory west of Arkansas since 1830. These Indians previously had lived throughout the South and had adopted a Southern lifestyle and Southern institutions, especially that of slavery. In 1830, the growing political pressure of land-hungry whites culminated in the passage of the Indian Removal Bill by Congress. The subsequent forced migration of the Five Civilized Tribes, their dealings with the United States government, and their Southern heritage helped shape the political, social, and economic conditions of Indian Territory in 1861. Also, these factors contributed to the differing sympathies of various Indian factions toward the white man's Civil War.[2]

On their arrival in Indian Territory, the Five Civilized Tribes faced extensive problems of restructuring their civilization. They had to heal the political divisions aroused by removal, rebuild their broken homes, and establish a new social and economic life. Fortunately for the Indians, they carried out this reconstruction relatively free of interference from the white man. However, contacts that existed between Washington and the Indians did not endear the Indians to the United States government. For example, private contractors, acting in behalf of Washington to fulfill the provisions of the removal treaties, supplied goods of poor quality to the needy tribes at irregular intervals. Under these conditions, it was no surprise that the Five Civilized Tribes were not enthusiastic about supporting the Union cause.[3]

Rebuilding their society and economy was not an easy task, but the Five Civilized Tribes pursued this end diligently and had achieved much success by 1861. The Indians brought their agricultural economy with them, their principal crops being cotton and corn; they also raised livestock and traded their surpluses down the rivers to New Orleans, Louisiana. By 1857, the territory stood on solid economic ground, with most

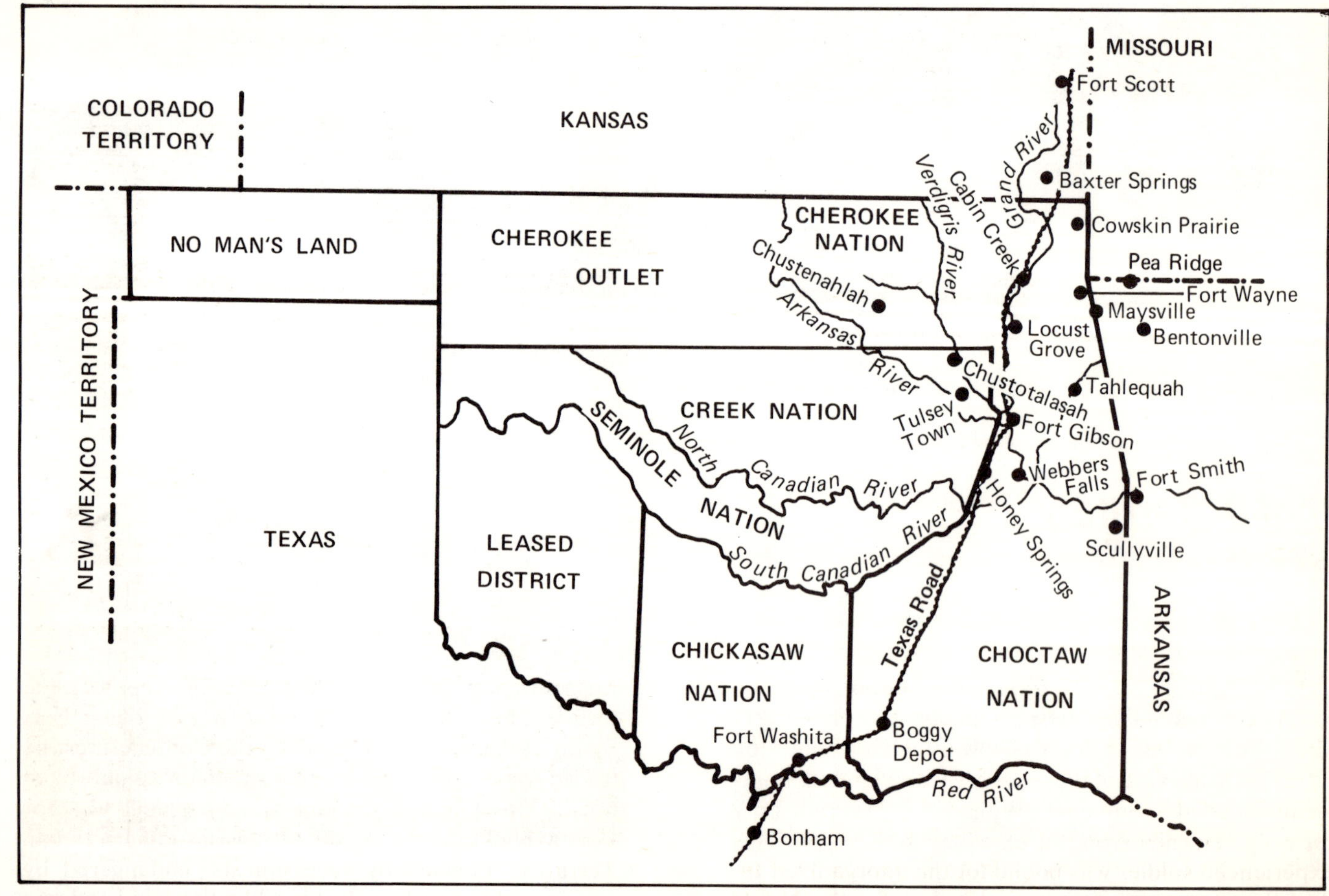

Indian Territory During the Civil War

Map Drafted by Georganne T. Bartow

South widened these divisions. The worst split occurred in the Cherokee tribe where the full-bloods under Chief John Ross formed a pro-Northern party known as the Pin Indians; the mixed-bloods, led by Stand Watie, started a Southern group called the Knights of the Golden Circle. Conflict between these two groups became commonplace, so that by 1861 the political crisis of the tribe mirrored that of the United States government in Washington.[6]

This was the situation in March, 1861, when Major Emory took command of the Union troops in the territory. Emory's new district contained four companies of the First Cavalry Regiment and five companies of the First Infantry Regiment scattered between three posts: Fort Washita, Fort Arbuckle, and Fort Cobb. Initially, Washington had ordered Emory to take command of Fort Cobb. But rumor of a planned Texan invasion of the territory changed those orders. Instead, Emory was to concentrate his troops at Fort Washita and contain the invasion. Union strategy changed again in April when Confederates cut direct supply lines to the territory. This act and the low status of the area among Washington's priorities forced another change in Emory's plans; Second Lieutenant Averall delivered these new instructions on May 2, 1861.[7]

The orders brought by Averall had not caught Emory unprepared. In fact, he had anticipated these instructions and departed from Fort Washita two days earlier.

Courtesy of National Archives

Major William H. Emory successfully evacuated United States Army forces located at three forts in the Indian Territory at the outbreak of the Civil War.

families living on their own self-supporting farms. The tribes also quickly demonstrated their long-standing interest in the social and cultural aspects of territorial life. The Indians reacted positively to the influx of missionaries into the area by accepting the white men's Christianity as their own and building places of worship. Since education had always played an important role in the life of the Five Civilized Tribes, it was not neglected on their arrival in Indian Territory; by 1861, the Indians maintained an extensive school system.[4]

The political system of the Indians had also reached a high level of development by the beginning of the war. All of the Indians except the Seminoles lived under a constitution and most had some type of elected representative government.[5] Although the system was desirable, political divisions caused by removal and race plagued the Indians, especially the Cherokees and Creeks. Tribal politics divided between full-bloods and mixed-bloods, and between those who had favored removal and those who had not. The rise of abolitionism and the growing conflict between the North and the

Courtesy of Smithsonian Institution

John Ross, the chief of the Cherokees, urged neutrality for his tribe at the outbreak of the Civil War, then allied briefly with the Confederate States.

Continuing its retreat, the Union column added the troops garrisoned at Fort Arbuckle and Fort Cobb to its numbers, and by May 4 was in full retreat toward Kansas. Invading Texas troops under Colonel William Young captured the posts only one day after Union evacuation; then the Confederates pursued Emory until May 5. That afternoon the Union troops captured the Texas advance column. Releasing the Confederates the next morning, the Union companies marched on to Kansas unimpeded. Major Emory led his command into Fort Leavenworth on May 9, 1861, having lost only two men by desertion. The successful Union retreat completed the first campaign of the Civil War in Indian Territory and left the advantage completely in the hands of the Confederacy.[8]

The Confederate government moved quickly in 1861 to win the allegiance of the Five Civilized Tribes and consolidate its control of the territory. On March 5, 1861, the Confederate Congress authorized President Jefferson Davis to appoint a commissioner to negotiate treaties with the Indians. Davis chose Albert Pike, an Arkansas newspaperman, to fill this post. The Confederate Congress specified its intentions toward the tribes on May 21 by passing an act which became the orders of Commissioner Pike. These instructions, largely financial in nature, included a promise that the Confederacy would finish paying the Five Civilized Tribes for their lands in the Southeast. The Southerners fully expected cooperation from the Indians because of their Southern background, United States withdrawal from the territory, and Washington's failure to pay the tribes for their land.[9]

With these expectations, Pike arrived in Indian Territory to open negotiations with the Cherokee Nation. The Confederate agent met with disappointment as Chief Ross adamantly insisted on the neutrality of his tribe. Discouraged but undaunted, Pike moved on to the land of the Choctaws and the Chickasaws where he was more successful. Both tribes assumed that disunion was an accomplished fact and concluded that their interests lay with the South. After these deliberations, the Choctaws and Chickasaws signed a treaty of alliance, on July 12, 1861. Two days prior to this the Creeks also had agreed to an alliance, although the respected Creek leader Opothleyahola led significant opposition to the treaty. On August 1, Pike concluded an agreement with the Seminoles, and on August 12 with the Plains Indians, leaving only the Cherokees unsigned.[10]

Since the Confederacy's initial proposals to Ross, the internal situation of the Cherokee tribe had changed significantly. The Southern faction eroded much of the tribal support of Ross by forming its own militia units and joining forces with the Confederates in Arkansas. As the other tribes signed treaties, the possibility of Ross maintaining neutrality dimmed. As a result of these events, Ross sent a message to Pike stating that the Cherokees were now prepared to negotiate an agreement. The Cherokee Executive Council ratified this

sentiment on August 1, 1861, and on October 7, the tribe signed a treaty of alliance with the Confederacy. This completed the mission of Albert Pike, an overwhelming and unquestioned success for the Confederate cause.[11]

Although the treaties of 1861 were an ultimate disaster for the Five Civilized Tribes, the agreements appeared to provide the Indians with many of the things they had wanted for years but failed to receive from the Union. The Confederate government promised to protect the tribes, to prevent invasion of Indian Territory by the United States, to grant the Indians their present lands without payment, to guarantee the continued legalization of slavery, and to allow the right of tribal self-government. In return, the Indians agreed to an offensive and defensive alliance with the Confederacy and to provide troops at the request of President Davis.[12] These provisions represented an ideal treaty for the Indians; they were lenient and favorable, and granted free land, annual monetary payments, and protection. Even the promise to raise troops and fight against the North did not seem too drastic; tribal leaders probably doubted that war would ever reach so far west.

With the withdrawal of Union forces north to Kansas, immediate conflict in 1861 seemed unlikely. But the Confederate government wanted its direct supply lines opened to the West, and that meant a military presence in Indian Territory. Such a presence had to be affected without removing troops from the more vital campaigns in the East. Using this strategy, Richmond created a separate military department for this area under the command of Pike, now a brigadier general. His command consisted largely of Indian regiments being formed among the Five Civilized Tribes. With the aid of some white units from Texas and Arkansas, the Indians would protect their land and the Confederacy's western strategy.[13]

While the Confederate government discussed its plans in Richmond, Virginia, the Indians established fighting units under commanders of their own choosing. The earliest to enter the war was the First Regiment of Choctaw and Chickasaw Mounted Rifles commanded by Colonel Douglas H. Cooper, a former Indian agent. On the same day, July 31, 1861, a Creek regiment organized and elected Colonel Daniel N. McIntosh as its leader. At the same time the Seminoles created their battalion under the command of Major John Jumper. The split among the Cherokees persisted as they formed their units on August 24. The First Cherokee Mounted Rifles led by Colonel John Drew consisted largely of allies of Ross, while the Second Cherokee Mounted Rifles commanded by Colonel Stand Watie was comprised of mixed-bloods.[14]

Signing the treaty with the Confederacy and raising troops had caused divisions within the Creek tribe; these splits finally led to the first battles of the war in the territory. The Upper Creeks (those loyal to the North) separated from the Lower Creeks (the Southern faction), elected their own chief, and pleaded with the United States government for help. Under the direction of the elder statesman Opothleyahola, the loyal Creeks sent a delegation north to Kansas, and later, another from there to Washington. These groups sought assurances that their treaties with the North would be fulfilled and they received promises of aid.[15]

While the Upper Creeks made overtures to Washington, two individuals were pressuring Opothleyahola to join the South. In a letter of September 19, 1861, Chief Ross urged the unification of all red men under the banner of the Confederacy. Opothleyahola did not believe that the Cherokee leader had written the note; however, a second letter from Ross on October 8 convinced the old Creek that he would have to fight alone. Colonel Cooper also asked that the Upper Creeks reach a reconciliation with the "constituted authorities of the Creek Nation."[16] Neither appeal had any influence on Opothleyahola's determination to remain loyal to Washington. When Cooper learned of this fact, he began a campaign to force the Upper Creeks back into the Confederate fold.[17]

Cooper's force, comprised of 1,400 men, including Choctaw, Chickasaw, Creek, and Seminole units and a detachment of the Fourth Texas Cavalry, began pursuit of the Creeks loyal to the United States on November 15, 1861. Closely following the fleeing Indians for several days, Cooper finally caught Opothleyahola on November 19 encamped somewhere between the present towns of Stillwater and Tulsa, Oklahoma. The two sides engaged in a brief, sharp encounter known as the Battle of Round Mountain from which the Upper Creeks retreated under cover of darkness. The first battle of the Civil War in Indian Territory had ended indecisively.[18]

Though Cooper seemed on the verge of victory, he could not pursue his advantage; he had received instructions ordering him east to prevent a Union invasion by troops under John C. Fremont. The Union forces retreated before Cooper could move toward Missouri, leaving him free to march again on Opothleyahola. The Confederates arrived at Chusto-Talasah on Bird Creek, north of Tulsey Town on December 8, 1861, and found the Upper Creeks occupying an easily defensible natural fortress. Across an open prairie and the deep waters and steep banks of the creek, lay a thickly wooded section of land where the loyal Indians awaited the Confederate attack. When it came, the battle raged back and forth for four hours with neither side able to achieve a decisive victory. Finally, the Upper Creeks retreated north and the Confederates pulled back to their camp.[19]

Desertion of many Cherokee troops and depleted supplies of ammunition forced Cooper to break contact once again. He immediately requested that Colonel James McIntosh send him white reinforcements from Arkansas. While he waited for their arrival, Cooper

Opothleyahola, leader of the Upper Creeks, attempted to remove about 6,000 Creeks and Seminoles loyal to the United States from Confederate-held Indian Territory.

tried to bolster the sagging morale of the Cherokees. Late in December, 1861, Cooper's command moved up the Arkansas River, while a mixed force of Texas and Arkansas troops under James McIntosh marched along the Verdigris River. The Confederates planned to catch Opothleyahola between the points of their pincer movement. But waiting for the arrival of supplies delayed Cooper, forcing McIntosh to enter the battle alone. On December 25, 1861, the Confederates caught the Upper Creeks at Chustenahlah and attacked. Again the loyal Indians had the advantage, defending a hill with 200 to 300 yards of open prairie in front of them. Colonel McIntosh did not use a complex battle strategy; instead, he sent his forces straight across the field and up the hill directly into the fire of the Upper Creeks. With the soon-to-be-famous Rebel yell sounding through the cold December air, the Confederates charged, topped the high ground, and in hand-to-hand combat broke the ranks of the Indians loyal to the United States. Routed, the Upper Creeks faded into the mountains and straggled north to a bleak refuge in

106

Kansas. The Confederates had won the first military campaign of the war and now completely controlled Indian Territory.[20]

By January 1, 1862, prospects for the Confederacy looked bright in Indian Territory. Yet the Southern command already faced problems that would plague it throughout the war; these included difficulties in obtaining supplies, conflicts over the area's commander, and providing a new life for Indian refugees fleeing their war-ravaged home lands. The most immediate problem faced by the Confederate troops in the territory was obtaining arms and ammunition. As early as December, 1861, Brigadier General Pike had complained to Richmond, Virginia, that his Indian troops were poorly armed and equipped. From this time on, the area's commanders pleaded with their government for more adequate supplies.[21]

The problem of Confederate command within the territory also was tied to that of supplies. Various commanders rose and fell because they could not win victories over invading Union forces; frequently these losses resulted from poorly armed troops. Brigadier General Pike resigned in July, 1862, disgusted with Richmond's deaf ear to the problems of the territory. Colonel Cooper succeeded Pike as the area's leader, but proved less than successful as a military strategist. In 1863, Richmond replaced Cooper with Brigadier General William Steele. But that choice proved unsatisfactory to the Indians, and early in 1864, Richmond again changed command, placing Brigadier General Samuel B. Maxey in charge. These wrangles over command and problems with supplies did not help the morale of the Confederate Indian troops. Given these conditions, it is a miracle that the tribes fought as well as they did.[22]

The devastating social and economic life of the non-combatant Indians living in the war zone was also a problem for the Confederate command. The tribes who remained loyal to the South found themselves refugees in every sense of the word. Because of the constant warfare raging across their lands, the Indians could not grow their crops and became dependent on supplies from the South. Taking care of these destitute people proved an overwhelming problem for the Confederate Bureau of Indian Affairs. To maintain control over the tribes, the Confederates constantly moved the Indians south as Union forces occupied more and more of the territory in 1864 and 1865. The Confederate command created refugee camps in the southern Choctaw and Chickasaw nations as well as at such northern Texas towns as Bonham and Sherman. Though never a pleasant existence, life became easier after moving into these camps; at least food was available from the grain fields of northern Texas. But Richmond never completely solved the refugee problem, and only with the end of the war would the lives of the tribes be returned to normal.[23]

In the relative calm of the early months of 1862, these problems seemed remote. The Union forces had retreated and their Creek allies had soon followed, leaving the victorious Confederate Indians in control of their home. Yet, a message ordering Indian troops east into Arkansas in March, 1862, shattered this tranquility and marked a turning point for the western Confederacy. The subsequent Battle of Pea Ridge began the South's decline in the West and in Indian Territory.

In preparation for this battle, Major General Earl Van Dorn, Confederate commander of the Trans-Mississippi District, ordered troops from Missouri, Arkansas, Louisiana, Texas, and Indian Territory to concentrate in northern Arkansas. Apparently Van Dorn hoped to carry the war to Missouri, but the movement of four Union divisions south into Arkansas thwarted that strategy. Instead, the Union troops, under Brigadier General Samuel Curtis, pushed the Confederate forces of Brigadier General Ben McCulloch and Major General Sterling Price back to Bentonville and Leetown, Arkansas. Here the combined Southern force of Van Dorn entered the fray, and on March 6 the three day Battle of Pea Ridge began. This running fight was a disastrous defeat for the Confederates; the Union forces crushed any hopes of the Confederacy reconquering Missouri and killed two of the South's best generals, Ben McCulloch and James McIntosh. Pike's command delivered a mixed performance during the battle. The Indians fought well in the wooded areas against individual Union units, but when United States artillery lent its booming voice to the battle's chorus, the red soldiers quickly retreated from the open fields. On March 8, Van Dorn ordered a general retreat; Pike gathered his scattered command and marched deep into Indian Territory. The Battle of Pea Ridge had ended and the rise of Union power in Indian Territory was about to begin.[24]

During the fall of 1861, Union leaders in Kansas planned an invasion of Indian Territory, but politics delayed the campaign until early summer, 1862. United States Senator James H. Lane of Kansas offered the first such proposal, persuaded President Abraham Lincoln to accept the plan, and was placed in command of the expedition. But Union military leaders opposed Lane as a leader of an invasion and succeeded in temporarily blocking such a move. Lane persistently lobbied for a commander in Kansas favorable to his point of view. Finally, in April, 1862, after three replacements, Lane succeeded with the appointment of Brigadier General James G. Blunt as the commander of the Kansas Department.[25]

Blunt brought ability and determination to his new post, and his first task was to get the so-called Indian Expedition out of southern Kansas and into Indian Territory. The new commander acted quickly and replaced Colonel Charles Doubleday with Colonel William Weer as the leader of the invasion force. In early June, 1862, Colonel Weer's army, including two regiments of infantry from Kansas and Wisconsin, three units of cavalry from Kansas and Ohio, and two artillery batteries gathered at Baxter Springs in southeastern Kansas. There, two regiments of Cherokees, Creeks, and Seminoles joined the force and the entire unit began training for the expedition. Finally, in mid-June, Weer slowly marched his army south, while news of his expedition preceded the invading forces like an advance guard.[26]

The Indian Expedition moved into northeastern Indian Territory in late June and quickly encountered resistance from Stand Watie's Second Cherokee Mounted Rifles. Weer led his units in an attack against detachments of Watie's command at Locust Grove on July 3. The Union forces won a complete victory and the demoralized Confederate Indians scattered south, convincing many Cherokees to desert to the Union side. Gradually the Indian Expedition cleared the Confederates out of the area north of the Arkansas and occupied Fort Gibson, a deactivated United States Army post. These Union victories convinced Chief Ross that his alliance with the South was a mistake. Consequently, early in August, Ross and his family moved to Kansas and then on to Washington, while over 2,000 Cherokees joined the Union cause.[27]

Unfortunately for the Indians who had changed sides, problems within the United States command dramatically changed the North's fortunes. Brigadier General Blunt became convinced that the expedition was in serious danger and communicated that feeling to Indian Territory. At the front, this fear spread and split the expedition's leaders. On July 18, second-in-command Colonel Frederick Salomon arrested Colonel Weer and ordered a general retreat north to Kansas. This action left the Indian units stranded without supplies or artillery and forced their unification into an Indian brigade under the command of Colonel R.W. Furnas. Finally, early in August all Federal troops, red and white, once again left Indian Territory for the refuge of Kansas. The Indian Expedition had not established permanent Union control of the territory, but it proved that the United States command could win victories over its enemy and that the apparent unity within the ranks of the Five Civilized Tribes was a fragile illusion dependent on Confederate success.[28]

On September 19, 1862, Washington changed the status of the Western command by consolidating Kansas, Missouri, Arkansas, and Indian Territory into the new Department of Missouri under the command of Major General Samuel R. Curtis. Brigadier General Blunt resented the subordination of his command and was angered even further when Kansas was combined with the troops of Brigadier General John Schofield into the Army of the Frontier, the latter commanding. Though bitterly dissatisfied with this arrangement, Blunt accepted his role long enough to lead the second invasion of Indian Territory. This came in response to a planned Confederate offensive against Kansas and Missouri by the commands of Brigadier General James Rains in Arkansas and Brigadier General Cooper in Indian Territory.[29]

Blunt moved his forces west into Missouri and then south to Bentonville, Arkansas, in October 1862. At that point he learned that Cooper's command was encamped at old Fort Wayne just over the border in Indian Territory. Planning a surprise attack, Blunt ordered an all-night forced march with an assault to begin at dawn. With Blunt in the lead, the Union troops set out across the rugged hills and through the dense forests of northern Arkansas. Blunt arrived near Fort Wayne just before daybreak, discovered the exact location of the Confederates, and fully expected his plan to succeed. But the Union leader soon discovered that he had only three cavalry companies present in his command; the remainder of his forces, straggling seven miles to the rear, had been delayed. Undaunted, Blunt attacked with a small force of Kansas cavalrymen. The surprise worked, keeping the Confederates engaged until more troops could appear. With the arrival of the delayed Union units and the capture of the only artillery battery of the Confederates, the battle turned into a rout for Cooper's command. Only the exhaustion of Union mounts prevented the complete annihilation of the Southern force, which did not stop running until it reached Scullyville, deep in the Choctaw Nation. Brigadier General Blunt had been completely successful in his first direct military contact with the Confederates.[30]

The Army of the Frontier, pleased with its performance, then settled in for the winter and underwent several changes in its command structure. In January, 1863, Brigadier General Schofield created a new unit, the Third Brigade. This organization was comprised of one battalion of the Sixth Kansas Cavalry, a battery of artillery, and the three Union Indian regiments. Schofield placed Colonel William A. Phillips in command of the new unit and ordered it to protect Union sympathizers living along the Arkansas-Indian Territory Border. In addition, Phillips was to provide food for the Indians and persuade the Confederate tribes to change their allegiance.[31]

Much to the dissatisfaction of Phillips, his movement into Indian Territory was delayed by problems and changes within the Union command. Feuds among the Missouri Department generals culminated in May, 1863, with the removal of Major General Curtis and his replacement by Schofield as the department's commander. Earlier, in March, Indian Territory had been placed under Blunt's District of Kansas. These two events finally freed Colonel Phillips for action.[32]

In early April, 1863, Blunt, recently promoted to major general, ordered the Indian Brigade into Indian Territory to fulfill its intended mission. Phillips occupied Fort Gibson, renamed it Fort Blunt, and consolidated his position north of the Arkansas River. Phillips soon learned of a planned meeting of the Confederate Cherokee Council at Webbers Falls on April 25.

Major General James G. Blunt of Kansas, the victor at the pivotal Battle of Honey Springs, which saved the Indian Territory for the United States.

Eager for action, he marched a 600-man force thirty miles deep into the Creek Nation. After an all-night trek, the Union unit struck the Southern camp at daybreak, caught the Confederates completely by surprise, and routed them. Withdrawing to Fort Blunt, the Union Indian Brigade had proved the strength of its position in the territory.[33]

The Confederate Indian Territory command responded very slowly to the Union threat north of the Arkansas River. For several months the Union position remained untouched while the lethargic Brigadier General Cooper built up his forces across the river at Honey Springs Depot. Finally, in June, a Confederate cavalry unit under Colonel D.N. McIntosh conducted a ten-day raid into Union territory, including a brief but indecisive skirmish at Greenleaf Prairie. This foray failed to cut Union supply lines between Kansas and Fort Blunt, but the tactic remained uppermost in the minds of Confederate commanders. In late June, Confederate Brigadier General William Steele ordered units under the commands of Watie and Brigadier General William Cabell to cross the Arkansas River and split the Union forces.[34]

The object of the Confederate raid was a Union supply wagon train en route from Fort Scott, Kansas, under the command of Colonel James M. Williams. It was escorted by the First Kansas Colored Infantry Regiment and reinforced by 600 men from Fort Blunt. Watie set up an ambush on the Texas Road at Cabin Creek, fifty-four miles northeast of Fort Blunt. The Confederates dug in on the south bank of the stream and awaited the arrival of the Union wagons. Meanwhile, Cabell's unit was unable to cross the swollen Grand River and, therefore, missed the impending engagement. The Union column arrived on July 1 and attacked the Confederate positions the next day. After two assaults, the Negro troops reached the high ground on the south bank and, with aid from the Ninth Kansas Cavalry Regiment, sent the Southerners running for their horses. The Confederate defeat at Cabin Creek permanently established Union control of Fort Blunt and set the stage for the most decisive battle of the Civil War in Indian Territory.[35]

Major General Blunt arrived at Fort Blunt on July 11, announcing, to everyone's surprise, that he intended to lead a major campaign against the Confederate troops south of the Arkansas. The Union commander hoped to catch Brigadier General Cooper by surprise, as he had done at Fort Wayne, and defeat him before he could receive reinforcements from Arkansas. Following brief preparations, the Union army began its march southward late in the afternoon of July 16. The 3,000-man Union force forded the Arkansas River and moved south along the Texas Road. Following an all-night march, Blunt struck Cooper's advance pickets in the early morning and drove them back into their encampment at Honey Springs Depot. Upon arriving a half mile from the Confederate camp which contained about 5,000 men, Blunt ordered a halt and rested his troops for two hours.[36]

During this rest period, Blunt organized his line of battle. The Union flanks contained unmounted cavalry and six pieces of artillery, while the center was held by Indian and Negro units and the remaining cannon. At 10:00 a.m., after a personal reconnaissance of the Confederate lines, Blunt ordered his forces to advance. As shouted commands rang through the warm summer air, the weary blue lines slowly moved forward, beginning the largest battle fought in Indian Territory during the Civil War.[37]

Through a series of problems, including bad luck and poor quality supplies, the Confederates found themselves in serious trouble from the beginning of the battle. When the Union troops came into view, the Southern artillery immediately opened fire. But their efforts were short lived, for the Union batteries pinpointed their position and blew them out of the battle. Confederate firepower, already seriously hampered, also suffered a problem with its gunpowder. It had rained most of the morning, and much of the Confederate gunpowder, imported from Mexico, turned to useless paste. Under these conditions, the Confederates had an uphill fight from the beginning of the battle.[38]

As the Union forces advanced, the Second Indian Regiment accidentally got between the First Kansas Colored Infantry Regiment and the Confederate Twenty-ninth Texas Cavalry Regiment. This mistake and the subsequent Southern response eventually cost Cooper the battle. Lieutenant Colonel John Bowles, commander of the Kansas troops, shouted to the Indians to withdraw. When the Texas units heard these orders, they thought the entire Union line was retreating. With shouts of victory, the Texans charged. Unfortunately for the Southerners, the Negro regiment stood calm under the assault and delivered a shattering volley into the Texas lines. The first series of shots destroyed the Confederate front line and the second volley sent the battered Texas soldiers into full, disorganized retreat. Elated by the success of the Negro regiment, the remainder of the Union line struck forward with renewed vigor, scattering Cooper's command before them. Defeated and demoralized, the Confederates rapidly fell back toward the Red River, not even stopping when Brigadier General Cabell arrived with 3,000 reinforcements at 4:00 in the afternoon.[39]

Two hours prior to Cabell's arrival, Major General Blunt had surveyed his troops and found them short of ammunition; he then ordered a halt to further pursuit of Cooper. Apparently unaware of the extent of his victory, Blunt withdrew from the battle site on Elk Creek, and returned to Fort Gibson on July 18. At the same time, Brigadier General Cabell returned his force to Fort Smith, the next target of the Union offensive. The Gettysburg of Indian Territory had ended, leaving the Union army in a commanding position and the Confederates able to conduct only guerrilla campaigns for the remainder of the war.[40]

Blunt next planned another sortie across the Arkansas River designed to destroy the command of Brigadier General Steele and capture Fort Smith. In August, 1863, Union troops slashed across the Arkansas River, once again sending their Southern enemies into rapid retreat. This time the Confederate withdrawal was planned; Steele hoped to draw Blunt into Southern territory so that Union supply lines could be severed easily. But the shrewd Union general refused to overextend his forces. Instead, meeting little resistance, Blunt returned the majority of his troops to Fort Gibson. Then, he led a small force comprised of his personal bodyguard and staff, the Second Kansas Cavalry Regiment, and the First Arkansas Infantry Regiment, and occupied Fort Smith without resistance on September 1. Blunt ended his campaign in control of western Arkansas and much of Indian Territory; after reporting to his superiors, the Union commander went to bed for some needed rest.[41]

Although the United States military successes seemed flawless in Indian Territory, Union leaders faced as many problems as their Confederate counterparts. These also centered on problems of supply, the politics of command, and relations with the loyal Indian refugees. Generally, the Union command in Indian Territory was better supplied than Southern forces, although it had difficulties providing the Indian troops with horses. Colonel Phillips continually complained to his superiors about inadequate numbers of mounts to supply his command.[42]

The major trouble that plagued the entire Union conduct of the war in Indian Territory was the politics of command. Lane's maneuvers for the appointment of Blunt as commander of the Kansas Department in 1861 were a part of this pattern. Later, in 1863, Schofield and Blunt carried on a running feud largely generated by ambition. Soon Schofield began a formal investigation of possible supply fraud in Blunt's Kansas District. Although no evidence of fraud was discovered, the allegation seriously impaired Blunt's reputation. Blunt replied in kind by accusing Schofield of incompetence in a letter to Secretary of War Edwin M. Stanton. There were also political wrangles within Blunt's command, and Colonel Phillips became the victim of these troubles. Several plots, apparently originating with Senator Land and Major General Blunt, were aimed at Phillips and finally resulted in his temporary removal in 1864. Such shifts in leadership disrupted the ability of the Union command to conduct an effective and efficient military campaign.[43]

The Indians who remained loyal to the United States also suffered much economic and social disruption, sometimes starvation, and often death. These tribes rushed north to Kansas after the retreat of the Union forces in 1861. Although their arrival was not unexpected by United States authorities, little was done to provide for them. Encamped on Fall River the first winter, the Indians suffered severely; ravaged by disease and living on the edge of starvation, the tribes were shuttled in 1862 from one camp in southern Kansas to another until they came to rest on the Sac and Fox Reservation, about twenty-five miles north of the Neosho Valley. There they barely survived the winter of 1862-1863. In the summer of 1863, the Union command, flushed with recent victories, moved their charges back home to Indian Territory. But the suffering of the loyal Indians had not ended; concentrated on the land around Fort Blunt, they presented even more of a supply problem than in Kansas. Just like its Confederate counterpart, the Union command never solved the refugee problem; only the end of the war brought salvation from danger and decimation to the loyal tribes.[44]

The Confederate military effort during the last two years of the war in Indian Territory aimed primarily at cutting the supply line between Fort Scott and Fort Blunt: hopefully, this and persistent guerrilla warfare might still result in Confederate victory. Brigadier

General Steele's resignation in December, 1863, marked the beginning of this change in strategy. Steele's replacement, Major General Samuel B. Maxey, recognized the difficulties of conventional war, given the conditions of his command and the military strength of the United States forces. Maxey also realized that his best military opportunity lay in using the ability of Watie, his most capable leader.[45]

The fall of 1863 brought the first taste of guerrilla warfare to Blunt's command, an experience that nearly proved disastrous to the Union. After his occupation of Fort Smith in September, Major General Blunt returned to Fort Scott, only to learn that Fort Smith was threatened by a superior Confederate force. Blunt gathered his staff and an escort of 100 men and marched toward Arkansas. On October 6, Blunt's column neared Baxter Springs, Kansas, and sighted a large body of men approaching from the direction of the Union post. Growing suspicious at their disorganized appearance and hearing of an irregular attack on Baxter Springs, Blunt went forward to get a closer look at the unidentified unit. Driven away by pistol fire, Blunt returned to find his troops running in all directions from the attack of William Quantrill's outlaw guerrillas. Quantrill carried the day, nearly annihilating the Baxter Springs command and the forces under Blunt. Barely escaping with his life, Blunt had suffered his first defeat at the hands of irregular Confederate troops and Indian Territory military personnel had tasted their first example of the guerrilla warfare that would prevail in the area until the conflict ended in 1865.[46]

During the remaining months of 1863, the Confederates conducted harassing raids into Union-held territory. In late October, Colonel Watie thundered into Tahlequah, killed several Union Cherokees, and broke up a meeting of the tribal council. On December 26, Watie led another sortie against the Northerners, this time threatening Fort Blunt. Captain Alexander Spilman and a 300-man Union infantry unit pursued the Confederates, caught them camped on the Barren Fork River, and defeated them in a sharp battle. This action secured the Union area of Indian Territory for the winter of 1863-1864.[47]

Colonel Phillips, commanding the United States forces at Fort Blunt, had decided not to sit idle during the cold winter months. Thus he planned and led a large expedition deep into the Confederate reaches of Indian Territory, hoping to pacify the region. Early in the morning of February 1, 1864, the 1,500-man column began its march along the Texas Road into the Choctaw Nation. Four days later, encamped on the North Fork River, Phillips sent out several small units to clear the area of Confederate troops. These scouting parties reported killing over 100 of the enemy and indicated that Cooper's command was in flight toward the Red River and the safety of Fort Washita. On February 9, Phillips marched his force south to Boggy Depot; there he concluded that scheduled reinforcements under Colonel Thomas Moonlight would not arrive. After destroying all major resistance in the area, Phillips wheeled his forces north and returned to Fort Blunt before the end of February.[48]

Although Union military action had not brought the war to a conclusion, Phillips' expedition accomplished part of its goal. It had spread demoralizing death and destruction over 400 square miles of Confederate territory. This campaign also proved that a concerted military effort by the Union Army easily could have pushed the weakened Confederates out of Indian Territory and into northern Texas.

While relative calm prevailed in Indian Territory during the spring of 1864, Colonel Phillips had time to reorganize and resupply his command. This peaceful interlude was brought on by the engagement of Major General Maxey's troops in the Confederate campaign near Camden, Arkansas. Here Indian troops played an important role in defeating a Union column at the Battle of Poison Spring on April 18, 1864. Colonel Tandy Walker's Choctaw Brigade was instrumental in the victory, helping capture 4 cannon and 170 wagons of supplies. This victory, as well as other Confederate successes, blocked Union Major General Frederick Steele's campaign against Shreveport, Louisiana; had Steele's move been successful, it would have severed Indian Territory from the rest of the Confederate command and probably brought defeat to Maxey's troops much sooner.[49]

During the summer and fall of 1864, Confederate strategy changed from conventional war to almost total guerrilla-style fighting; Watie, now a brigadier general, commanded almost all Confederate actions of this type until the end of the war. Watie had his first success in the intensified Confederate guerrilla effort in June, 1864. The Union command had decided to experiment by shipping provisions aboard the steamer *J.R. Williams* up the Arkansas River to Fort Blunt. Carrying supplies worth $120,000, the Union ship departed from Fort Smith escorted by twenty-six United States soldiers under the command of Second Lieutenant Horace Cook. Watie surprised the *J.R. Williams* at Pleasant Bluff, raking it with artillery and musket fire. The boat beached on the opposite shore of the river and, after brief resistance, Cook retreated with his men to Fort Smith; this left the entire cargo in the hands of Watie's guerrillas.[50]

Watie's successful capture of the *J.R. Williams* bolstered the morale of the Confederate forces and encouraged them to increase their military activity. Brigadier General Cooper made several feints at Fort Smith and the outlying area in the late summer months. Brigadier General Richard M. Gano of Texas attacked a Union outpost at Massard Prairie on July 27. The Confederate troops swept down on Major David Mefford's four companies of the Sixth Kansas Cavalry Regiment, drove them from their positions, and captured or killed the entire command. Again, on July 30,

Brigadier General Stand Watie, noted Cherokee guerrilla leader in the Indian Territory, was the last Confederate general to surrender.

Cooper moved against Fort Smith, maneuvering his forces into position in front of the post and stinging the Union troops with his artillery and Watie's cavalry. But when night fell, the cautious Cooper withdrew to a safer camp at Cedar Prairie.[51]

In September, 1864, the Confederate troops returned to the campaign in Indian Territory, harassing the area around Fort Blunt and attacking the Union supply line to that post. Brigadier General Watie and Brigadier General Gano marched 2,000 men into Union-held territory on September 15, the largest Confederate raid since 1863. Their first objective was the Union haying station at Flat Rock, which the Confederates struck the following day. The small Negro force protecting the Union operation, outnumbered ten to one, fought bravely for over two hours until finally crushed by the overwhelming Confederate forces.[52]

Disrupting Union haying operations was not the central Confederate objective. Instead, Watie and Gano aimed at cutting the Texas Road in order to starve Fort Blunt. To achieve this, the Confederates marched toward Cabin Creek on September 17, hoping to quickly locate and destroy an expected Union supply column. En route from Fort Scott, Kansas, Major Henry Hopkins and a force of 360 men had left Baxter Springs with the Union supplies several days earlier. On September 17, Colonel Stephan Wattles (commanding at Fort Blunt since the removal of Phillips in July) ordered

Hopkins to move his command to Cabin Creek and await the arrival of reinforcements. When the Confederates topped the high ground above the stockade on the following day, they looked down on the supply column, seeing the Union wagons circling the post and the Union soldiers secure behind its walls. Watie attacked twice, the second wave successfully driving the Union forces out of their position and capturing the bulk of the wagon train. The Confederates completed the victory the next day, scattering the remainder of the Union troops. To avoid contact with the Union relief column, Watie and Gano retreated south, carrying their much needed supplies back to the safety of Confederate Indian Territory.[53]

This Confederate victory marked the last major engagement of the war in Indian Territory. As action subsided both sides reorganized their commands and prepared for attacks that never came. On May 26, 1865, Lieutenant General Edmund Kirby-Smith surrendered the white Confederate command for Indian Territory and, on June 23, Brigadier General Watie did the same for his Indian command; he was the last Confederate general to lay down his arms.[54]

The Civil War had a major impact on life in Indian Territory. Military command during the conflict mirrored all the frustrations and successes of the United States and the Confederate States. Political wrangling among ambitious army officers and the difficulty of obtaining qualified leaders plagued both commands. Neither the Union forces nor the Confederate forces could obtain the supplies they needed from their governments. Yet, the war had its positive side for Indian Territory troops. The military ability of some of the commanders, such as Blunt, Phillips, and Watie was excellent; these men were as capable as any who led troops during the war. And the common soldiers — Indian, Negro, and white — who carried the burden of the war on their shoulders, fought as bravely and as capably as their counterparts in the East. The hit-and-run tactics developed so well by Watie and others provided a textbook for the successful guerrilla of the future.

In addition to these contributions to the military aspects of the conflict, the Civil War in Indian Territory significantly affected Union and Southern strategies in the West. Through their intervention in the territory, the Union forces helped block Confederate expansion westward, breaking a direct link between the South and New Mexico. Although the principal effort of the South was blocked, Confederate troops in Indian Territory prevented an invasion of Texas and the severance of that important supply state from the rest of the Southern war effort.

For the Five Civilized Tribes, the war devastated almost all that they had built and developed in Indian Territory since their removal from the South and Southeast. The Indians had not only to reconstruct their society and their economy, but heal their political divisions as well. The second reconstruction of the tribes also had to be conducted under the terms of their treaties with the United States government. These agreements included living on lands half the size of their original area, structuring an economy without slavery, being governed by a unified council under the watchful eye of Washington, and living with the penetration of the territory by the railroad.[55] The Civil War had completely changed Indian Territory geographically, socially, economically, and politically. The changes the conflict had created left a land that was an easy target for the future expansion of the white man's frontier.

NOTES

1. United States Department of War, *War of the Rebellion: A Compilation of the Official Records of the Union and Confederate Armies* (70 vols., 128 books, Washington: Government Printing Office, 1880-1901), Ser. I, Vol. LIII, pp. 493-496; *ibid.*, Vol. I, p. 667; Muriel H. Wright, "Lieutenant Averall's Ride, 1861," *Chronicles of Oklahoma*, Vol. XXXIX, No. 1, Spring, 1961), pp. 2-14.

2. United States, *Statutes at Large* (87 vols., Boston: Little, Brown, and Company, 1850-1973), Vol. IV, pp. 411-412.

3. United States House of Representatives, 27th Congress, 3rd Session, *Executive Document No. 219* (Washington: Gales and Seaton, 1843), pp. 182-183.

4. United States House of Representatives, 33rd Congress, 1st Session, *Executive Document No. 1* (Washington: A.O.P. Nicholson, 1854). p. 382; Grant Foreman, *The Five Civilized Tribes* (Norman: University of Oklahoma Press, 1934), pp. 58-64; Charles Francis, "Confederate Ascendency in Indian Territory" (Master of Arts Thesis, Stillwater: Oklahoma State University, 1963), pp. 4-6.

5. *Ibid.*, p. 6; United States House of Representatives, 33rd Congress, 1st Session, *Executive Document No. 1*, pp. 407-408.

6. Francis, *op. cit.*, p. 7; Annie H. Abel, *The American Indian as Slaveholder and Secessionist* (Cleveland: Arthur H. Clark Company, 1915), pp. 86, 50; Edward E. Dale and Gaston Litton, eds., *Cherokee Cavaliers* (Norman: University of Oklahoma Press, 1939), pp. 57-58.

7. Dean Trickett, "The Civil War in Indian Territory," *Chronicles of Oklahoma*, Vol. XVII, No. 3 (September, 1939), p. 318; *Official Records*, Ser. I, Vol. I, pp. 659-660, 650, 656, 647.

8. *Ibid.*, pp. 648-649, 652.

9. James D. Richardson, comp., *A Compilation of the Messages and Papers of the Confederacy, 1861-1865* (2 vols., Nashville: United States Publishing Company, 1905), Vol. I, p. 149; United States Senate, 58th Congress, 2nd Session, *Executive Document No. 234* (Washington: Government Printing Office, 1904), p. 244; United States Senate, 37th Congress, 1st Session, *Executive Document No. 1* (Washington: Government Printing Office, 1862), p. 682.

10. *Official Records*, Ser. IV, Vol. I, pp. 445-446, 426-443, 513-527, 542, 554.

11. Dale and Litton, eds., *op. cit.*, pp. 99-100; James Thoburn, "The Cherokee Question," *Chr9,ic****Oklahoma*, Vol. II, No. 2 (June, 1924), p. 175; *Official Records*, Ser. IV, Vol. I, pp. 669, 686.

12. *Ibid.*, pp. 669-686.

13. *Ibid.*, Ser. I, Vol. VIII, p. 690; United States Senate, 58th Congress, 2nd Session, *Executive Document No. 234*, p. 343.

14. *Official Records*, Ser. I, Vol. III, pp. 614, 625, 624; *ibid.*, Vol. VIII, p. 5; *ibid.*, Vol. III, p. 673, 690, 692.

15. Abel, *The American Indian as Slaveholder and Secessionist*, pp. 245-246; United States House of Representatives, 37th Congress, 3rd Session, *Executive Document No. 1* (Washington: Government Printing Office, 1863), p. 282; *Official Records*, Ser. I, Vol. VIII, p. 25.

16. Thoburn, *op. cit.*, pp. 170-172; *Official Records*, Ser. I, Vol. VIII, p. 5.

17. *Ibid.*

18. *Ibid.*, pp. 5-7, 14-15.

19. *Ibid.*, pp. 7, 9-10, 16.

20. *Ibid.*, pp. 11-12, 22-24, 26-27.

21. *Ibid.*, p. 720.

22. *Ibid.*, Vol. XIII, pp. 857-858; *ibid.*, Vol. XXII, Pt. 2, pp. 771-772; Dale and Litton, eds., *op. cit.*, p. 151.

23. Angie Debo, "Southern Refugees of the Cherokee Nation," *Southwestern Historical Quarterly*, Vol. XXXV, No. 2 (April, 1932), pp. 256-258; Edward E. Dale, "The Cherokees in the Confederacy," *Journal of Southern History*, Vol. XIII, No. 2 (May, 1947), pp. 164-165, 182-183.

24. *Official Records*, Ser. I, Vol. VIII, pp. 763-764; Annie H. Abel, *The American Indian as Participant in the Civil War* (Cleveland: Arthur H. Clark Company, 1919), pp. 26-27, 34; *Official Records*, Ser. I, Vol. VIII, pp. 217, 232-234, 298-299; *ibid.*, Vol. XIII, pp. 954, 824-825.

25. Barney K. Neal, "Federal Ascendency in Indian Territory, 1862-1863" (Master of Arts Thesis, Stillwater: Oklahoma State University, 1966), pp. 26-31.

26. *Ibid.*, p. 35; Wiley Britton, *The Union Indian Brigade in the Civil War* (Kansas City: Franklin Hudson Publishing Company, 1922), p. 62; *Official Records*, Ser. I, Vol. XIII, pp. 441, 444, 595.

27. *Ibid.*, pp. 137-138, 160-161, 551-552; Neal, *op. cit.*, p. 46.

28. *Official Records*, Ser. I, Vol. XIII, pp. 482-483, 475-476, 551-552.

29. *Ibid.*, pp. 653, 730, 754-755; Albert Castel, *A Frontier State at War: Kansas, 1861-1865* (Ithaca: Cornell University Press, 1958), p. 154.

30. *Ibid.*, pp. 324-327; Neal, *op. cit.*, p. 64.

31. *Ibid.*, p. 73; *Official Records*, Ser. I, Vol. XXII, Pt. 2, pp. 61-62.

32. *Ibid.*, pp. 277, 290-292; Castel, *op. cit.*, p. 110.

33. Neal, *op. cit.*, pp. 82-83; *Official Records*, Ser. I, Vol. XXII, Pt. 2, p. 315; Britton, *The Union Indian Brigade in the Civil War*, p. 222.

34. *Official Records*, Ser. I, Vol. XXII, Pt. 1, pp. 32-33.

35. Wiley Britton, *The Civil War on the Border* (2 vols., New York: G.P. Putnam's Sons, 1890-1904), Vol. II, pp. 95-96; *Official Records*, Ser. I, Vol. XXII, Pt. 1, pp. 378, 380-381.

36. *Ibid.*, Pt. 2, p. 367; Britton, *The Civil War on the Border*, Vol. II, pp. 116-117.

37. *Ibid.*, pp. 114, 118-119; *Official Records*, Ser. I, Vol. XXII, Pt. 1, pp. 447-448.

38. *Ibid.*, p. 458; Britton, *The Civil War on the Border*, Vol. II, p. 119.

39. *Ibid.*, p. 120; *Official Records*. Ser. I, Vol. XXII, Pt. 1, pp. 450, 448, 459.

40. Neal, *op. cit.*, pp. 110-112.

41. *Ibid.*, p. 112; *Official Records*, Ser. I, Vol. XXII, Pt. 1, pp. 601-603; *ibid.*, Pt. 2, pp. 525-526; Castel, *op. cit.*, p. 159; James G. Blunt, "General Blunt's Account of His Civil War Experiences," *Kansas Historical Quarterly*, Vol. I, No. 3 (May, 1932), p. 277.

42. Sharon D. Wyant, "Colonel William A. Phillips and the Civil War in Indian Territory" (Master of Arts Thesis, Stillwater: Oklahoma State University, 1967), p. 69; Britton, *The Union Indian Brigade in the Civil War*, p. 381.

43. Neal, *op. cit.*, pp. 89-90; Lary C. Rampp, "The Twilight of the Confederacy in Indian Territory, 1863-1865" (Master of Arts Thesis, Stillwater: Oklahoma State University, 1968), pp. 75-78.

44. Abel, *The American Indian as Participant in the Civil War*, pp. 79-89; United States Department of the Interior *Report of the Commissioner of Indian Affairs for the Year 1862* (Washington: Government Printing Office, 1863), pp. 151-152, 130; Dean Banks, "Civil War Refugees from Indian Territory in the North, 1861-1864," *Chronicles of Oklahoma*, Vol. XLI, No. 3 (Autumn, 1963), pp. 293-295, 297-298; Jerry L. Gill, "Federal Refugees from Indian Territory, 1861-1867" (Master of Arts Thesis, Stillwater: Oklahoma State University, 1973), pp. 195-197.

45. *Official Records*, Ser. I, Vol. XXII, Pt. 2, p. 1094; Abel, *The American Indian as Participant in the Civil War*, p. 326.

46. LeRoy H. Fischer and Lary C. Rampp, "Quantrill's Civil War Operations in Indian Territory," *Chronicles of Oklahoma*, Vol. XLVI, No. 2 (Summer, 1968), pp. 163-164; *Official Records*, Ser. I, Vol. XXII, Pt. 1, pp. 688-689.

47. Dale and Litton, eds., *op. cit.*, pp. 144-145; *Official Records*, Ser. I, Vol. XXII, Pt. 1, pp. 781-782.

48. Wyant, *op. cit.*, pp. 57-61; *Official Records.*, Ser. I, Vol. XXXIV, Pt. 1, p. 108; *ibid.*, Pt. 2, p. 272.

49. *Ibid.*, pp. 785, 849, 841-844.

50. Rampp, "The Twilight of the Confederacy in Indian Territory, 1863-1865," pp. 35, 88-93.

51. Britton, *The Union Indian Brigade in the Civil War*, pp. 425-426; *Official Records*, Ser. I, Vol. XLI, Pt. 1, pp. 34, 35.

52. *Ibid.*, pp. 780-782; Lary C. Rampp, "Negro Troop Activity in Indian Territory, 1863-1865," *Chronicles of Oklahoma*, Vol.

XLVII, No. 1 (Spring, 1969), pp. 550-553.

53. *Official Records*, Ser. I, Vol. XLI, Pt. 1, pp. 766-767, 786-791.

54. Lary C. Rampp and Donald L. Rampp, *The Civil War in the Indian Territory* (Austin, Texas: Presidial Press, 1975), p. 120; Gayle Ann Brown, "Confederate Surrenders in Indian Territory," LeRoy H. Fischer, ed., *The Civil War Era in Indian Territory* (Los Angeles: Lorrin Morrison, 1974), pp. 124-130.

55. M. Thomas Bailey, *Reconstruction in Indian Territory: A Story of Avarice, Discrimination and Opportunism* (Port Washington, New York: Kennikat Press, 1972), pp. 55-83.

SELECTED READINGS

Annie H. Abel, *The American Indian as Participant in the Civil War* (Cleveland: Arthur H. Clark Company, 1919).

Annie H. Abel, *The American Indian as Slaveholder and Secessionist* (Cleveland: Arthur H. Clark Company, 1915).

Wiley Britton, *The Civil War on the Border* (2 vols., New York: G. P. Putnam's Sons, 1890-1904), Vol. I, pp. 164-174, 214-278, 295-312, 347-375; Vol. II, pp. 1-43, 74-100, 112-126, 237-252, 340-352, 519-535.

Wiley Britton, *The Union Indian Brigade in the Civil War* (Kansas City: Franklin Hudson Publishing Company, 1922).

Edward E. Dale, "The Cherokees in the Confederacy," *Journal of Southern History,* Vol. XIII, No. 2 (May, 1947), pp. 160-185.

Edward E. Dale and Gaston Litton, eds., *Cherokee Cavaliers* (Norman: University of Oklahoma Press, 1939), pp. 98-228.

Angie Debo, "Southern Refugees of the Cherokee Nation," *Southwestern Historical Quarterly*, Vol. XXXV, No. 2 (April, 1932), pp. 255-266.

LeRoy H. Fischer, ed., *The Civil War Era in Indian Territory* (Los Angeles: Lorrin Morrison, 1974).

LeRoy H. Fischer and Lary C. Rampp, "Quantrill's Civil War Operations in Indian Territory," *Chronicles of Oklahoma*, Vol. XLVI, No. 2, (Summer, 1968), pp. 155-182.

Lary C. Rampp and Donald L. Rampp, *The Civil War in Indian Territory* (Austin, Texas: Presidial Press, 1975).

James Thoburn, "The Cherokee Question," *Chronicles of Oklahoma*, Vol. II, No. 2 (June, 1924), pp. 141-242.

Dean Trickett, "The Civil War in Indian Territory," *Chronicles of Oklahoma*, Vol. XVII, No. 3 (September, 1939), pp. 315-327, Vol. XVII, No. 4, (December, 1939), pp. 401-416, Vol. XVIII, No. 2 (June, 1940), pp. 142-153, Vol. XVIII, No. 3 (September, 1940), pp. 266-280, Vol. XIX, No. 1 (March, 1941), pp. 55-69, Vol. XIX, No. 4 (December, 1941), pp. 381-396.

JOURNAL *of the* WEST®

Index
By LeRoy H. Fischer